Writing
FOR MEDIA AUDIENCES

A Handbook for
Multi-platform News,
Advertising, and Public Relations
Second Edition

TOMMY G. THOMASON
ANDREW CHAVEZ

*Schieffer School of Journalism
and Strategic Communication*

Kendall Hunt
publishing company

Photo of Paula LaRocque in "A Visit with Your Writing Coach" sections are by Mei-Chun Jau.

Cover images © Shutterstock, Inc.

Kendall Hunt
publishing company

Send all inquiries to:
4050 Westmark Drive
Dubuque, IA 52004-1840

Copyright © 2012, 2013 by Kendall Hunt Publishing Company

ISBN 978-1-4652-3011-9

All rights reserved. No part of this publication may be reproduced, stored in a retrieval system, or transmitted, in any form or by any means, electronic, mechanical, photocopying, recording, or otherwise, without the prior written permission of the copyright owner.
Printed in the United States of America
10 9 8 7 6 5 4 3 2 1

Acknowledgments

The authors are grateful to the great team of media writing faculty members in the Schieffer School of Journalism and Strategic Communication at Texas Christian University, from whom they have learned (and stolen) much. Some members of that team wrote chapters in this book. We are also grateful to Jim Witt, executive editor of the Fort Worth Star-Telegram, who has made available to us many stories written for that newspaper to use as examples in this book.

But most of all, we're thankful to the people who have actually taught us how to teach media writing: our students.

~ TOMMY THOMASON AND ANDREW CHAVEZ

Contents

Chapter 1	**Reader-Friendly Writing:** A Mass Media Approach to Media Writing	1
Chapter 2	**Newsthinking:** What's the News?	29
Chapter 3	**Getting Started:** Shaping the News Story	41
Chapter 4	**The Associated Press Stylebook:** Bringing Consistency to Media Writing	53
Chapter 5	**Writing Leads:** Capturing the Reader's Interest in the First Graf	63
Chapter 6	**Copy Editing:** Improving Writing One Sentence at a Time	87
Chapter 7	**Organization Issues:** The Body of the Story	101
Chapter 8	**Using Quotes:** Enlivening and Humanizing the News	113
Chapter 9	**Attributions:** Showing Readers Where We Got Our Information (Geoff Campbell)	129
Chapter 10	**The Speech Story:** A Media Writing Basic	137

Chapter 11 **More Common News Story Types:**
Localization, Advances, Follow Stories 157

Chapter 12 **Writing Headlines:**
Hooking Readers, Summarizing Stories 165

Chapter 13 **Another Approach to News:**
The What, When and How of the Alternative Lead
(Robert Bohler) 173

Chapter 14 **Long Story Short:**
Writing News for Broadcast
(Suzanne Huffman) 183

Chapter 15 **Writing and Fairness:**
Avoiding Bias When Writing about
Minority Groups 193

Chapter 16 **Public Relations Writing:**
A Different Approach to Media Writing
(Maggie Thomas) 209

Chapter 17 **Writing for the Web:**
Stories for People Who Skim and Scan 223

Chapter 18 **Writing Advertising Copy:**
Oz, Magic, Rock 'N' Roll
(Carol Glover) 229

Chapter 19 **Is That Legal?**
What Writers Need to Know about Media Law
(Chip Stewart) 239

Chapter 20 **Final Thoughts:**
On Learning to Write for the Media 251

Appendix:
A Media Writer's Guide to Grammar 253

An AP Styleguide 265

Chapter One
Reader-Friendly Writing: A Mass Media Approach to Writing

So let's start at the beginning: Why do university mass communications programs offer courses in media writing? Doesn't everyone already take freshman English? Do mass communications practitioners—online and print and broadcast journalists, public relations practitioners, advertising copywriters, and the like—really write differently from other professional writers?

Yes.

There are other types of writers—novelists, technical writers, speechwriters, movie scriptwriters. But mass communications professionals approach writing in a unique way. They know that much of what they write will be read by busy people who do more skimming than reading. If you buy a book, for instance, you intend to read it. You put aside time to curl up with the book or the electronic device you downloaded it on.

But think about the products of writers in mass communications. You may whiz past an advertising message on a billboard at 70 miles an hour. You scroll through a webpage, scanning headlines or blogposts for something that will arrest your attention. You thumb through newspaper pages, glancing at headlines and leads and ads, only occasionally stopping to read one. You watch TV news while you eat and talk with friends.

Media writers produce writing that must compete for attention—and then hold the attention of those who start to read. If you buy a mystery novel, you probably finish it unless it sucks. But how often do you finish news stories or ads you start to read? Media writers know that they must seek to engage their audience.

A "mass media" writing style uses techniques that make text-reading easier and more accessible to an on-the-go audience. There are indeed many other approaches to writing, approaches that may differ from a mass media style but still are appropriate for their audiences.

Legal briefs, for instance, are documents written by attorneys to convince a judge of an argument by citing statutory law, court decisions and policy arguments. Here is a sample:

> *This rule of public policy has been relaxed only in those instances where the legislature for sufficient public reason has seen fit by statute to extend the stimulus of a reward to the public without distinction, as in the case of* United States v. Matthews, 173 U.S. 381, *where the attorney-general, under an act for "the detection and prosecution of crimes against the United States," made a public offer of reward sufficiently liberal and generic to comprehend the services of a federal deputy Maggiel. Exceptions of that character upon familiar principles serve to emphasize the correctness of the rule, as one based upon sound public policy.* (Gray v. Martino, 1918)

Scholars, on the other hand, write primarily for other scholars. The writing is frequently dense with specialized jargon and allusions to the history of the field and to previous research. Scholars write to present their research to others with advanced degrees, and they assume their readers will have the specialized knowledge to follow their arguments, as in the following example:

> *An element of a shared symbolic system which serves as a criterion or standard for selection among the alternatives of orientation which are intrinsically open in a situation may be called a value ... But from this motivational orientation aspect of the totality of action it is, in view of the role of symbolic systems, necessary to distinguish a "value orientation" aspect. This aspect concerns, not the meaning of the expected state of affairs to the actor in terms of his gratification-deprivation balance but the content of the selective standards themselves. The concept of value-orientations in this sense is thus the logical device for formulating one central aspect of the articulation of cultural traditions in the action system.* (Lanham, 1974)

To see a history of Volkswagen's ad campaign for the Beetle, scan the QR code or go to http://bit.ly/cusZ2K.

A judge will take time to read a brief, and scholars might pore over a journal article that may confirm or contradict their own research. But mass media writers can assume no such specialized knowledge or commitment to consume the printed word. We have to fight to get our audience and to keep it. And there's no better example than advertising copywriters.

The following advertising copy is some of the most famous ever written. It was part of ad agency Doyle Dane Bernbach's 1959 campaign that introduced the Volkswagen Beetle® to an American market dominated by big cars that were seen by the public as part of the American dream.

The Doyle Dane Bernbach copywriters focused on the Beetle's compact size and affordability in brilliantly written print ads that are still considered by many to be among the best ads ever written. The following ad illustrates a mass media approach to writing:

> *Our little car isn't so much of a novelty any more. A couple of dozen college kids don't try to squeeze inside it. The guy at the gas station doesn't ask where the gas goes. Nobody even stares at our shape. In fact, some people who drive our little flivver don't even think 32 miles to the gallon is going any great guns. Or using five pints oil instead of five quarts. Or never needing anti-freeze. Or racking up 40,000 miles on a set of tires. That's because once you get used to some of our economies, you don't even think about them anymore. Except when you squeeze into a small parking spot. Or renew your small insurance. Or pay a small repair bill. Or trade in your old VW for a new one. Think it over.**

Mass media writing uses techniques that make it reader friendly, whether it's an ad or a newspaper article or website copy written by a public relations practitioner. These techniques include everything from sentence structure to vocabulary to the use of traditional language conventions. Let's look at the techniques media writers use to engage readers.

The Techniques of Mass Media Writing

A Simple Vocabulary

We write to express, not impress. Most readability formulas measure the number of multisyllable words, awarding better reading-ease scores to writing that uses shorter words. The three writing samples you read earlier in this chapter are great examples:

- The legal brief had 19.27 percent complex words and 1.61 syllables per word.
- The scholarly writing had 21.85 percent complex words and 1.78 syllables per word.
- The VW ad had 2.86 percent complex words and 1.24 syllables per word.

Longer sentences are harder to read and understand. Good writers use sentence variety—they balance longer sentences with shorter ones so the writing does not seem choppy. So even media writers occasionally use a longer, but well-crafted sentence. Overall, however, we keep sentences shorter. In the excerpts above:

- The average words per sentence in the legal brief was 21.8.
- The average words per sentence in the excerpt from the scholarly book was 29.75.
- The average words per sentence in the Volkswagen ad was 10.

---

*Used with permission of Volkswagen Group of America, Inc.

Graf Length

High school English teachers often define paragraphs (we typically call them *grafs* in mass comm writing) as units of thought. They teach that paragraphs should develop an idea and include a topic sentence, supporting details and a summary sentence. For purposes of the rest of your career in mass comm, you can forget that.

Media grafs are units of typography, not units of thought.

And they are short. Sometimes, even one sentence. In advertising copywriting and feature copywriting, occasionally even one word.

Whether it's for newspapers, television, advertisements or the Internet, writing for mass media shares several important qualities.

Media writers keep grafs short for one reason: They are more readable. Long paragraphs, along with long words and long sentences, intimidate readers. Your high school English teacher may have taught you that you start a new paragraph when you change topics or introduce new ideas. But in media writing, how do you know when to start a new graf? When the old one gets too long to be readable—typically several lines of text. You start new grafs when you introduce new ideas or new speakers in a story that contains quoted matter. But you can also start a new graf just because you want to—to make the text more inviting-looking for your readers.

Overall Brevity

Media writers say what they want to say and then stop. They have learned to edit themselves ruthlessly and to delete unnecessary words—to keep the best and cut the rest. You can still find long-form journalism in some newspapers, magazines and news sites, but it's longer because it includes in-depth information that readers want, not because the writer would not take time to edit.

Blaise Pascal, a French mathematician and philosopher, once said, "I am sorry I have had to write you such a long letter, but I did not have time to write you a short one." That statement puzzles only nonwriters. Writers realize that to write briefly, you have to focus the piece and make every word count. That won't necessarily happen when you first put words on a screen, but media writers follow writing with editing and revision. They aren't afraid to cut, to re-focus, to move sentences and paragraphs around, and to delete everything that doesn't contribute to the piece.

Michelangelo is supposed to have explained his famous sculpture of David by saying that he began with a piece of stone and chipped away everything that didn't look like David. Writers relate to that. It may be a journalist telling the story of a shooting or an ad copywriter extolling the virtues of a product—the writer crafts the piece and then chips away everything that doesn't contribute substantially to the message.

Starting Right

Media writers start sentences with a subject and its modifiers, instead of "backing in." Paula LaRocque (2000) explains the issue in *The Book on Writing:*

> *We back into a sentence when we begin it with a preposition, verb, verbal, or with certain conjunctions and adverbs. Such a sentence is easy to recognize: It begins with a dependent phrase rather than with a sentence's subject, thereby delaying the subject and failing to make a clear point immediately.*

If someone asks how you did on your history test, do you answer, "Having studied all night in a marathon review session with several friends, I scored in the top echelon on the examination"? Or would you say, "I made an A. I pulled an all-nighter"? Don't make readers wade through long phrases or dependent clauses before they get to the subject. That's like someone showing up at your door to tell you that you have just won the sweepstakes, but first insisting on going through 10 minutes of limitations and conditions on the prize before telling you that you have won. It wouldn't make sense, and chances are you would slam the door on the contest representative before he ever got to the part about your winning the sweepstakes. And that, figuratively, is what readers do when writers make them wade through a lot of words before they get to the subject. Readers "slam the door" by moving on to the next story or ad.

Obviously, sentences are more readable when they begin with a subject, followed quickly by a verb. Another way to back into a sentence is by starting it with "there is" or "there are." *There* is a conjunctive adverb, not a subject. In the sentence *There are 15 students in this class*, the subject is *students*. A stronger sentence would be *Fifteen students are enrolled in this class*. Here are some more examples:

Correct, but weak: There is research that shows that studying results in higher grades
Better: Research shows that studying results in higher grades.
Correct, but weak: There was an incident in 2011 of a journalism student caught plagiarizing a story.
Better: A journalism student was caught plagiarizing a story in 2011.

Sentence Structure

Media writers use a number of techniques to make writing more readable. Remember, we're talking ease of reading here, not correctness. If you look back at the legal brief and the scholarly excerpts above, you'll note that the grammar, spelling and punctuation are perfect—but they're still hard to read. Here's what media writers routinely do to enhance the readability of their work:

They avoid putting too many ideas into a single sentence. Writer William Zinsser (1990) explained it this way:

> *One thought per sentence. Readers only process one thought at a time. So give them time to digest the first set of facts you want them to know. Then give them the next piece of information they need to know, which further explains the first fact. Be grateful for the period. Writing is so hard that all of us, once launched, tend to ramble. Instead of a period we use a comma, followed by a transitional word (and, while), and soon we have strayed into a wilderness that seems to have no road back out. Let the humble period be your savior.*

Although this seems similar to keeping sentences short, it's more than that. Media writers control the number of concepts or thought-chunks they introduce in a sentence.

Media writers prefer simple, Anglo-Saxon words to Latinized constructions. Words we borrowed from Latin tend to be longer and to end in *ion* or *ent*—maximization, implementation, communication, fulfillment. As the *Random House Guide to Good Writing* (Ivers 1991) explains, Anglo-Saxon words "tend to sound earthy and concrete, while Latin-derived words seem lofty and abstract." The Anglo-Saxon *rise* becomes *ascend* in Latin, *ask* becomes *interrogate*, fire becomes *conflagration*, fear becomes *trepidation* and *goodness* becomes *probity*. And you end up saying things like "prior to the implementation of the mandates" instead of "before the rules went into effect."

For more on readability formulas, scan this QR code or go to http://en.wikipedia.org/wiki/Readability

Beware of zombie nouns! They suck the life out prose like zombies suck out brains.

Scan this QR code or go to: http://bit.ly/SmpAKt

Media writers prefer active constructions to passive. The active voice of verbs emphasizes the agent of the action (The governor signed the bill). The passive voice emphasizes the receiver of the action (The bill was signed by the governor). Note that active sentences are more direct and concise. The passive voice uses a form of the verb *to be* followed by a past participle (in this case, *signed*) and a *by* phrase. If the *by* phrase is omitted, the reader will not know who or what performed the action (The bill was signed). There are times, of

A VISIT WITH YOUR WRITING COACH
Perspective: Good Writing in a Nutshell

Paula LaRocque

Introduction

http://snd.sc/LoURqG

course, when writers want to emphasize the recipient of the action over the actor—but when there is a choice, media writers typically prefer the active voice. It's tighter, clearer and easier to read.

Media writers sometimes violate the norms of traditional conventions. Notice we didn't say that media writers break grammar or punctuation rules. Not real rules anyway—only some of the conventions that we're sometimes taught in high school English. Like not beginning sentences with *and, but* or *or*. Like avoiding one-sentence grafs or even one-word grafs. Occasionally, you will find intentional sentence fragments or sentences with no verb in news or advertising or public relations copy.

Grammar and Style

Ever wonder why media writing teachers put so much emphasis on grammar and spelling and punctuation and Associated Press style—probably more emphasis on the conventions than you will find anywhere else at the university? It's not because media writers are fixated on *correctness*; it's because we're fixated on *readability*. The reason for all the emphasis on "getting it right" is that we don't want readers to notice anything but the writing. Grammar and spelling errors are distracting—if the reader stops even for a second to notice an error, the reading flow has been interrupted.

What media writers fixate on is grabbing a reader and holding him or her, pulling that reader into the story or ad. We don't want readers to notice that the grammar and punctuation were perfect—we don't want them thinking about those elements at all. So the emphasis in media writing classes on conventions is really an emphasis on avoiding distractions and anything that detracts from readability.

Word Choice

Writers are word people. They pay attention to the words they use, in the same way master chefs pay attention to the ingredients in their dishes. A nonwriter might slap words on the screen to fill space, but writers pay careful attention to words because their goal is to communicate meaning and to arrest and hold the attention of the reader. We see this in several ways:

A preference for concrete over abstract nouns and verbs. A novice writer might say *The woman bought a pet at the store*. But note the improvement when you make a simple noun substitution: *The woman bought a dog at the store*. And watch the improvement in the sentence as you continue to substitute more specific nouns and adjectives:

- *The woman bought a poodle at the store.*
- *The woman bought a French poodle at the store.*
- *Maggie Ballard bought a French poodle at Pet Land.*
- *Maggie Ballard bought a white French poodle at Pet Land.*
- *Maggie Ballard bought a fluffy white French poodle at Pet Land.*

Paula LaRocque

A VISIT WITH YOUR WRITING COACH
Overview of Tips for Good Writing

What is good writing?

http://snd.sc/LoV25z

Let's say the Volkswagen ad you read earlier was written like this:

In fact, some people who drive our car aren't impressed with our fuel economy.

Or savings on oil and engine fluids. And how you can drive farther on each set of tires.

That's because once you become accustomed to the various ways you can save money by driving our car, you don't even give consideration to them anymore.

Except when you park the car or buy cheaper insurance or save on repairs or trade in your VW.

Re-read the original copy below and compare it to what you just read. The "real" copy is more readable because it's concrete, not abstract:

In fact, some people who drive our little flivver don't even think 32 miles to the gallon is going any great guns.

Or using five pints oil instead of five quarts. Or never needing anti-freeze. Or racking up 40,000 miles on a set of tires.

That's because once you get used to some of our economies, you don't even think about them anymore.

Except when you squeeze into a small parking spot.

Or renew your small insurance. Or pay a small repair bill. Or trade in your old VW for a new one.

Avoiding wordiness, redundancies and clichés. Media writers need to make every word count. Writing guru William Zinsser (1990) put it this way: "Clutter is the disease of American writing. We are a society strangling in unnecessary words, circular constructions, pompous frills and meaningless jargon."

Speech is naturally wordy because we compose as we talk. But writing gives us the luxury of revision, so we need to make sure that we have chosen the most reader-friendly ways to express ourselves. This is really an editing issue more than a writing issue—because we are thinking on the screen as media writers, unnecessary words will inevitably find their way into our writing. That's only natural. But as media writers, we have to find them—and delete them.

Here are some everyday expressions that media writers routinely cut from their copy in favor of more efficient wording:

Pretentious words
- Utilizes (uses)
- Optimal (best)
- Assiduous (industrious)
- Cupidity (greed)

Wordy phrases
- In regard to (about)
- At this point in time (now)
- In the event that (if)
- Prior to (before)

Redundant adverbs
- Completely finish
- Connected together
- Totally destroyed

Redundant adjectives
- Time schedule
- Alternative choices
- Component parts
- All-time record
- Annual anniversary

Clichés
- Bitter end
- Calm before the storm
- Fall on deaf ears
- Nipped in the bud
- Witch hunt
- Worst-case scenario

For more on wordiness and clutter in your writing, scan this QR code or go to http://bit.ly/Hca2l0

You get the idea—but if you want lots more examples, scan the QR code in the box to the left. We inevitably use these inefficient and wordy constructions when we talk, and because media writers write like they talk, that wordiness creeps into our writing. Be on the lookout for it when you edit. Your writing will be leaner and stronger and easier to read when you take it out.

The Bottom Line

Media writers write everything from ad copy to news copy to the various forms of copy generated by public relations practitioners. And they do it across all media platforms. The types of writing may vary widely, but the basic techniques are much the same—they emphasize readability and reader-friendliness. This chapter has outlined several techniques you will find among all these professions. And as you can see, writing simply isn't always simple—it involves a number of techniques that writers employ to make text more accessible. Or as 19th-century novelist Nathaniel Hawthorne put it, "Easy reading is damn hard writing." In the coming chapters, you will see how media writers apply these techniques in different types of writing across a wide range of media.

Writing Simply

"Try to write like you're having a conversation with your best friend."
~ PHIL LAVELLE

"Clarity is crucial to good writing of any kind. Whether the communication is a news story, press release, letter, memo or report, its merit rests on its understandability. If it's unclear, it can only bewilder, annoy or mislead."
~ PAULA LAROCQUE

Nonwriters often believe complicated is better than simple, long is better than short, and wordy is better than terse. They write to impress, not to express. But they only impress other nonwriters. Writers are never impressed by needless complexity.

Typically, muddy or pretentious prose hides sloppy or careless thinking. Nonwriters will sometimes even say, "You're oversimplifying" or "You're dumbing down that idea." Actually, the best communicators have usually been the clearest communicators. Think of the straightforward prose of Ernest Hemingway or F. Scott Fitzgerald or Winston Churchill or Joan Didion or even Abraham Lincoln. President Lincoln spoke only two minutes at Gettysburg; the main orator, Edward Everett, spoke almost two hours. Everyone remembers the lean prose of the Gettysburg Address, but who remembers Everett or what he said?

Good writing avoids long, uncommon words, sentences and paragraphs that go on forever, and constructions that hide meaning rather than expose it. In fact, that type of writing is probably copied from bureaucrats who want to hide behind language rather than use it to communicate. So they talk about collateral damage rather than casualties, revenue enhancements rather than tax increases, ongoing highway maintenance programs rather than roadwork and technical adjustments rather than market drops.

A physics professor at New York University, Alan D. Skokal, once showed that pretentious language could hide the sloppiest of thinking. He wrote an article, published as serious scholarship in an academic journal, in which he said, among other things, that scientific discourse "for all its undeniable value, cannot assert a privileged epistemological status with respect to counter-hegemonic narratives emanating from dissident or marginalized communities" (Skokal, 1996). The thesis of his long-winded article? There's no real world; we made it up. No one caught on to the fact that Skokal had perpetrated a hoax on the academic community—a gag—until he confessed.

Too many nonwriters are victims of what writing coach Paula LaRocque calls the Diamond Jim Brady theory of communication. Brady, an American financier in the 1800s, became a millionaire by selling for a railroad supply company and investing his profits. Diamond Jim became known for his tasteless display of jewelry. When asked why he wore so many gaudy gems, he is said to have replied, "Them as has 'em wears 'em." LaRocque (2002) calls this "the paradox of good taste":

> *Good taste shows restraint and simplicity: Them as has 'em wears just one or two—but the right one or two. The rest stay in the safe for another occasion. It's the same with words. Owning many words informs and enriches our communication even when we leave most of them in the safe. And the more words we know, the surer and freer we are to choose the plainest, simplest words. After all, having knowledge is useful only if we can convey it clearly and briefly—and that means translating the complex into the simple. (p. 38)**
>
> For media writers, the antidote for obfuscation is simple: Write like you talk. When you write, instead of worrying about the "correct" way to frame a sentence, just put down the ideas as they come to you. When you finish, read it out loud. If you stumble over clauses and end each sentence out of breath, your sentences are too long. Make them shorter.
>
> When writers make something more complicated than it needs to be, they force readers to "translate" into understandable language. Too many readers give up.

References

Gray v. Martino. 103 (A. 24, 1918).

Ivers, M. 1991. *The Random House Guide to Good Writing.* New York: Ballantine.

Lanham, Richard. 1974. *Style: An Anti-Textbook.* New Haven, CT: Yale University Press.

LaRocque, Paula. 2000. *Championship Writing: 50 Ways to Improve Your Writing.* Oak Park, IL: Marion Street Press.

———. "Use Large Words Sparingly." *Quill* (December 20, 2002).

Schuster, E. H. "A Fresh Look at Sentence Fragments." *The English Journal* (May 2006): 78–83.

Skokal, A. "Transgressing the Boundaries: Towards a Transformative Hermeneutics of Quantum Gravity." *Social Text* (Spring/Summer 1996): 217.

Zinsser, William. 1990. *On Writing Well.* New York: HarperCollins.

———. "Writing English as a Second Language." *The American Scholar* (Winter 2010). http://bit.ly/qgjB7z.

---

* From "Use Large Words Sparingly" by Paula LaRocque, in *Quill*, December 20, 2002. Reprinted by permission of Paula LaRocque.

Skills Development: Practice in Media Writing

Exercise 1.1

Words and phrases in this exercise and the ones to follow are admittedly out of context. They will, however, give you an opportunity to think about conciseness in writing and eliminating wordiness. Some words and phrases can be improved in more than one way. Don't worry about looking for *the one right answer* so much as finding a way to improve each item. The goal here is to help you think about the many ways you can eliminate wordiness in writing. Replace each word or phrase with more concise wording.

1. a bigger/greater/higher/larger degree of: _____
2. a decreased number of: _____
3. a majority of: _____
4. a total of seven: _____
5. absolutely essential: _____
6. all of: _____
7. close proximity: _____
8. consensus of opinion: _____
9. despite the fact that: _____
10. due to the fact that: _____
11. few in number: _____
12. first and foremost: _____
13. for the purpose of: _____
14. for the reason that: _____
15. has (or needs) to: _____
16. in point of fact: _____
17. in reference to: _____
18. making a determination (decision): _____
19. past history: _____
20. small in size (number): _____
21. subsequent to the use of: _____

22 whether or not: _____

23 absolutely essential: _____

24 added bonus: _____

25 advance reservations: _____

26 advance planning: _____

27 advance warning: _____

28 all of: _____

29 all of a sudden: _____

30 all of these: _____

Exercise 1.2

Replace each word or phrase with more concise wording.

1. all-time record: _____
2. almost never: _____
3. any and all: _____
4. armed gunman: _____
5. as a means to: _____
6. as a result of: _____
7. assemble together: _____
8. at a later date: _____
9. at the conclusion of: _____
10. at the present time: _____
11. at this point in time: _____
12. autobiography of his [or her] life: _____
13. bald-headed: _____
14. based in large part on: _____
15. basic fundamentals: _____
16. basic necessity: _____
17. because of the fact of: _____
18. being that: _____
19. best ever: _____
20. blend together: _____
21. both of these/them/the: _____
22. by means of: _____
23. by the use of: _____
24. by virtue of [the fact that]: _____
25. came to a realization: _____

26 came to an abrupt end: _____

27 careful scrutiny: _____

28 classify into groups: _____

29 clearly articulate: _____

30 close down [up]: _____

31 close scrutiny: _____

Exercise 1.3

Replace each word or phrase with more concise wording.

1. collaborate together: _____
2. combine together: _____
3. come to the understanding: _____
4. common similarities: _____
5. compare and contrast: _____
6. complete stranger: _____
7. completely eliminate/destroy/annihilate: _____
8. conduct an investigation into: _____
9. connect[ed] together: _____
10. consensus of opinion: _____
11. continue on: _____
12. crisis situation: _____
13. depreciate in value: _____
14. despite the fact that: _____
15. disappear from sight: _____
16. during the course of: _____
17. each and every [one]: _____
18. economically deprived: _____
19. eliminate altogether: _____
20. emergency situation: _____
21. end result: _____
22. enter into: _____
23. exactly identical: _____
24. fall down: _____
25. few in number: _____

26 filled to capacity: _____

27 final destination/outcome: _____

28 first priority: _____

Exercise 1.4

Replace each word or phrase with more concise wording.

1. for the purpose of: _____
2. foreign imports: _____
3. free gift: _____
4. future plans/prospects: _____
5. gather together: _____
6. general consensus: _____
7. general public: _____
8. give consideration to: _____
9. grave crisis: _____
10. grow in size: _____
11. has had an effect upon: _____
12. heat up: _____
13. in excess of: _____
14. in light of the fact that: _____
15. in order to: _____
16. in the course of: _____
17. in the vicinity of: _____
18. in today's society: _____
19. inadvertent error: _____
20. is aware of the fact that: _____
21. joint collaboration: _____
22. joyous celebration: _____
23. kneel down: _____
24. lag behind: _____
25. large [small] in size: _____

18 Writing for Media Audiences

26 later on: _____

27 local residents: _____

28 look ahead to the future: _____

29 made/make an effort: _____

Exercise 1.5

Replace each word or phrase with more concise wording.

1. major breakthrough: _____
2. make a decision: _____
3. make contact with: _____
4. make/made reference to: _____
5. meet together: _____
6. mental attitude: _____
7. merge together: _____
8. mix together: _____
9. mutual agreement: _____
10. necessary prerequisite: _____
11. never before: _____
12. new invention/innovation: _____
13. new record: _____
14. new recruit: _____
15. nodded his head: _____
16. none at all: _____
17. nostalgia for the past: _____
18. old adage/custom: _____
19. on a daily basis: _____
20. on account of the fact that: _____
21. on the grounds that: _____
22. open up: _____
23. over and over again: _____
24. over exaggerate: _____
25. overall goal: _____

26 overall structure: _____

27 past experience: _____

28 past history: _____

29 past memories: _____

30 personal friend: _____

Exercise 1.6

Replace each word or phrase with more concise wording.

1. personal opinion: _____
2. plan ahead: _____
3. polar opposites: _____
4. previous/prior to: _____
5. protest against: _____
6. readily apparent: _____
7. refer/reflect/reply back: _____
8. scrutinize carefully: _____
9. serious danger: _____
10. shout loudly: _____
11. shrugged her shoulders: _____
12. small in size: _____
13. subsequent to: _____
14. sudden impulse: _____
15. sum total: _____
16. summarize briefly: _____
17. surrounded on all sides: _____
18. sworn affidavit: _____
19. take action: _____
20. terrible/horrible tragedy: _____
21. the final result: _____
22. the final conclusion: _____
23. the month of September: _____
24. the overall plan: _____
25. the reason why: _____

Exercise 1.7

Replace each word or phrase with more concise wording.

1. to make a plan/decision: _____
2. to make an acquisition: _____
3. to make an arrangement: _____
4. total destruction: _____
5. true fact: _____
6. 2 a.m. in the morning: _____
7. ultimate fate: _____
8. ultimate objective: _____
9. unexpected emergency: _____
10. unexpected surprise: _____
11. useless in function: _____
12. valuable asset: _____
13. very unique: _____
14. violent explosion: _____
15. visible to the eye: _____
16. warn in advance: _____
17. were in attendance: _____
18. will have an effect on: _____
19. with regard to: _____
20. witnessed firsthand: _____
21. young in age: _____

Exercise 1.8

Each of the following sentences contains a "be" verb that could easily be replaced by a simpler verb, making the sentence more reader friendly. We've done the first; you do the rest.

1. The law is applicable to working reporters.
   The law applies to working reporters.

2. Students are benefited by the policy.

3. The agreement is binding on both parties.

4. The negotiators are desirous of an answer by Friday.

5. The senator is in agreement with the president.

6. He will be in attendance at the meeting.

7. Their response is indicative of what you can expect from them.

8. The agreement has been in existence since 1979.

9. That professor is influential on many media writing students.

10. She is in receipt of the document.

11. The reactor will soon be operative.

12. The company was in violation of several clean-air regulations.

13. The committee was productive of a comprehensive report.

14. They are supportive of the candidate's position on the flat tax.

Exercise 1.9

Later on, we look specifically at advertising copywriting. But for now, let's play with ad copy as an example of readable writing.

Your assignment is to write 120–140 words of advertising copy. Re-read the ad copy for Volkswagen in this chapter—it's exactly 137 words. Your assignment is to write a block of ad copy for a product: scissors.

You can name the product yourself. Your selling proposition here is that your scissors are sharp and easy to handle, allowing you to finish your cutting work in less time than ever before.

Assume you have a headline and some art—a picture of some happy consumer using your scissors—and a copy block with a minimum of 120 and a maximum of 140 words (remember that Microsoft Word will count the words for you). Or to make this a more real-world exercise, go to Google Images (www.google.com/images) and find some art to use with the ad. Try to make it look as much like a typical magazine ad as possible. Use the principles of readable writing found in this chapter for your 120-140 word copy block.

Exercise 1.10

Assume you are the PR director for Acme Widget. Your new CEO calls you into the office and gives you the following memo. He says that he knows it's wordy and stilted, and he wants you to rewrite it. His instructions: "Rewrite it so it's something our employees will want to read, something everyone can understand."

Rewrite the memo, leaving out or adding what you need to. Use Microsoft Word to check the readability level of the document below, and see how much you can improve the readability when you rewrite.

Note: You may need to do a little Internet research on TQM before you write.

To: All Acme Widget Employees
Date: 1 May 2012
From: Mr. Preston Holloran, CEO
Re: New Procedures

I wish to express to one and all employees that I am tremendously exhilarated by the tremendous opportunity afforded to me as the CEO of Acme Widget. Employees will find the author's management style emphasizes the implementation of optimum operationalization, which, of course, leads to ultimate productivity and fiscal liquidity! Promotion of an effective working environment, based on the latest principles of Total Quality Management, will help launch the Acme brand to the top of our industrial milieu. As part of the new TQM strategy, a new, more open worker-manager communication strategy has been implemented, EFFECTIVE IMMEDIATELY. Issues or suggestions may now be brought to the management's attention via two avenues: a cork-product bulletin board in the break room and direct, interactive appointment. Suggestions may be anonymously posted in the break room as the board will be used as an interactive, division-wide interchange, with employees and the manager being offered the chance to interface in a public forum. The procedures for using the appointed board are as follows: Obtain an anonymous suggestion form from the author's secretary. Use the writing instrument of your choice to write the date and subject of the suggestion in the top lines provided on the form. Then legibly print the issue at hand within the parameters of the space thus provided. Commentary which is illegible will be disregarded. Employees who wish to discuss an issue with management directly may also do so via person-to-person appointment. Fifteen minute appointments will be available for assignment each Friday morning from 9 to 11 o'clock. You may also, should you prefer this method of communication, send an email to me at the following electronic address: holloran@acme.com. I welcome any and all interaction or discussion regarding ideas for the further improvement of Acme Widget.

Chapter Two

NEWSTHINKING: WHAT'S THE NEWS?

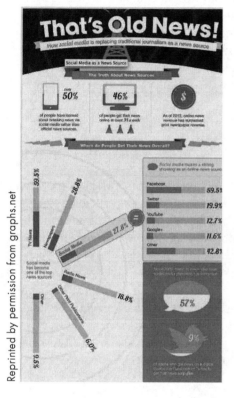

We'll start our journey toward developing competency at media writing where many professionals have started: newswriting. Over the years, writers in many fields have started as reporters. They ended up in sports promotion or corporate public relations or political PR or novel-writing or speechwriting or digital communications or fundraising or advertising, but they started as newswriters. In effect, they learned to write as reporters and then moved on to other types of writing.

Writers like Mark Twain, Ernest Hemingway, Tom Wolfe and Gay Talese all started as journalists. Even Stephen King's first writing gig was with his school newspaper.

No matter where you're ultimately heading with your career, newswriting is one of the best ways to develop a mass media style. Newswriting can be an important part of your writing training, even if you *never* want to work as a journalist. Why? Because newswriting teaches you how to find the most important information and to present it readably, in simple sentences and paragraphs, to people who will read it on the go—readers whose attention you must grab and hold.

Or look at it this way: Ever been to a track and seen runners running backward? Why were they doing that? There are, after all, no backward races. If you talk with one of these backward-runners, you'll find out that it's a valuable training regimen. People who can run miles without even breaking a sweat can try for the first time to run once around the track backward and feel that their legs are about to give out. That's because running backward uses a different set of muscles than running forward. Even though there will never be an opportunity to demonstrate their backward-running skills or participate in a backward race, they still do it—because it develops muscles they will use when they are running forward.

And that's why it's important to study newswriting, no matter what media career you are preparing for. The skills you learn are transferable to many other types of writing.

The movie "Karate Kid" demonstrates how we can learn something without realizing we're learning it. The old Karate master had his young student do some tasks he thought were irrelevant to learning to fight. Later on, he realized that he was learning important skills without being aware of it. Watch the clips at http://bit.ly/wYWG0r and you'll see why newswriting can be important, even for those students who don't plan journalism careers.

Finding the Story

The first step in newswriting isn't writing. It's identifying the news. The question of What's the news? is the most basic and most controversial part of newsgathering and writing. How do you decide—whether you're a journalist or a PR practitioner sending news releases to the media—whether something is newsworthy?

The definition of news has changed over the years. In the early days of American journalism, news was defined as something that happened in Europe several months previous. Communities were small and they learned about a lot of local goings-on by word of mouth, so what they wanted to know was what was happening in London and on the European continent. Much of their news came from London newspapers, so the news would have to be written and printed in London, put on a ship, and brought to an American newspaper where it was then turned into news for an American audience. It took months. But there were no other places to get the news from Europe (unless you met a traveler who had just returned), so this old news was still new to Americans.

But over the years, transportation speeded up, technology improved the speed at which news could be typeset and printed, and most important, the telegraph could take news anywhere telegraph wires could be strung. By the Civil War, readers could learn about a battle the day after it had been fought.

Changes in newspapers also affected the definition of news. For the first 150 or so years of American journalism, most crime news was not considered that important. Then, in the 1830s, the New York Sun began covering crime news as a beat. Following a trend that had become popular in London, the Sun sent a reporter to the police station, and a new genre of news was born—police/crime news. In the 1820s, the answer to the question *What is news?* was "mostly politics and government." But by 1840, the answer to that question was "anything readers are interested in—especially crime."

News Definitions

The definitions of news keep changing, along with changes in society. (The question of whether the news *reflects* changes in society or *brings about* changes in society is one you can discuss in a sociology class.) Let's look at some of the factors that currently determine whether news media see something as newsworthy. Look up *news* in the dictionary and you'll find it described as "a report of recent events or previously unknown information." But most of the things that happen in the world every day don't find their way into the newspaper or onto the air in a newscast. So what makes an *event* into *news*?

Timeliness. News is what happened recently. But it all depends on how you define *recently*. For some weeklies, if they are the only news medium in town, recently could be something that happened several days ago. (But the advent of social media is changing this definition even for weeklies. No longer are the weeklies "the only game in town," even if they are the only news medium in town. Weekly newspapers are discovering that Facebook has usurped much of their market for breaking news, forcing these newspapers to develop a social media presence themselves, as well as an online edition. They are discovering that they may be a weekly in print, but they need to be a daily online.)

For a daily newspaper, the definition of *timely* has traditionally been anything that happened since the last paper came out. But with people spending more and more time online, daily newspapers are finding that they cannot cover events as if they are breaking news if people are watching those events unfold on television or listening to them on radio or interacting with their friends about them on Facebook. We can now watch news occurring in real time, so the meaning of "timely news" now means virtually "news as it's happening."

College newspapers deal with this almost every day, as campus groups bring in information about events that may have been legitimately newsworthy—if the info hadn't been brought in 24 hours after it happened. An event that might have been newsworthy on Tuesday is barely worth a mention on Wednesday and ancient history by Thursday. The people who brought the announcement to the newspaper see it as newsworthy, but according to journalism's definition of timeliness, it's now irrelevant.

Impact. How many people are affected by the event? A gas tanker truck that overturns in a rural area and causes a road closure and the evacuation of a few farm families may not get much news coverage. But let that same truck overturn in an urban area, with the evacuation of a subdivision and a school and major traffic tie-ups, and you'll see an army of reporters and several news helicopters. If a local man is diagnosed with tuberculosis, that's news only to his family; but if he teaches in an elementary school and has exposed a lot of children, the impact on the community makes it major news.

Proximity. People are most interested in what happens close to home. If it's a community newspaper in a rural area, proximity might be the small town or the county. For that paper, what happens in the next county isn't news. For a metro area, proximity may be what happens in the city and the surrounding suburbs. But those suburbs may have newspapers or online news sites of their own that define *proximity* as only what happens in that suburb. For national TV shows, proximity is what happens in the United States (subject to the other definitions of news in this section) or anything that happens involving Americans.

Thus, we may never see news about Somalia on American TV because it doesn't meet the proximity test—it's too far away. But if what happens involves an American, it may be covered extensively. Few news events meet just one definition of news. Most news events involve several of these characteristics of newsworthiness. But proximity is important to newsworthiness. You may see nothing about an airplane crash in Siberia or central Africa, even if several people die. But a crash close to home, or involving people from your area, may dominate news coverage for days.

Conflict. Arguments and disagreements make news. It's human nature to be interested in stories that involve controversy or public debate. Imagine a political debate where the candidates were mostly in agreement on the issues. Then imagine another where the room was full of tension that erupted into arguments, finger-pointing, and charges and counter-charges.

Conflict makes news because conflict makes a story. In fact, that's the very definition of a story. A chronological account of happenings is a narrative. Add a problem—conflict—and you have a story. You read a novel because there is a conflict or problem and you want to see how it is resolved. In every murder mystery, someone is killed and the detectives spend the rest of the book or movie or TV show trying to resolve the "problem" of finding the killer.

The ultimate conflict, of course, is war—which is the biggest news that the media ever cover. Conflict doesn't always pit one person or group against another against another. Sometimes it is people against nature, as in the Hurricane Katrina stories, or people against disease, as in the coverage of the SARS outbreak. Individuals battling the bureaucracy or the legal system are also examples of stories involving conflict.

Prominence. Is a well-known person involved? If the event involves a celebrity, it is probably newsworthy. Do journalists write stories about divorces? Not usually. But if the couple is Katie Holmes and Tom Cruise, the divorce becomes major news. How about the robbery of a convenience store where the robber takes $100 from the cash register and a wallet and watch from a customer? Probably not news … unless the customer is the mayor of your city. Now the "probably not news" has become a front page story. And prominence can boost the newsworthiness of any story. A plane crash near your city is news already, but if well-known people are on board, it can go from being an important news story to a major news story, followed for many days by local media.

Oddity. Perhaps the most famous news proverb ever uttered is this one: "If a dog bites a man, that is not news. But if a man bites a dog, it's news!" The extraordinary and the unexpected appeal to human curiosity. See the "missing monkey" story below for a local editor's defense of his paper's coverage a missing monkey over a story about a local politician.

News values of the Web. Every new medium affects the news values of the media that were previously dominant. When radio joined newspapers as a news medium in the 1920s, it took away some of newspapers' dominance as a breaking news medium. People came to rely on radio's ability to get the news out first; radio announcers could read the news instantly on the air, without having to go through a lengthy writing, editing, production, and distribution process. Radio could not challenge newspapers' completeness of coverage or depth. But when it came to timeliness, newspapers could not complete.

Paula LaRocque

A VISIT WITH YOUR WRITING COACH
Less Really Is More: Keeping It Short

Keeping sentences short

http://snd.sc/LoV3q0

Then came TV, which presented the news with video in a way that captured the American imagination. But still, newspapers delivered the bulk of the news. Newspaper journalists reminded their readers that an entire 30-minute newscast, if set in type, would not cover the entire front page of a newspaper.

The missing monkey... should it have been featured on the front page of the newspaper? This editor defends his news Choices. Scan the QR code or go to http://bit.ly/z0gp0J.

The Web added a whole new dimension: podcasts like radio, video like television, and stories long and short. And all searchable and mostly free. All major print and broadcast media are also on the Web, along with many other small and large Web-only operations.

The Web redefined only one aspect of newsworthiness: timeliness. But it cornered the market on that. Now, when newspapers go to press, editors know there is a good chance that virtually every news item has already appeared on the Web, along with hypertext links that allow readers to explore the news in depth and comment boxes that allow them to interact with others about the news event and coverage of that event. All media have had to rethink which of the news values they will emphasize and reconsider what unique perspectives they can bring to the news.

Appeal to social media platforms. This new definition of news has been created by the growing popularity of social media. What makes events newsworthy for older media also makes them important on social media, but there they take on a life of their own. Traditional media have to take into account the fact that stories have already broken on Facebook and Twitter. Legacy media are one-way transmissions—journalists and editors publishing for the consuming public. Social media are interactive—news consumers reading and reacting to the news or occasionally even adding to it and becoming news disseminators themselves.

Traditional media prided themselves as being gatekeepers. They used the news values discussed earlier in this chapter to determine newsworthiness and passed on to the public what they determined to be news. And what about the events that were never written about, the stories that were never covered? Obviously they weren't news by the gatekeepers' definitions.

Social media changed that. Traditional gatekeepers are no longer the only game in town. Facebook and Twitter can now determine what's news. Social media are a jumble of all kinds of news, from what someone is having for dinner to YouTube videos of cute kittens to listicles to traditional national and international news stories. The *New York Times* explained the phenomenon of news on social media: "Hit the right note, and your readers become like bees, stopping by your site to grab links and heading back out on the Web to pollinate other platforms" (Carr 2012).

The Bottom Line

The question of *What is news?* is not only a debate for a graduate seminar in journalism; it's the daily dilemma of newspapers and TV news and radio news and Internet news sites. Only the Internet has the space for all the news that it could carry, but no medium has the professional staff to cover it. (This has led to the phenomenon of citizen journalism on the Internet, with readers becoming newsgatherers and writers, thus helping to determine news values.) Every day, editors and news directors must make decisions about what to cover and what to ignore. Those decisions remain the most controversial aspect of journalism.

References

Carr, David. "Significant and Silly at Buzzfeed." *The New York Times*, 6 Feb. 2012, sec. B.

Skills Development: Practice in Media Writing

Exercise 2.1

Pick up a print edition of your student newspaper. List each headline, and next to it write the news value that story represents. Many will have more than one.

Exercise 2.2

Look at a week's worth of articles in your campus newspaper or online news site. Tell what news is being left out. How is *news being defined in the medium you chose*? After the class compiles a list of the types of news the paper or news site seems to be neglecting, invite the editor in to react to your class list.

Exercise 2.3

Many news media have adopted a *digital first* philosophy—perhaps your campus media are among them. Basically, *digital first* is a process that puts digital delivery over print delivery. When news breaks, it immediately goes onto the Web, rather than being held for print. *Digital first* means media prioritize audience over content, and they get the news to their audience immediately—perhaps first on Twitter, then on Facebook, then on their website, and finally in print. If your campus media, or local media, have adopted a *digital first* philosophy, investigate what that means and how it affects their news definitions.

Exercise 2.4

Do some personal research among friends and acquaintances outside journalism and mass communications. Ask about how they use Twitter and Facebook to get news. Do they "like" news organizations on Facebook and use it to keep up with current events? Do they follow the news on Twitter?

Exercise 2.5

Each of the following stories appeared over a period of a week in the Fort Worth Star-Telegram. Under each lead, identify the news value(s) represented in the story.

1. Tarrant County is the 24th-healthiest county overall in Texas but ranks worse than the state average in several specific areas that affect health, including air pollution and sexually transmitted infections, according to a new report. (Branch 2012)

    News value(s): _____

2. Authorities appealed for help on Tuesday in locating an ex-convict who escaped from police and deputies in Johnson County on Monday after attempting to run over one of them, the sheriff's office said. (Ramirez 2012b)

    News value(s): _____

3. A former Texas Wesleyan University chemistry professor was in federal custody Monday, accused of downloading and trading child pornography for about 10 years, according to federal authorities. (Ramirez 2012a)

    News value(s): _____

4. A Mississippi traveling evangelist who often spoke to Texas youth groups—including several times at a Southlake church—is accused of secretly filming women and girls as young as 17 as they undressed in bathrooms, police agencies said. (Barbee 2012)

    News value(s): _____

5. Retired Airman Colton Read and his wife sued the U.S. government for millions of dollars in federal court Friday, asserting that military surgeons botched a routine gallbladder procedure so badly that civilian doctors had to amputate his legs to save his life. (Vaughn 2012)

    News value(s): _____

6. For the first time in history, the U.S. military hosted an event for soldiers and others who don't believe in God, with a gathering sort of like a county fair Saturday on the main parade ground at one of the world's largest Army bases. (Breen 2012)

    News value(s): _____

7. A man was taken to John Peter Smith Hospital for a mental evaluation Friday after police say he stripped off his clothes at a downtown Fort Worth church, sped off in his car and crashed. (Boyd 2012)

    News value(s): _____

Exercise 2.6

For each potential news story, give the news value(s) that might cause that event to be treated as news on your campus. When the events are similar, like 2-4, tell which is the bigger news—and why.

1. The president of your university changes places with a freshman biology major as part of his President for a Day program. The student goes to the president's office for meetings and other official functions and the president attends all the student's classes.

    News value(s): _____

2. City police arrest a college freshman and charge him with possession of marijuana.

    News value(s): _____

3. City police arrest the chairperson of your Faculty Senate and charge her with possession of marijuana.

    News value(s): _____

4. City police arrest the director of your campus Drug and Alcohol Abuse Program and charge her with possession of marijuana.

    News value(s): _____

5. The women's soccer coach at your university is named Coach of the Year by your athletic conference.

    News value(s): _____

6. The women's soccer coach at your university is chosen to referee at the World Cup.

    News value(s): _____

7. Former Secretary of State Condoleezza Rice will visit your campus to speak at Honors Day next month.

    News value(s): _____

8. Oprah Winfrey will visit your campus to speak at Honors Day next month.

    News value(s): _____

9. A history professor reports that two laptops, an iPad and an iPhone were stolen from his office a week before Thanksgiving.

    News value(s): _____

10. A history professor reports that a 1914 Babe Ruth rookie card was stolen from his office a week before Thanksgiving.

    News value(s): _____

11 A history professor reports that a 1949 Babe Ruth rookie card was stolen from his office the day before the World Series starts.

News value(s): _____

12 A Native American graveyard is discovered by workers as they prepare to build a new parking garage on your campus.

News value(s): _____

13 A Native American graveyard is discovered by workers as they prepare to build a new football field on your campus.

News value(s): _____

14 Food poisoning outbreak closes dining hall on your campus.

News value(s): _____

15 Food poisoning outbreak closes dining hall on a nearby campus.

News value(s): _____

16 Food poisoning outbreak closes dining hall on nearby campus – a dining hall operated by the same company that operates your campus dining hall.

News value(s): _____

17 Truck stops for gas near campus. Back gate is left ajar and three pigs escape and run through the center of your campus. Campus police give chase.

News value(s): _____

18 Trustees raise tuition by 10 percent.

News value(s): _____

19 Faculty senate passes resolution urging trustees to rescind tuition hike.

News value(s): _____

20 Students protest tuition hike with a sit-in at administration building.

News value(s): _____

References

for Chapter 2 exercises

Barbee, Darren. *Fort Worth Star-Telegram*, April 2, 2012. http://www.star-telegram.com/2012/04/02/3855183/traveling-evangelist-accused-of.html#storylink=cpy.

Boyd, Deanna. *Fort Worth Star-Telegram*, March 30, 2012. http://www.star-telegram.com/2012/03/30/3848244/naked-man-crashes-car-in-downtown.html#storylink=cpy.

Branch, Alex. *Fort Worth Star-Telegram*, April 3, 2012. http://www.star-telegram.com/2012/04/02/3855288/how-healthy-is-tarrant-county.html#my-headlines-default#storylink=cpy.

Breen, Tom. *Fort Worth Star-Telegram*, March 31, 2012. http://www.star-telegram.com/2012/03/31/3850753/military-holds-event-for-atheists.html#storylink=cpy.

Ramirez, Domingo. *Fort Worth Star-Telegram*, April 2, 2012a. http://www.star-telegram.com/2012/04/02/3855108/former-texas-wesleyan-chemistry.html#storylink=cpy.

———. *Fort Worth Star-Telegram*, April 3, 2012b. http://www.star-telegram.com/2012/04/03/3856908/ex-con-escapes-from-johnson-county.html.

Vaughn, Chris. *Fort Worth Star-Telegram*, April 1, 2012. http://www.star-telegram.com/2012/04/01/3850919/former-airman-sues-us-after-losing.html#storylink=cpy.

Chapter Three

GETTING STARTED: SHAPING THE NEWS STORY

Once a media writer decides that something is newsworthy, the next step is to take the information and present it as a news story—concise, readable, tightly focused and in a format that meets the requirements of the medium for which it is being written. In the next chapter, we begin at the beginning, with the lead. But first let's look at some newswriting conventions. The following principles will guide your writing the rest of this semester and throughout your career in media writing.

The basic news questions. Square 1 in any journalism class is typically the still-relevant basic news questions. Rudyard Kipling said it poetically in his poem "I Keep Six Honest Serving Men":

I keep six honest serving-men

(They taught me all I knew);

Their names are What and Why and When

And How and Where and Who.

Two of these questions (*who* and *what*) are found in virtually every story. Two more (*when* and *where*) are also typically important, though not the focus of the story in most cases. The last two (*how* and *why*) sometimes make it in, and are occasionally even central to the story, but also can require special handling by the writer.

Most stories are *who* stories or *what* stories. They feature who did something, or something that happened. Here's a *who* story from the Fort Worth Star-Telegram:

First lady Michelle Obama will visit North Texas next week on a three-day tour marking the second anniversary of her Let's Move! initiative to address childhood obesity. (First lady 2012)*

That's both a *who* story and a *what* story, but since it involved the first lady, the emphasis is on the *who*. Sometimes it's a *who* story and the person is not well known, so media writers use a general description of the *who* and then move on to the *what*, as in this example from the Star-Telegram:

One man was stabbed with a golf club shaft and was "close to death" after a brawl last month at a golf course at Eagle Mountain Lake. Clay Carpenter, 48, of Springtown said he is recovering from a punctured femoral artery and massive blood loss. He said the brawl broke out when his group of three tried to play through the group in front of them. (Mitchell 2012)*

The news value here is oddity—people fighting and one suffering a serious injury in a fight about who would play first on a golf course. The news is the *what*, a serious injury, but the man who was injured was not well known, so note that he was not identified until the second graf.

Most news is about what happened. A person might be mentioned, but the story is about what happened to that person:

Arlington police have arrested a suspect in the stabbing death of a woman found inside her apartment Saturday. (Branch 2012a)

Fire investigators ruled that an arsonist started a blaze Saturday night that killed a 90-year-old man and his 67-year-old nephew who used a wheelchair, authorities said Sunday afternoon. (Ramirez 2012)*

---

* From the *Fort Worth Star-Telegram*, 2012. Reprinted by permission.

The basic questions of who, what, when, where how and why are crucial pieces in just about any story. While not every news story has all six, many do.

Tarrant County Republicans favored Rick Santorum over the other remaining presidential candidates at a straw poll and candidates fair Saturday. (Batheja 2012)*

Note that each of the previous leads has a time element: *when* something happened. In the first lady story, the *when* element isn't something that has already happened, but news of when something will happen next week.

How and *why* elements are a little trickier. To describe how something happened, journalists who were not present at a news event have to use an authoritative source for the *how* or *why* elements and attribute them to their information source. In the fire story above, the *why* is the featured element: The story tells why a house burned down, killing two people, and attributes the news to an arson investigator.

The inverted pyramid. The first stories you ever heard were the bedtime stories that inevitably began, "Once upon a time …" These stories proceeded in traditional narrative fashion, beginning at the beginning and moving—quickly or slowly, depending on the storyteller—toward a climax. In the beginning of the story you found out there were three little pigs with different personalities and work ethics. And then you found about the houses they built, and so forth. The storyteller then introduced the Big Bad Wolf, who wanted to make a meal of the pigs. The story proceeded through the wolf's success in gaining entry to houses made of straw and sticks and his eventual attempt to break into a house made of stone. Bad mistake. He ended up dead in a pot of boiling water. The organizational pattern of those stories, and most novels, is chronological—following a time sequence from beginning to end.

But let's say you lived across the street from the third pig and saw the action go down. You saw the wolf huffing and puffing to blow the house down and then climbing onto the roof in frustration so he could gain entry through the chimney. You heard him yelp in pain as he hit the boiling water and saw the paramedics and police arrive soon after. If you were telling someone else what happened in your neighborhood that day, would you begin with *Once upon a time there were three little pigs*?

Or would you begin by saying "This wolf got killed across the street today. Dude tried to crawl down my neighbor's chimney"? Important breaking news is often told in what journalists call an "inverted pyramid." We tell news beginning with the most important information. Then we proceed to give more important information before less important information. If you look at the traditional story format as a metaphorical pyramid, beginning with introductory information and ending with a climax, the inverted pyramid begins with the climax—or at least the information most important to the reader.

That's been the norm in journalism since roughly the 1860s, when newspapers began to cover battles not as stories of approaching armies and initial skirmishes and eventual conflict, but beginning instead with the battle's outcome. That's much the same way we would cover another kind of battle today, say, a sports battle between two teams. Note the beginning of this account of a college basketball game:

LaMarcus Reed scored 20 of his 22 points in the second half to lead UT Arlington to its 13th win in a row, 69-61 over Central Arkansas on Saturday. (UTA Men 2012)*

The most important thing in a basketball game is the outcome, which is featured in this lead. But note that the writer also made it into a *who* lead to feature the player who led his team to victory. The following article by writing coach Chip Scanlan (Scanlan 2003) examines how today's journalists view the inverted pyramid.

---

* From the *Fort Worth Star-Telegram*, 2012. Reprinted by permission.

Writing from the Top Down
The Pros and Cons of the Inverted Pyramid

~ Chip Scanlan

Developed more than a century ago to take advantage of a new communications technology, the inverted pyramid remains a controversial yet widely used method of reporting news and will have a future in the 21st century, journalists in all media agree.

The inverted pyramid puts the most newsworthy information at the top, and then the remaining information follows in order of importance, with the least important at the bottom.

Historians argue over when the form was created. But they agree that the invention of the telegraph sparked its development so that it had entered into common use by newspapers and the newly formed wire service organizations by the beginning of the 20th century.

Journalism historian David T. Z. Mindich argues that one of the first inverted pyramid leads was written by an Associated Press reporter after Abraham Lincoln was assassinated in April 1865:

To The Associated Press

Washington, Friday, April 14, 1865

The President was shot in a theater to-night and perhaps mortally wounded.

The pyramid has to be big at the top because it must answer all the questions that readers have. Remaining information is arranged in diminishing order of importance.

The conventions of the inverted pyramid require the reporter to summarize the story, to get to the heart, to the point, to sum up quickly and concisely the answer to the question: What's the news? The pyramid approach addresses the most important questions at the top of the story. It states the thesis and then provides supporting material.

According to one journalism historian, one of the first inverted pyramid news leads was written about the death of Abraham Lincoln. That means the inverted pyramid is well over a century old.

Journalism has a love-hate relationship with the inverted pyramid. Its supporters consider it a useful form, especially good for breaking news. The inverted pyramid, or at least its most substantial element "the summary lead," is used widely and is one of the most recognizable shapes in communications today. You'll find it on the front and inside pages of most newspapers, as well as in stories distributed worldwide by The Associated Press, Reuters and other news services elsewhere on the Internet.

"The inverted pyramid organizes stories not around ideas or chronologies but around facts," says journalism historian Mitchell Stephens in "A History of News." "It weighs and shuffles the various pieces of information, focusing with remarkable single-mindedness on their relative news value."

Critics of the inverted pyramid say it's outdated, unnatural, boring, artless, and a factor in the declining readership that newspapers have been grappling with for decades.

The inverted pyramid, its critics say, is the anti-story. It tells the story backward and is at odds with the storytelling tradition that features a beginning, middle, and end. Rather than rewarding a reader with a satisfying conclusion, the pyramid loses steam and peters out, in a sense defying readers to stay awake, let alone read on.

Despite decades of assaults, the pyramid survives.

In the memorable phrase of Bruce DeSilva of The Associated Press, "The inverted pyramid remains the Dracula of journalism. It keeps rising from its coffin and sneaking into the paper."

There are good reasons for this staying power.

Many readers are impatient and want stories to get to the point immediately. In fast-breaking news situations, when events and circumstances may change rapidly, the pyramid allows the news writer to rewrite the top of the story continually, keeping it up-to-date.

It's also an extremely useful tool for thinking and organizing because it forces the reporter to sum up the point of the story in a single paragraph. Journalism students who master it and then go on to other fields say it comes in handy for writing everything from legal briefs to grant applications.

The inverted pyramid and summary lead can be a challenging form for some journalists. At least, it was for me when I began reporting. Summing up three hours of a school board meeting or trying to answer the five W's about a fatal car accident in a single paragraph, then deciding what other information belonged in the story—and in what order—was arduous and frustrating, especially with the clock ticking to deadline.

Also, as a beginner, I usually didn't have the knowledge of the subjects I covered to easily answer the central question posed by the event: What was newsworthy about it, and in what order of importance? I resisted the disciplined thinking the pyramid demands, and like many reporters, scorned the form as uncreative and stilted. I preferred the storytelling approach of the fiction writer to the "just the facts" style of the reporter.

Over time, it became easier, and I came to see that the form helps develop the powers of critical thinking, analysis, and synthesis that are the foundation of clarity in thinking and writing. The inverted pyramid is a basic building block of journalistic style.

In the days of "hot type" printing, when stories had to be trimmed to fit a finite space, the inverted pyramid allowed editors, even the compositors who made up the pages in the back shop, to cut stories from the bottom up: no news judgment required. Technology continues to wield its influence. With studies showing that those who get their news from computers don't want to look at more than a screen at a time, it's not surprising that the inverted pyramid is widely used by online news organizations.

Like it or not, reporters in the 21st century have to be familiar with the form.

From *Reporting and Writing: Basics for the 21st Century*, by Chip Scanlan (1999). By permission of Oxford University Press, Inc.

Leads and lead length. The lead (some journalists spell it lede) is the first graf of your news story. Most journalists believe it's the most important graf because many readers look only at the lead to determine if they will read a story. It's a little like a department store window—you have to display something to entice the customer into the store.

The first step toward writing a good lead is to find the story's focus. Sometimes it helps to use the "tell-a-friend" technique: If you were telling this story to a friend, where would you start? If you covered your university's board of trustees meeting, and the board voted to raise tuition next year by 10 percent, would you call a friend and say: "The board met today at 2 p.m. to consider several controversial funding issues, including a tuition increase and a proposal to build a new parking garage"? Of course not. You'd say, "The board just raised tuition by 10 percent!"

That tells you where the focus of your lead needs to be. Leads should get to the point and tell the most important news. Writing coach Donald Murray (quoted in Hall), author of "Writing for Your Readers," said: "Three seconds and the reader decides to read or move on to the next story. That's all the time you have to catch the reader's glance and hold it; all the time you have to entice and inform."*

Let's assume you are writing a story about a residence that burned down last night. The house was destroyed. Here's what you have:

Who: we don't have one in this story

What: an empty house burned down

When: last night (but use the day of the week to avoid confusion on the when)

Where: 2000 block of West Berry Street (People typically want to know where something happened. Remember the proximity principle: It's bigger news to them if they live or work near there, or they know someone in the area.)

That will give you a lead like this:

Passive voice lead: A house in the 2000 block of West Berry Street was destroyed by fire Tuesday night.

Or using the active voice to get to the point quicker: Fire destroyed a house in the 2000 block of West Berry Street Tuesday night.

But let's assume a person in the house was killed in the fire. The news is now that a person died, not that property was destroyed.

So: *An 80-year-old Fort Worth man died when his home in the 2000 block of West Berry Street was destroyed by fire Tuesday night, fire department officials said.*

Why the attribution when the man died, but not when the house was destroyed? We discuss this more in a later chapter, but basically because you could have driven by the house on Tuesday night and seen that it was destroyed. But you couldn't have driven by and known that an 80-year-old man had died in the fire.

Let's look at another:

What: a 52-year-old Tioga man arrested by Denton County Sheriff's deputies

More about what: man found with an open bottle of wine and smelling like alcohol

When: early Monday/just after midnight

Why: suspicion of public intoxication

Where: outside the First Baptist Church on South Fifth Street in Sanger

Your source: Tom Reedy, spokesperson, Denton County Sheriff's Department

Your lead may look something like this:

A 52-year-old Tioga man was arrested early Monday on suspicion of public intoxication outside a Sanger Church in Denton County, authorities say.

But what if the man was well-known country singer Randy Travis? Here's the way the story read in the online edition of the Star-Telegram (Branch 2012b) later on the day of his arrest:

Country music singer Randy Travis was arrested early Monday on suspicion of public intoxication outside a Sanger church in Denton County, authorities said.

---

* Reprinted from *Beginning Reporting*–http://www.courses.vcu.edu/ENG-jah/BeginningReporting/Writing/newslead.htm. Copyright © Jim Hall. Reprinted by permission.

Just after midnight, a Sanger police officer investigating a suspicious vehicle at First Baptist Church on South 5th Street reportedly found Travis with an open bottle of wine and smelling like alcohol, said Tom Reedy, spokesman for the Denton County Sheriff's Department.

Travis was booked into Denton County Jail about 1:30 a.m., he said. He was released several hours later with a Class C misdemeanor citation.

Travis owns property in nearby Tioga.*

When writing a lead, there are several principles to guide you:

Principle #1: First, find the news. If there are several news elements, find the most important one.

Principle #2: Begin your lead with that important news.

Principle #3: Write an active voice lead unless you need to emphasize *who* or *what* something happened to, rather than the active agent. For example: If you had been writing news the day President Kennedy was shot, you would not have written an active voice lead that started, "Dallas resident Lee Harvey Oswald shot and killed President John F. Kennedy …" You would have written a passive lead that emphasized the president: "President John F. Kennedy was shot and killed by an assassin Thursday."

Principle #4: Keep the lead short. Different newspapers and news sites have different philosophies on this, but most try to keep leads somewhere in the 25-word range. You will note that The Washington Post and The New York Times routinely write much longer leads. You will also see two-sentence leads occasionally in the media, but for now, since you're starting your media writing career, keep them shorter. Writing short, once-sentence leads will ensure you get the most important facts high in the story.

Graf length. Remember that news grafs are not at all like the paragraphs your English teacher taught you about. In English composition classes, perhaps you were taught that paragraphs were units of thought and should develop, support, and summarize ideas. That's a technique of formal and academic writing, not media writing.

In media writing, a graf is a unit of typography. When do you start a new one? You'll love this answer: Anytime you want to, typically when the graf you're writing looks a little long. Shorter paragraphs look more inviting to readers. And online and with mobile devices, that's even truer. Ever tried to read a long graf on an iPhone screen?

Opinion. When writing news, leave out your opinion. The possibility of objectivity is hotly debated in journalism circles today, because there are many ways to slant the news. The people you choose to interview can reflect a bias, as can the amount of space or time a medium gives to reporting the story. Even the placement of quotes can reflect bias: If the pro-abortion quotes are near the top of the story and the anti-abortion quotes are near the end, that reflects a bias because many readers never read the second half of stories.

Most problems in this area are actually unintentional, rather than the effort of a writer to slant the news. Unattributed opinion can make it appear the writer is taking a position that the source is actually taking. It may seem natural to say that "a tragic accident took the lives of two students Saturday night," but it's not the newswriter's call to label something as "tragic." The events should speak for themselves. Writing that a "large crowd of demonstrators" greeted the president is actually an opinion, because who is to determine the meaning of "large"? In some places, 20 demonstrators might be a large crowd; in other places, 50 would be a small crowd.

---

* From the Fort Worth Star-Telegram, 2012. Reprinted by permission.

What else? There are other common news lead conventions, like these:

- Leads are typically written in past tense, unless they refer to a future event.
- Attribution is common, so readers can know where the information presented comes from, and thus judge its veracity on their own.
- Time elements are used in almost every lead to tell the reader when the event occurred.
- News is written in third person. Newswriters make it "the United States," not "our country," and "the growing deficit faced by the nation," not "the growing deficit we face."
- Media writers use names in leads when the names are widely recognizable, and other descriptors when they are not. In the story above about the 80-year-old Fort Worth man who died in the fire, the name would typically be used at the beginning of the second graf. But if the man had been a city council member, the name would have been used in the lead. In the Randy Travis lead above, when we thought he was an anonymous 52-year-old Tioga man, his name was not in the lead. But since he was singer Randy Travis, we used his name in the lead.

The Bottom Line

When Milton Bradley introduced the board game Othello in the 1970s, the advertising slogan was "A minute to learn, a lifetime to master." And that could almost be said of news leads. You can read this chapter in only a few minutes. And the principles of writing news leads are basic: Decide what the news is, put it in the lead, begin the lead with that information, keep it short. Simple. But it takes practice to do it well.

So let's get started. You understand the basics now—and there's probably nothing wrong with your lead-writing style that actually writing a lot of leads won't fix.

Paula LaRocque

A VISIT WITH YOUR WRITING COACH
Be Wary of Fad, Cliché and Jargon

Avoiding fad, cliché and jargon

http://snd.sc/LoV5ye

References

Batheja, Aman. "Santorum Wins in Straw Poll of Republicans in Tarrant." *Fort Worth Star-Telegram*, February 4, 2012. http://www.star-telegram.com/2012/02/06/3715873/man-nearly-killed-in-brawl-at.html#storylink=omni_popular#storylink=cpy.

Branch, Alex. *Fort Worth Star-Telegram*, February 6, 2012a. http://www.star-telegram.com/2012/02/06/3714606/singer-randy-travis-arrested-in.html#storylink=cpy.

———. "Randy Travis Arrested, Cited for Public Intoxication." *Fort Worth Star-Telegram*, February 7, 2012b. http://www.star-telegram.com/2012/02/06/3715889/randy-travis-arrested-cited-for.html.

"First Lady Will Visit Fort Worth Next Week." *Fort Worth Star-Telegram*, February 6, 2012. http://www.star-telegram.com/2012/02/03/3710679/first-lady-to-visit-fort-worth.html#storylink=cpy.

Hall, Jim. *Beginning Reporting*. n.d. http://www.courses.vcu.edu/ENG-jeh/Beginning Reporting/Writing/newslead.htm.

McFarland, Susan. "Man Arrested in Woman's Stabbing Death in Arlington Apartment." *Fort Worth Star-Telegram*, February 4, 2012. http://www.star-telegram.com/2012/02/06/3715873/man-nearly-killed-in-brawl-at.html#storylink=omni_popular#storylink=cpy.

Mitchell, Mitch. "Man Nearly Killed in Brawl at DFW Golf Course." *Fort Worth Star-Telegram*, 2012. http://www.star-telegram.com/2012/02/06/3715873/man-nearly-killed-in-brawl-at.html#storylink=omni_popular#storylink=cpy.

Ramirez, Domingo. "House Fire in Fort Worth Was Set by Arsonists, Investigators Say." *Fort Worth Star-Telegram*, February 5, 2012. http://www.star-telegram.com/2012/02/06/3715873/man-nearly-killed-in-brawl-at.html#storylink=omni_popular#storylink=cpy.

Scanlan, Chip. "Writing from the Top Down: Pros and Cons of the Inverted Pyramid." *Poynter* (June 20, 2003). http://www.star-telegram.com/2012/02/06/3715873/man-nearly-killed-in-brawl-at.html#storylink=omni_popular#storylink=cpy.

"UTA Men Outlast Central Arkansas 69-61." *Fort Worth Star-Telegram*, February 5, 2012. http://www.star-telegram.com/2012/02/06/3715873/man-nearly-killed-in-brawl-at.html#storylink=omni_popular#storylink=cpy.

Skills Development: Practice in Media Writing

Exercise 3.1

Pick up both a local newspaper and your college newspaper. Choose five stories from each. For each story, fill in the following. The *who* may be a person, an animal, an organization, or any "actor" causing results, like a tornado. There may be more than one *who* and more than one *what*, and not all stories will contain each of the news elements.

Who: _____

What: _____

When: _____

Where: _____

Why: _____

How: _____

Exercise 3.2

Write leads only for the following stories. Your instructor may choose to have you write the second graf, too. The story facts, like all fact sets you will find in this book, include errors in AP style. You will need to correct those when you write.

Who? First Baptist Church in your city

Another who: stained glass artist was Johnny Devine of Missoula, Montana

What? FBC is having a dedication this Sunday. What they are dedicating is four absolutely stunning stained glass windows that will be a credit to this church, to our city, and to the Lord himself. The windows depict the miracles of Jesus. Miracles shown in glorious display in the windows are the feeding of the 5000, the turning of water to wine, the raising of Lazarus, and Jesus walking on the water. The windows will be on the west side of the church, facing Rosemont Avenue.

Where: FBC is proudly located at 4332 Church Street.

When: The dedication will be at the 11 AM worship service of the church this coming Sunday.

Another when: The windows were installed last week.

Also: Everyone is invited. This should be a highlight of our year and a really uplifting time for all who attend.

Who? A local woman, Juanita Ramirez, a 30-year-old nail technician; also two paramedics, Randy Embry and Carl Presley, who work for Central City Ambulance Service.

What? A 911 caller said a pickup truck had flipped over on Interstate 30. The truck went into the center median and flipped, coming to rest upright on top of the steel cable that divides the westbound and eastbound lanes, the caller said. The paramedics were only one mile away when they got the call about the accident. They rushed to the scene and found the pickup truck in flames. They pulled Ramirez out. You could say she was one lucky woman

When? The call came in at 9:15 a.m. The paramedics pulled her out of the burning truck minutes later.

Where? The accident was at the 7th St. exit off interstate thirty.

When? Assume that today is May 10. The record low occurred at 2 a.m. The previous record for May 10 had been set in 1913.

What? A record for low temperatures on May 10 occurred last night. It hit 32 degrees. That's freezing. The previous low for May 10 was 38 degrees. You can blame an Alaskan cold front that passed through the county. Temps are warming today, with a predicted high in the Sixties.

Who? Dr. Mansour is associate professor mathematics. Students are Francine McIntosh, a senior from Miami, Florida; Zeno Forbush, a junior from Atlanta; Rylie Poston, a junior from Aberdeen, Washington; Josh Mann, a senior from Seattle. All of these people are math majors.

What? The campus Math Society elected officers last night. McIntosh is president; Forbush is vice president; Poston is secretary; and Mann is treasurer. After the election, the advisor to the society, Dr. Alfred Mansour, presented an informative talk on proposed changes in the math curriculum for the Department of Mathematics. After Dr. Mansour's informative PowerPoint presentation, everyone enjoyed pizza and soft drinks. Members said it was one of the best meetings all year!

When? Election was held at 8 p.m.

Where? Room 244 of the Masterson Technology Center on campus.

Who? Emma Smith, senior, biology major; Taylor Smith, senior, English major; Sam Pitcock, senior, history major; Rufus Jones, senior, PR major; Maxine Albright, senior, Kaitlyn Breese, senior, modern dance major; Maxine Jacobs, senior, sociology major.

What? These students from your campus chosen as Fulbright scholarship winners. This is a record. Top number chosen for anyone year previously is four. 25 students at the university applied. 12 were finalists. These were actually chosen. The Fulbright program chooses top American university students to travel all over the world. These students will travel, do research, and serve as teaching assistants.

When? chosen yesterday

Who? Clyde – an elephant owned by the Ramirez Bros. Circus. Clyde is one of eight elephants owned by the circus.

What? Clyde was shot in a drive-by shooting. Clyde was hit by a bullet in his shoulder. Bullet was fired by a white SUV that slowed down on Collins Avenue, which runs past the parking lot where the elephants were being exercised. Only one bullet was fired, hitting Clyde. The circus veterinarian says Clyde should make a full recovery. Ramirrez Bros. is offering a $10,000 reward for information about the shooter.

When? This morning.

Where? Outside the Hoskins County Arena downtown, where the Ramirez Bros. Circus was camped. The circus is performing this week in the arena. The elephants were being exercised in the parking lot of the arena this morning.

Why? Police said they have no motive and no suspects in the shooting.

Chapter Four

The Associated Press Stylebook: Bringing Consistency to Media Writing

Students learning how media writing works are sometimes confused by the word *style*, a word often used differently by media practitioners than by other professional writers. At the university, when you hear professors talk about style, they generally use it in the sense of the unique approach of every writer. Perhaps you have heard Hemingway's style contrasted with Faulkner's style—referring to the length of sentences and paragraphs and the pace of their prose. That's probably the most common use of *style*.

But media writers use *style* to mean the writing rules of the road. Is the word capitalized or lowercased? Is the number in numeral form or spelled out as a word? Is that word abbreviated? Should that be set off by commas? All those are issues of style for media writers. And they are important because we never want to distract readers by handling something one way in one paragraph and another way somewhere else.

Style is important for the same reason that consistency is important in any art form. If you are painting a mural, you don't want to mix your colors differently on one section of the wall. People will notice and they'll wonder why the sky was deep blue in one section of the mural and almost-deep blue in another section. You don't want them to take even a couple of seconds to wonder about the colors. You want them to focus on the overall image. If a writer says FBI in one paragraph and F.B.I. in another, or Senator Harry Reid at the beginning and Sen. Mitch McConnell at the end, readers wonder (even if subconsciously) why the titles are different.

If you are writing an academic paper, you might use APA or MLA or Turabian style. But if you're a media writer—either in news or in strategic communications—your style bible is "The Associated Press Stylebook and Briefing on Media Law." It's typically called the AP Stylebook, and almost universally just *the stylebook*.

Indeed, whether you're in the newsroom of a major metropolitan daily, a community weekly, an online news site, or an advertising/PR agency, if you ask a style question, the answer comes from *the stylebook*.

The AP Stylebook has been around since 1953, though it becomes more comprehensive with every edition. Indeed, it's more than a guide to capitalization, abbreviation, numbers, punctuation, and the like. It's a veritable treasure-trove of information needed by writers on all kinds of topics, organized in alphabetical order.

And like the dictionary, the stylebook is not a static document. A new edition comes out every year, and there are always new entries and changes in the old entries. E-mail is now email, Web site is now website, and CEO is allowed on first reference to a chief executive officer. Every summer, veteran media writers wait eagerly to see what additions have been made to the stylebook and what rules they'll have to re-learn because the stylebook has changed.

All media do not use the AP Stylebook exclusively. Many publications have their own styleguides, but typically even these publication-specific guides are based on AP, with some exceptions. The publication might use courtesy titles for people in the news, or it might italicize the names of newspapers and magazines instead of capitalizing them, or it may even use two-letter Postal Service state abbreviations instead of the traditional abbreviations favored by the stylebook (OK instead of Okla., for instance). But even in these cases where publications have well-known exceptions to the AP Stylebook, these styleguides are usually more like the traditional AP Stylebook than they are different.

The stylebook contains a lot of information you will find useful throughout your career, but it's best to think of it in two categories: stuff you need to memorize and stuff you need to look up. The last category, thankfully, is much larger. Some media writing teachers require students to memorize sections of the stylebook ("Tomorrow, a test on the letter C."). But everyone realizes that ultimately, you will end up searching the stylebook for most of your queries. Some things really do need to be memorized: You don't need to look up common titles to see if they are capitalized before a name, or check every number to see if it is spelled out or used as a numeral, or check the rules for placing commas every time you use them. In the appendix of this book, we have excerpted some of the major rules that you need to know—and if you take time to memorize them, you'll save a lot of time and a lot of style mistakes. The style rules in the appendix are all found in the AP Stylebook, but they are so common that you really want to have them memorized rather than look them up every time you need them.

The Bottom Line

The AP Stylebook is so important because it is used across media platforms and in all media professions. News people use it and PR people use it. And media writers know that a story written in perfect AP style is not necessarily a good story, but at least the reader can focus on the story itself, the content we are trying to convey, rather than being distracted by inconsistencies in the way words and punctuation are used.

Paula LaRocque

A VISIT WITH YOUR WRITING COACH
Pretensions: Don't Try to Impress

Writing with clarity and simplicity

http://snd.sc/LoVbWD

Revising the AP Stylebook: Q&A with Editor David Minthorn

~ Sue Burzynski Bullard

David Minthorn, the deputy standards editor of the Associated Press, answered questions in an email interview about how the "AP Stylebook" comes together. Minthorn has been a correspondent or editor with The Associated Press for more than 40 years. He has worked on style issues at the news cooperative since 2000. Minthorn is one of three editors of the AP Stylebook and answers questions on the Ask the Editor website.

Q: Why is style important? And is it less important as more readers move to the Web?

A: Standardized style provides a framework of proper word usage, punctuation, spellings, definitions and story formats for accurate and credible journalism. By using a standard style, journalists don't have to agonize over basics such as how to present the news. The answers are at hand in an authoritative reference known as a stylebook. For The Associated Press, standard style applies to all forms of newsgathering and distribution. The guidance holds across all platforms, including news on the Web, where our standard style is equally important.

Q: How do you decide to change a style entry (like the 2010 change from Web site to website)? What's the process?

A: The AP Stylebook editors—Deputy Managing Editor Sally Jacobsen, Editor at Large Darrell Christian and I—discuss style and usage issues throughout the year and consult with other senior AP editors on potential new entries or amendments of existing entries. We accepted the one-word spelling of website this spring after several years of discussions. Stylebook users, including persistent voices in the AP staff, argued that the popular spelling, website, has overtaken the original term, Web site, which derives from World Wide Web. It was noted that the stylebook's main dictionary reference—Webster's New World College Dictionary, Fourth Edition—adopted website as its preference. So we became convinced that the time had come to formalize the one-word spelling in the 2010 edition of the AP Stylebook.

Q: What about new entries? What criteria do you use to decide to add something like "unfriend" to the stylebook or "Great Recession"? Who comes up with the new ones?

A: The term "unfriend" was a logical entry in 2010 stylebook's new Social Media Guidelines section, which includes about 50 terms and Instant Message abbreviations ranging from aggregator to LOL to YouTube. Great Recession was added with the advice of AP's business and economics specialists because it is widely used in government, commerce and academia to describe the longest and deepest recession since the Great Depression of the 1930s. The floor is always open to proposals for new terms, tweaks of existing entries or deletions of outdated entries.

Q: What are the most common questions about style that you get? Have the kinds of questions changed much over the years? And how often do you get questions?

A: Spelling questions, including compounds and hyphenated words, are among the most frequent questions posed at Ask the Editor, the online stylebook's help site, which I run. A lot of questions concern composition titles, personal titles, capitalization and numerals. Quite a few involve writing-phrasing advice. On average I answer about 35-40 style questions a week at the blog. There's a certain amount of repetition, so I refer some questioners to the site archive for answers. Fresh topics of wide relevance are likely to get prompt attention.

Q: How should students learn AP style? And do they really need to know it all or just how to use the book?

A: The way to become knowledgeable about AP style is by reading into the alphabetical entries and practicing the advice in daily journalism. We provide some guidance and instruction online. Go to http://www.apstylebook.com … in the left side, click on Ask the Editor FAQ for my compendium of some basic style points. The 2009 and 2010 stylebooks have a Quick Reference Guide of important terms and page numbers for guidance, a refinement I suggested for highlights. Students should also read into the specialty sections on business, sports, social media, media law, etc. By becoming familiar with the contents, students will know where to look for answers and cross-references. The public site of Ask the Editor—with a week's worth of Q-and-A on style—can also be helpful to students.

Q: Copy editors are often passionate about style. Do you see that passion in the kinds of requests for changes/updates you get?

A: People can get emotional about word usage, writing and grammar. They care about proper English and generally appreciate having a forum to air their suggestions or complaints. One recent example: A member editor strongly objected to the use of "busted" as a modifier, as in "busted well" used in an AP story about the Gulf oil spill. While we agreed that it's informal and slangy, Webster's sanctions the adjective form. So we expressed sympathy with the viewpoint but said we wouldn't be very successful making it a stylebook exception to the dictionary. Such exceptions take a lot of policing.

Q: What's been the most controversial change you've made in AP style?

A: Although the change to "website" was widely hailed by AP Stylebook readers, there was considerable criticism of our decision to stick with "the Web" (capped) and "Web page" (two words), just like Webster's. Perhaps surprisingly, we've gotten some criticism at the AP Stylebook Twitter account from "traditionalists" who were disappointed by the change to "website." The discussion goes on … (Bullard 2010).

References

Bullard, Sue Burzynski. "Revising the AP Stylebook: Q&A with Editor David Minthorn." *American Copy Editors Society* (November Q4, 2010). http://www.copydesk.org/512/ap-qa/.

Skills Development: Practice in Media Writing

Exercise 4.1
Brushing Up on the AP Stylebook

One of the best ways to brush up on style rules, and learn some new ones, is through the website Newsroom 101 (http://www.newsroom101.com/newsroom101.net/). You'll find online exercises in both AP style and grammar. You can do them on your computer and see them graded immediately. The more time you spend at the Newsroom 101 site, the more your style will improve. There's a nominal cost, but it's well worth the price to get this practice in AP style.

Exercise 4.2
Getting to Know the AP Stylebook
An AP Find-it Exercise

Edit the following sentences for style mistakes. You can find all the errors in your AP Stylebook. Do not change or rewrite the sentences in any way. Take out no words. Add no words. Re-arrange no words. Every mistake here can be fixed by changing spelling, capitalization or internal punctuation or marking through a word to substitute another. None of the items below is "common knowledge," so you may need to go through the sentences word-by-word looking to find the style issue.

1. Hannah's parents have scheduled her bar mitzvah for next March at a Dallas synagogue.

2. Obama said the House Republicans, who refused to consider his budget without spending cuts, were adverse to change.

3. CBS newsman Bob Schieffer was honored with his own bobble-head by the Fort Worth Cats at a game in 2005.

4. Police said the robber shot the homeowner and took $250 in cash and a Diner's Club card.

5. Kirk Franklin, a Gospel singer from Fort Worth, has won several Grammy awards.

6. The band asked the visiting musician to come to the stage, take the mike and sing his latest hit ballad, "Lovin' You."

7. Gov. Rick Perry, speaking to a Future Farmers of America convention in Midland, called the Texas economy "recession proof."

8. The Taliban is one of the groups that formed to oppose the Russian occupation of Afghanistan.

9. The rein of Queen Elizabeth II began in the 1950s.

10. The mayor said Aledo would continue to spray for mosquitos in the summer, despite allegations from his election opponent that the insecticide contains carcinogens.

11. The archaeology professor insisted that his research indicates that early Greek ships would not sail past the Straits of Gibraltar.

12. The senator criticized American oil companies like Conoco Phillips, which still gets much of its crude from Venezuela despite the human rights violations alleged against President Hugo Chavez.

Exercise 4.3
Another AP Stylebook Find-it Exercise

On 1 through 12, edit the sentence. On 13 through 16, answer the question. Don't guess on anything. Look up the rule or the information in your AP Stylebook. Nothing on this page is "common knowledge."

1. Police found the body in a dumpster behind a convenience store at Front and Broad streets.

2. Do they eat chilies in Chili when it's chilly in the winter?

3. The book of Revelation in the Bible says the Anti-Christ will be involved in the battle of Armageddon.

4. Jones, a New York restauranteur, will open a new French restaurant in Fort Worth this December.

5. The launching of Sputnik I on Oct. 4, 1957, began the space age.

6. You can find a social security number on voter registration documents.

7. Tony the Tiger and Smokey the Bear are two well-known advertising symbols.

8. She thinks female students at TCU wear too much make-up.

9. Was Yuri Gagarin the first Cosmonaut to orbit the planet?

10. The students at Glenwood School are no longer allowed to sell daffodil seeds as part of their PTA fund raiser.

11. He flouted his wealth in front of his friends when he showed up in Manhattan driving his new Jaguar convertible.

12. Mike Huckabee, former governor of Arkansas, was considered a front runner in the race for the GOP nomination in 2012.

13. How many liters in two gallons? _____

14. Is Columbus Day a legal holiday? _____

15. Which is larger, the Vatican or Monaco? _____

16. In a story about the president, can you say President Obama on first reference, or do you need to say President Barack Obama on first reference? _____

Chapter Five
Writing Leads: Capturing the Reader's Interest in the First Graf

American journalist Gene Fowler once explained writing in this way: "Writing is easy. All you do is stare at a blank sheet of paper until drops of blood form on your forehead."

Since the sheet was blank, Fowler no doubt had a lead in mind.

Journalists and other writers have agonized over leads since the craft was invented. They are important because they are the first thing a reader sees. And in the mass media, they often determine whether the reader goes into the news article or moves on to something else.

Many book chapters have been written on crafting good leads. And here comes another one. Writing about lead-writing is frustrating, because we can't tell you how to write a good lead. Remember Supreme Court Justice Potter Stewart who said he couldn't define pornography—he just knew it when he saw it? The same is true for leads.

Here's what we *can* do: We can share a process that will help you to know what to do when you approach lead-writing; we can tell you what to put into a lead and what to leave out; we can give you examples of what are generally considered good leads; and we can show you some ineffective leads. But when all that's over, you're left pretty much on your own, facing a blank screen and trying to come up with a lead.

At that point, you may relate to Gene Fowler's line about the drops of blood on your forehead.

The only way you learn to write good leads is to write them. So we'll go through our lead-writing checklist of dos and don'ts and here's-how-you-do-its. And then we'll leave you to that blank screen and the practice that will ultimately help you learn to write good leads. Get used to it; no matter what direction media writing may take you, there's a beginning point—a lead—for every written product.

Let's get started. We've already talked about the way mass media products are written, about news values and about how we approach news stories. Now it's time to talk turkey. Let's look at how media writers put together leads.

It starts simply enough: You have to understand the news event and decide what readers really want to know. The lead typically presents the most important information, what you would say if you were telling someone the news and had only one sentence to do it.

Here are three ways to begin to wrap your mind around a news event:

1. **Tell someone else.** If you have a minute, turn to someone and tell him or her what the news event is about. That person may ask questions. Pay attention to those questions. Telling the news out loud helps you frame it mentally.

2. **Write a headline.** Later on, we look at the mechanics of headline writing, but for now, any kind of head will do. You know that the headline should tell the news in as few words as possible. When you have done that, write the lead using the same idea.

3. **Decide if this will be a *who* lead or a *what* lead.** Will it feature an individual or will it be about something that happened?

Once you have an idea of what the lead will be about, it's time to start writing. You may have taken composition classes where your teacher said you should always know what you are going to say—and perhaps even have an outline—before you start to write. In media writing, we typically think on the screen because deadlines loom constantly and because we know we can always revise what we write. Get an idea of what you want to feature and just start writing. The more you write, the more you will find yourself able to compose as you write. Your brain will seem to connect directly to your fingertips and the writing flows from your thinking.

That may not happen at first. But don't let yourself sit at your screen and over-plan so that you want to know exactly what you will write before you start. Instead, consider the focus of the story. Tell someone else about the story or write a headline in your mind if that will help. Then start writing.

Let's apply these principles to a story:

Who: Fort Worth Zoning Commission

When: Wednesday morning

What: voted to deny zoning application to Walmart

More what: The application had asked the commission to rezone a site at Hemphill and Berry streets. Walmart wanted to raze a community center owned by a church to build a Walmart Neighborhood Market. Commission voted 7–2 to deny the application.

Here are some possible leads:

1. Earlier this year, Walmart applied to the Fort Worth Zoning Commission for the re-zoning of a site at Hemphill and Berry streets to build a Walmart Neighborhood Market. The commission voted 7–2 Wednesday morning to deny Walmart's application.

    Comments: The writer "backed into" this lead. Leads should begin with a subject, not a time element. Is the news that Walmart had earlier applied for the rezoning? That could have been written six months ago. Why does this lead contain two sentences? More important, why is the main news in the second sentence of the lead?

2. On Wednesday, the Fort Worth Zoning Commission voted to deny a re-zoning request from Walmart.

    Comments: Leads should not start with a time element. This lead does not tell the reader enough. Why did Walmart make the request? Where was the rezoning to take place? Remember the "proximity" news value. Knowing the location of the request makes it newsworthy for many readers.

3. The Fort Worth Zoning Commission met Wednesday to consider a re-zoning request from Walmart. The commission voted to deny Walmart's request to rezone a site at the corner of Hemphill and Berry streets to allow the building of a new Walmart Neighborhood Center.

    Comments: Remember the inverted pyramid. Is the fact that the commission met the most important thing in this story? It is, according to the way this lead is constructed. The main news is in the second sentence.

Paula LaRocque

A VISIT WITH YOUR WRITING COACH
Cut Wordiness

Making every word count

http://snd.sc/LoVron

Here's the lead the way it actually appeared in the Fort Worth Star-Telegram (Nishimura 2012) with the second and third grafs included to show you how the writer continued to develop the story after the lead:

> *The Fort Worth Zoning Commission voted 7–2 Wednesday morning to deny Walmart the rezoning of a site at Hemphill and Berry streets, where it wants to raze a church-owned community center and build a Walmart Neighborhood Market.*
>
> *Commissioners said they were troubled by the idea of setting a "precedent" in granting Walmart waivers it wants on the site, after neighborhood leaders said the company's overall plan would hurt the city's Hemphill/Berry Urban Village design for the area. Walmart is the first developer to seek waivers in the district since the city approved the urban village several years ago.*
>
> *Neighborhood leaders said they want the Walmart Neighborhood Market, but want it to better fit the urban village plan, which calls for old-style buildings that hug street fronts and sport lots of windows that highlight activity inside and draw pedestrians in.**

The hardest part of lead *writing* is the *thinking* part: deciding what the story is about, then deciding which element is most important for the reader to know. With many readers, you will have only one shot, the lead, or the first half of the lead, or maybe only the headline. So you have to make it count.

The zoning story writer thought the most important element was the fact that the commission had turned down Walmart for the Berry at Hemphill rezoning, which would have torn down a church's community center and replaced it with a Walmart Neighborhood Market. That's a lot, and the writer took 38 words to convey all that information.

Is that lead too long? Is it loaded with too much information, or is that information needed to make sense of the story? Here's a shorter version:

> *The Fort Worth Zoning Commission turned down Walmart's request Wednesday to rezone property at Berry and Hemphill streets to build a Walmart Neighborhood Store.*

That's only 24 words, but we had to leave out some information you may consider important to the story. Compare the two leads. Which do you prefer? If you lived in that neighborhood, which would you prefer? Did the second lead leave out information the reader needs? Media writers who write news must always deal with this balancing act. We want to write short, and that always involves deferring information to the second or even third grafs. But when we push info into a later graf in the interest of brevity, have we left out something the reader needs to know? Indeed, have we failed to interest readers because we left out something that would have hooked their attention? That's the choice media writers must make every time they craft a news lead. Writers constantly have these kinds of discussions in their heads. There are no right answers, only options.

As you write your leads, here are some other principles to guide you:

Start with a noun and a verb. When you've figured out the most important element of the story, start there. And don't back into the story with a date or a prepositional phrase; start with a noun. Here are examples of backing in:

> *Tonight at 6:30, the TCU baseball team will hold its third annual Frogs for the Cure Women's Baseball Clinic at the Sam Baugh Indoor Practice Facility.*

> *Hoping to instruct female fans on the finer points of baseball while raising money for a good cause, the TCU baseball team will hold its third annual Women's Baseball Clinic at 6:30 p.m. tonight at the Sam Baugh Indoor Practice Facility.*

This is a simple story involving a *who* (the baseball team) and a *what* (holding a women's clinic). You could start with either, as below:

---

* From the *Fort Worth Star-Telegram*, 2012. Reprinted by permission.

The TCU baseball team will hold its third annual Frogs for the Cure Women's Baseball Clinic at 6:30 p.m. tonight at the Sam Baugh Indoor Practice Facility.

A baseball clinic for women sponsored by the TCU baseball team is scheduled at 6:30 tonight at the Sam Baugh Indoor Practice Facility.

William Caldwell (Hall n.d.), a Pulitzer Prize-winning reporter, recalled the best lead he ever heard. The year was 1922.

I was on my way home from school and my stint at the local weekly. My little brother came running to meet me at the foot of the street. He was white and crying. A telegram had come to my mother. "Pa drowned this morning in Lake George," my brother gasped. I was ashamed to admit my inner response. Before I could begin to sense sorrow, despair, horror, loneliness and anger, before all the desolation of an abandoned child could well up in me, I found myself observing that the sentence my brother had just uttered was the perfect lead. Noun, verb, period, and who-what-when-where to boot.*

Time elements. Most leads include some type of time element, typically the day of the week. The time element answers the question of when something happened, so it is always used as an adverb and, as such, should be as close to the verb as possible. Use the day of the week for days within seven days before or after the date of publication. Use the month and a figure for dates beyond this range. Avoid redundancies such as *last Tuesday* or *next Tuesday*.

Websites typically use *today* as a time element for events that occurred that day because stories on news websites are date-stamped.

If the verb takes a direct object, the object should follow the verb, and then give the time element, for example, Provost Nowell Donovan ordered campus police Tuesday to ticket students who ride their bicycles on sidewalks.

If your placement of the time element gives you an awkward construction, you can add *on* before the day of the week.

Occasionally, you will not put the time element in the lead. This typically happens when you are reporting nonbreaking news or when the exact time of the news event is not known. Always use a perfect tense of the verb if you have no time element. Here's an example (Cox 2012):

Nissan North America has opened a new $2 million, 25,000-square-foot training facility in Irving that will enable the company to double the number of Nissan and Infiniti service technicians it trains.†

The writer used *has opened* because there was no time element. If there had been a time element, the verb would have been the simple past tense: opened. But using a specific time element lead creates a dilemma on where the time element would go. Here are some options:

Option 1: *Nissan North America* **Thursday** *opened a new $2 million, 25,000-square-foot training facility in Irving that will enable the company to double the number of Nissan and Infiniti service technicians it trains.*

Option 2: *Nissan North America opened a new $2 million, 25,000-square-foot training facility in Irving* on **Thursday** *that will enable the company to double the number of Nissan and Infiniti service technicians it trains.*

What to do about names in the lead. When you have a *who* lead, you have to make a decision: Do you name the person in the lead or do you describe the person in some way and name him or her in the second graf?

---

* Reprinted from Beginning Reporting–http://www.courses.vcu.edu/ENG-jah/BeginningReporting/Writing/newslead.htm. Copyright © Jim Hall. Reprinted by permission.

† From the *Fort Worth Star-Telegram*, 2012. Reprinted by permission.

How do you know which to do? The rule is simple: If the name is recognizable to readers, use it. Otherwise, use some other type of descriptor, like a *32-year-old Dallas man or a sophomore art history major or a 9-year-old third grade boy.*

Some examples:

FORT WORTH—The parents of a toddler mauled by dogs were arrested Thursday morning, accused of failing to provide adequate safety for the boy and failing to supervise him.

Deputies arrested Chance Walker Sr., 25, and his wife, Patricia Walker, 23, without incident shortly after 11:30 a.m. at a residence in the 900 block of Hackamore Street in White Settlement. (Ramirez 2012)*

An Arlington man was convicted of murder Thursday in the fatal stabbing of his ex-girlfriend's boyfriend.

A Tarrant County jury deliberated two days before convicting Henry Hernandez, 27, in Criminal District Court No. 1. (Hunt 2012)*

These so-called *blind leads* cut the length of the lead because writers do not have to include the unfamiliar name and an identifier in the opening graf. Instead, we can briefly identify someone and move on to the *what*, saving the *who* (the name) for the second graf. Use blind leads when using the name would require an immediate identification of who that person is.

Datelines. You'll notice in some newspapers and on some websites that leads sometimes begin with the name of a city, or a city and state, in all-caps. These datelines originally included the location (city) and the date of the story. Over time, the date was dropped by most newspapers, and now the dateline is only the story's point of origin. Most newspapers use a dateline when the story originates outside the city where the paper is published. Datelines also appear on all stories originated by The Associated Press.

Check out the "datelines" entry in your Associated Press Stylebook for the rules on whether to include the city and state in the dateline or only the city.

Paula LaRocque

A VISIT WITH YOUR WRITING COACH
Don't Back In

Backing into the news
http://snd.sc/LoVD75

Some Things to Watch For

This chapter has been about how to write leads, but as you might guess, there are a few things to avoid, too.

Question leads. News leads should make a statement, not ask a question. Even most feature writers think question leads for features are a poor way to start their stories. Your job is to give information, not ask questions, because after the question is asked, you still haven't presented any news.

---

* From the *Fort Worth Star-Telegram*, 2012. Reprinted by permission.

Quote leads. Quotations can be an important part of a news story, so much so that we devote an entire chapter to talking about how to handle them effectively in your story. But remember, quote leads are, by definition, out of context. If the first thing readers see is a quotation, they don't know who said it or what it applied to. You have to follow up the quote by telling why you quoted it. And where's the news in all that? Quote leads may occasionally have a place in feature treatments, but they have no place in hard news story leads. An old journalism joke is that the only appropriate hard news direct quote lead may be this one:

"I'm back," Jesus said.

Multisentence leads. One word about multisentence leads: Don't. Beginning writers, especially, should keep leads to one sentence. But, you say, you have seen a number of two-sentence leads in The New York Times and other publications. That's true, but writing a two-sentence lead is something best left to the pros. Beginning media writers who write multisentence leads tend to bury the news in the second sentence. And besides, many writers don't like multisentence leads anywhere, even in The New York Times. For now, keep your leads to one sentence and keep that one sentence as close to 25 words as you can.

Clothesline leads. These are leads where the writer tries to hang everything on the lead, like hanging clothes on a line. This lead type, popularized initially by The Associated Press early in the 20th century, tried to get all the five w's (and maybe the h) into the lead. You don't hear much about clothesline leads today, but you do see leads where it's obvious the writer tried to pack in a lot of information. Look at the following two leads, the first from McClatchy News Service and the second from The Los Angeles Times, both reporting the same event:

> WASHINGTON—*A decade after the United States launched two wars that put women at the front lines of unconventional fighting, the Pentagon crept closer Thursday to formally allowing them to serve in combat by announcing an additional 14,000 combat-related jobs for women. (Youssef 2012)**

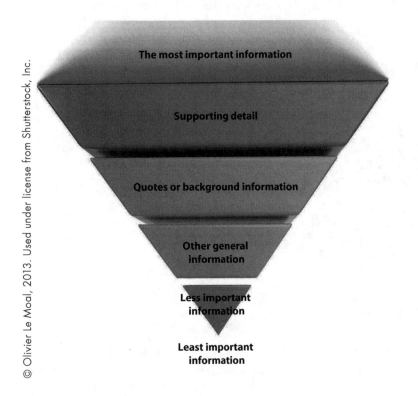

> *Reporting from Washington—The Pentagon plans to ease restrictions on women serving in combat, which will open 14,000 new and potentially more dangerous jobs to female troops, mostly in the Army and Marine Corps. (Cloud 2012)*

The McClatchy lead has 42 words, includes more background and backs into the news that the Pentagon is adding new combat-related jobs. The Los Angeles Times lead has 30 words and puts the news peg right up front.

---

* From the *Fort Worth Star-Telegram*, 2012. Reprinted by permission.

And after the lead? What next?

So you have a lead that grabs the reader. What next? How do you organize the rest of your story?

Chapter 3 introduced the organizational structure called *the inverted pyramid*. We'll develop this technique more in Chapter 7, but the basic idea behind the inverted pyramid is that it tells a story in order of importance, not by chronology (time sequence).

People are not committed to reading the whole story to get to the eventual payoff at the end. They want a headline that summarizes the story and a lead that tells it briefly. Then they may read on. They may read three grafs or five grafs or eight grafs. But when was the last time you read an entire news article in any medium? You know that if you read the lead, or half the story, there is nothing more important further on in the story than what you have already read. That's our unwritten contract with the reader.

You wouldn't buy a murder mystery and read half the first chapter and feel disappointment that the killer had not yet been revealed. For novels, we're interested in the reading *process*. We want to be fooled and led down blind alleys on our way to the payoff in the last chapter. For news readers, the contract is different – we want to be able to read as much or as little as we choose, confident that we have at least read the most important part of the story.

We put the most important information in the lead, the next most important information in the second graf, and so on. As you work on the exercises at the end of this chapter, you can practice organizing the way media writers do. When you finish writing a story, put your finger on any paragraph past the lead. Then look at the grafs below where your finger is—is any of the information south of your finger more important than the information north of your finger? Would a reader who stopped after, say, three grafs have missed anything in graf four or seven or nine that's more important than what he or she just read?

This style of organization will seem unnatural at first, but it will help you write for today's reader. It also helps editors who have to cut stories for length. They don't have to trim a sentence here and a word or phrase there—they know they can always trim from the bottom and cut the less-important information.

The Bottom Line

When you begin to write leads, it may seem like you're trying the old trick of patting your head and rubbing your stomach at the same time. We've given you a lot of dos and don'ts. Remember: The key is to understand what the news is about and what the reader wants to know first. Tell that news as a *who* or *what* lead. Then stop. Start a new graf and tell the next most important thing. You'll probably never be able to pat your head and rub your stomach simultaneously, but as you read more good leads and get more experience as a writer, you'll see your leads improve.

Alternatives to the Hard News Lead

There's another way to write this?

As you read news in newspapers or online, you'll notice that many stories aren't written like those we're talking about here. In fact, it seems that some leads written by professional media writers violate pretty much every rule in this chapter. The news peg isn't in the lead at all: It's often in the second or third or fourth graf.

And the lead? It's the beginning of an anecdote or part of a description or maybe an attention-getting statement. What gives?

Actually, you've discovered a different approach to newswriting. These alternative leads and story forms are explained in chapter 10. You frequently find these leads when the writer is presenting news that's not exactly new to the reader, and there's no better example of that than sports.

Gone are the days when you opened a newspaper sports page to find out who won or lost or what the score was. Newspapers are no longer a breaking news medium for many types of news. If you read a news story about your favorite college or pro football team, for example, do you read it to find out how the game came out?

Nope. You already know. You saw it on TV or heard it on radio or maybe even followed a live blog of the game. So why would you even read a game story if you saw the game? You want more. You want news about player reactions and coaching strategy and the implications of the game.

It would be useless to write a lead like this about an NBA game that most fans already knew about:

> *The Dallas Mavericks beat the Denver Nuggets 105–95 Wednesday to snap a three-game losing streak.*

Note that this "useless" lead actually follows the lead guidelines in this chapter. But it's like watching a rerun on TV; you already know what's going to happen. So instead, lead writers frequently take a more creative approach, an approach that signals to you that this article will contain information you don't already have. You get this type of approach (Price 2012) in the following story:

> *Dirk Nowitzki put in one last eye-popping performance in an attempt to get himself in the All-Star game.*
>
> *And what a performance.*
>
> *Nowitzki scored a game-high 25 points—passing Adrian Dantley along the way—as the Dallas Mavericks carved up the Denver Nuggets 105–95 on Wednesday before 15,970 at the Pepsi Center. The Mavericks (15–11) snapped a three-game losing streak by sending the Nuggets to their fourth consecutive loss.**

Note the third graf. That's the nutgraf—the paragraph that gives you the real hard-news nut of the story.

But certainly you haven't seen all the games written about in the sports pages. Some stories cover games in other parts of the country. And if you look closely, you will see that those leads are typically written with the approach you learned about in this chapter. The lead will talk about who won, who lost and the significance of the game.

You will find this approach in other parts of the newspaper or online. More on that in chapter 13. Students frequently like alternative leads more than hard news leads, but it's important to master the hard-news approach first. The types of leads in this chapter put the most important information in the lead. After you've learned to write good hard news leads, we let you try your hand at some alternative approaches.

* From the *Fort Worth Star-Telegram*, 2012. Reprinted by permission.

References

Cloud, David S. "Pentagon to Ease Restrictions on Women in Combat." *Los Angeles Times*, February 9, 2012. http://www.latimes.com/news/nationworld/nation/la-na-pentagon-women-20120209,0,5107352.story.

Cox, Bob. "Nissan Opens New Training Center in Irving." *Fort Worth Star-Telegram*, February 9, 2012: 3B.

Hall, Jim. *Beginning Reporting*. n.d. http://www.courses.vcu.edu/ENG-jeh/Beginning Reporting/Writing/newslead.htm.

Hunt, Dianna. "Briefs: Arlington Man Is Convicted of Murder." *Fort Worth Star-Telegram*, February 9, 2012. http://www.star-telegram.com/2012/02/09/3724454/briefs-arlington-man-is-convicted.html.

Nishimura, Scott. "Fort Worth Zoming Commission Denies Walmart's Hemphill/Berry Rezoning." *Fort Worth Star-Telegram*, February 8, 2012. http://www.star-telegram.com/2012/02/08/3720448/fort-worth-zoning-commission-denies.html#storylink=cpy.

Price, Dwain. "Dirk Helps Mavericks Snap Skid in Denver." *Fort Worth Star-Telegram*, February 9, 2012: 2C.

Ramirez, Domingo. "Parents of Toddler Mauled by Dogs Face Injury to a Child Charge." *Fort Worth Star-Telegram*, February 9, 2012. http://www.star-telegram.com/2012/02/09/3723259/deputies-arrest-parents-of-tarrant.html#my-headlines-default.

Youssef, Nancy A. "Pentagon to Open More Service Jobs to Women." *Fort Worth Star-Telegram*, February 10, 2012: 3A.

Skills Development: Practice in Media Writing

Following are facts for news stories. Write the stories for publication in a local newspaper or online. Assume that factual information and names are correct, but fact sets may contain grammar, spelling and AP style mistakes.

Exercise 5.1

- This happened Friday
- Source for all information: police
- Police officer Frank Smith was en route to an assault call late Friday afternoon.
- He was driving west on Poindexter Street.
- He had his emergency lights and sirens activated.
- As he drove down Poindexter, another driver made a left turn in front of Smith's car and struck the patrol car.
- Smith lost control of his car; it rolled and struck two other vehicles.
- One car was parked and unoccupied.
- The other car he hit had pulled over to the side of the road as the driver heard Smith approaching on the emergency call.
- The car that was pulled over had two occupants; neither was injured.
- Smith was taken by helicopter to John Peter Smith hospital.
- He is there right now, in the intensive care unit.
- Det. Lucy Cifuentes of the Fort Worth Police Department said the officer, who has been with the department for 4 years, is in stable condition and expected to improve.
- The driver of the vehicle that hit the patrol car was taken to Harris Hospital and treated for non-life threatening injuries.

Exercise 5.2

- Assume you are writing this for a Texas newspaper during the 2012 presidential primary season.
- You are reporting campaign fundraising statistics released yesterday by the Center for Responsive Politics.
- Assume you are writing this during the presidential primary season; all candidates mentioned are still in the race for their party's nomination.
- Here's how much each candidate has raised so far in Texas: Rick Perry—$10.8 million; Mitt Romney—$5 million; Barack Obama—$4.67 million; Ron Paul—$1.67 million; Rick Santorum—$1.3 million; Newt Gingrich—$1.1 million.
- Top states giving to candidates: California—$34.4 million; Texas—$26.4 million; New York—$23 million; Florida—$17.5 million; Illinois—$11.2 million.
- The five Texas communities that donated the most to presidential candidates: Houston, $8 million; Dallas, $5.7 million; Austin-San Marcos, $3.2 million; San Antonio, $2 million; and Fort Worth-Arlington, $1.8 million.
- Larry Sabato, director of the Center for Politics at the University of Virginia, said: "Texas is rich in political donors, big givers who want the prizes that come to contributors—returned telephone calls, appointments and influence. There's a concentration of wealth in a large population of people who have lots of excess cash."
- Allan Saxe, associate professor of government at the University of Texas in Arlington, said: "Our donor tradition is old. We are the second most populous state in the Union with lots of wealthy donors, both Democratic and Republican and other parties as well. Oil, lots of highways, ranching and farming have both fueled and been recipients of campaign cash. The big donors still can and will give in the presidential campaign as it begins in earnest."*

---

* From the *Fort Worth Star-Telegram*, 2012. Reprinted by permission.

Exercise 5.3

- Texas has had a long-running dispute with Amazon.com.
- The state has wanted the Internet site to collect state sales tax when it sells to Texas consumers.
- The online retailer has said it did not want to collect sales taxes for the state.
- Susan Combs, the Comptroller for the state of Texas, has been in negotiation with Amazon.
- She had claimed that Amazon should have been collecting sales taxes from Texas consumers for the past five years.
- Six months ago, she sent Amazon a tax bill for $269,000,000 for unpaid taxes.
- Amazon had claimed the Texas tax assessment was "without merit."
- Amazon had even closed a distribution center in Irving because of the continuing dispute with Texas.
- But today, the two sides settled the disagreement.
- Looks like Amazon caved.
- Amazon will start collecting Texas sales taxes on July 1.
- This agreement was announced jointly by Texas and Amazon.
- As part of the agreement, Amazon said it will create at least 2,500 jobs in Texas and make at least $200 million in capital investment. Amazon said it will announce details later.
- Combs said: "The agreement resolves all sales tax issues between Texas and Amazon."*
- Paul Misener, Amazon's vice president for global public policy said: "Amazon looks forward to creating thousands of new jobs in Texas, and we appreciate Comptroller Combs working with us to advance federal legislation. We strongly support the creation of a simplified and equitable federal framework, because congressional action will protect states' rights, level the playing field for all sellers, and give states like Texas the ability to obtain all the sales tax revenue that is already due."
- Combs said: "We thank Amazon for partnering with us to find a solution that works for our state. This is an important step in leveling the playing field in Texas. It's a smart business decision. They know where their customer base is and Texas has been a large growth state and will continue to be."*

---

* From the *Fort Worth Star-Telegram*, 2012. Reprinted by permission.

Exercise 5.4

- Announcement came today from Rob Busfield, superintendent of the public schools in your city.
- He said that he is beginning medical leave on Monday.
- He said the leave is necessitated by his having to have one of his kidneys removed.
- Busfield said he will be on medical leave for three months.
- He said he would be replaced by the district's associate superintendent for curriculum and instruction, Mavis Henry.
- Busfield said: "I have no doubt that Dr. Henry will bring the same leadership qualities to the district as a whole that she has brought to her job as head of curriculum and instruction. She is an excellent leader and motivator, and I know that the superintendent's office will be in excellent hands during my absence."
- Henry's title will be Acting Superintendent.

Exercise 5.5

Write a news story on this research study published yesterday in the "Psychological Bulletin."
- The Bulletin reported research that was funded by the Robert Wood Johnson Foundation.
- The research was conducted in the Harvard School of Public Health.
- The research was looking into the effects of mental outlook on health.
- Scientists have known for a long time that Type A personalities and people who are short-tempered and often angry or depressed or anxious have a higher risk of heart attacks.
- This research looked into the effects of positive mental attitudes.
- The findings: Being optimistic or generally upbeat can help protect against heart disease.
- Here is a link to a short blogpost written by one of the researchers: bit.ly/1Yuz14. Go to that blog and pull some quotes from the researcher, Julia Boehm. Treat that blogpost just as you would the text of an interview you conducted with Boehm.

Exercise 5.6

- There was bad news at the Rachel Carson Middle School.
- This case involved a diagnosis of Hepatitis A.
- A student has been diagnosed with the disease.
- Parents of students in the school got a letter Friday telling them of the diagnosis, according to Sylvie Batchelor, school spokesperson.
- (Check online to see what Hepatitis A is, and include a brief explanation in this story.)
- The diagnosis was confirmed by school officials and your county health department.
- Debby Presley of your county health department told you that the student in question and close companions have all been vaccinated. The case is not considered infectious.
- Batchelor said this: "All indications are that the infection did not originate here at the school, but we sent a letter home Friday to parents."

Exercise 5.7

You have just received a statement from Berkshire Hathaway CEO Warren Buffett. You need to write a news release based on that announcement. The time element here is Tuesday, which was the day of the release. The statement itself can be found at http://bit.ly/J692Vz. Do some Internet research to find and include the following:

- Background on Berkshire Hathaway
- Background on Warren Buffett
- Background on Stage 1 prostate cancer

Exercise 5.8

- The Conference Board has been conducting research on the effects of the recession on employment.
- Today, the CB announced the results of the study.
- Most economists consider the recession to have ended in 2009. But there are lingering effects on employment.
- Various study results announced today:
    - Average wages for women are still lower than those for men by nearly 20%.
    - Men's wages have been slower to rebound from the recession because of the recession's impact on male-dominated industries like construction.
    - Men are taking a bigger hit in their paychecks than women because of lingering effects of the recession.
    - In terms of number of jobs, women are hurting: they got only 23% of the new jobs created over the past 2 years.
    - Although the recession ended in 2009, men's wage growth had rebounded to half the average rate of the previous decade by last year. Meanwhile, the growth in wages for women had almost fully recovered.
    - Wages for men and women each grew an average of about 3% annually from 1998-2008. But from 2008-2010, men's wages stayed constant while women's wages grew about 1% a year.
    - Gad Levanon, director of macroeconomic research at the CB and co-author of the study, said: "While there were signs of modest overall wage improvements in 2011, the severe depression of wage growth during the Great Recession is likely to impact consumer spending, inflation, corporate profits, income inequality, and employee engagement for many years to come.

Exercise 5.9

- Last year was the worst single-year drought in the state's history.
- Hot and dry weather this summer caused high water use and evaporation throughout the Smithville area and produced very little rainfall to replenish the lakes.
- This resulted in lakes Lafayette and Miller, the region's water supply reservoirs, falling to their third lowest combined storage level in history. The lowest combined storage last year was 736,047 acre-feet (or 37 percent full) on Dec. 1. An acre-foot is 325,851 gallons.
- This year's rains have increased combined storage by 243,257 acre-feet since Jan. 1. But Lake Lafayette is almost 31 feet below its normal level for April, and Lake Miller is about 16 feet below normal for April.
- Mayor Sarah Lawrence said this yesterday: Smithville will continue to ask its wholesale customers to implement drought restrictions aimed at reducing water use 10 to 20 percent and encourages all residents to use water as wisely and efficiently as possible.
- Ralph Elliot, professor of meteorology at the local university, said: "Weather patterns could be favorable for more rain. Last year's exceptionally dry weather began with the development of La Niña in the Pacific Ocean during the fall of 2010. La Niña typically causes a pattern of drier than normal weather across all the state, especially during the fall and winter. This La Niña was one of the strongest in the last century. Recently, La Niña has faded and a neutral Pacific is forecast for the remainder of spring and summer. Near normal to slightly above normal rain is forecast this spring and summer. Many long-range climate models indicate the Pacific will trend toward a weak El Niño this fall. El Niños typically cause a pattern of above normal rainfall across the state in the fall and winter months."

Exercise 5.10

Assume you work for a newspaper or news site in this community where Franklin State University is located. Rewrite the following information into a news story.

Franklin State University here has some great news! They have just chosen a new president. Her name is Wanda Jackson and she is currently the provost and executive vice president for academic affairs at Western State University in Las Vegas, NE. She will replace Marvin Forbes, who is retiring at the end of this semester. Her academic field is English Literature and she holds a Ph.D. from Harvard. The Franklin board of trustees met last night and they voted to name Dr. Jackson as president. The President of the board, Joe Bob Tansill, had this to say: "We are fortunate to name a leader of Dr. Jackson's caliber to take over the reins at Franklin State. We know she is the perfect fit to make sure excellence remains the priority at FSU."

Exercise 5.11

You got the following bulletin from your university police department. Use the information to write a news story for campus media. Attribute information to your university police.

Today the city Police notified the University Police that the Shell Station one block from campus located at the corner of W. Berry and University Drive was robbed. Suspect is described as a Black male with a slim build, about 5'10" tall wearing a brown hoodie. Suspect was covering his face with a type of surgical or dust mask.

Suspect demanded that the clerk give him all of the money. Suspect then asked for clerk's wallet and clerk told suspect that he did not have a wallet. Suspect left the store walking toward Bowie St. No weapon was shown during the robbery, but suspect continued to pat the pocket of his hoodie as if something was in his pocket.

Additionally, the University Police took a suspicious persons report at about 05:49 am today. A student who lives in the 2600 block of Boyd Ave. stated that three unknown males and two unknown females entered into his backyard wearing white and black hoodies. We searched thoroughly and no one was found. Another student who lives in the 3800 block of Lambert Ave. reported that unknown suspects were hitting his windows and the side of his residence. At this time we do not know if these incidents are related.

Exercise 5.12

This happened at a local meat packaging plant yesterday.

Police and paramedics were called to the plant at 10:41 a.m.

It seems an accident happened to a new employee, He was Hector Veloz, and he had worked at the plant (Acme Meat Products, 4232 Avenue F in your city) for less than a week.

Veloz was cleaning an industrial size meat blender when he fell in. The blender was used to regulate the fat content in ground beef. Source for this information is Jennifer Clinton, spokesperson for Acme.

Another employee was the horrific accident and pressed the emergency button. It was too late.

Paramedics pronounced Veloz dead at the scene of the accident. Paramedic Wilson Rogers told you that Veloz died of "blunt-force injuries and chopping wounds."

After Veloz's body was extracted, the plant continued normal operations.

Exercise 5.13

It is now one day after the horrible accident described in 5.12.

Joe Don Patterson, director of the local office of OSHA, said today that the agency is investigating Acme Meat Products. Patterson said the investigation could take up to six months. He said it is "way too early" to speculate on whether or not Acme had committed workplace safety violations.

You investigate and find out that Acme was cited in February of last year for multiple violations of worker safety standards. Among the violations for which Acme was cited was that a table saw did not have a hood to protect against arm injuries and that there was no protective device around a rotating blade to prevent inadvertent contact.

Write the story of the investigation, using information from 5:12 to update readers who may not be familiar with the story.

References

for Chapter 5 exercises

Nishimura, Scott. "Texas Comptroller Sees Reasons to Be Confident, Cautious About State Economy." *Fort Worth Star-Telegram*, April 16, 2012. http://www.star-telegram.com/2012/04/16/3888551/texas-comptroller-sees-reasons.html#storylink=misearch.

Tinsley, A. "Presidential Candidates Raise Millions in Texas." *Fort Worth Star-Telegram*, April 27, 2012. http://www.star-telegram.com/2012/04/27/3918896/presidential-candidates-raise.html#storylink=misearch.

Chapter Six

Copy Editing: Improving Writing One Sentence at a Time

© Pixsooz, 2013. Used under copyright from Shutterstock, Inc.

Understanding copy editing is essential, whether the editing is taking place digitally or by hand, as in the photo above.

For media professionals, writing is only the first step. Indeed, writing is only a part of a process that culminates with editing. Since media writing is intended for an audience, writers must make sure that nothing distracts from their prose.

A well-edited news story or ad or direct-mail piece or blogpost is not necessarily a high-quality piece of writing. But copy editing removes the mistakes that distract readers and keep them from focusing on the message. Professional writers see editing as part of the writing process. They inevitably edit as they write, but they do their most thorough editing after they finish the piece they are working on.

After they write they immediately move on to editing, which really consists of two discrete actions: revising the writing and cleaning up the writing. Writers revise by looking back over what they have written to improve the wording or the flow of their sentences. Sometimes they find sentences that don't make sense and they re-word them. Sometimes they find sentences that include too much information for readability and they turn one sentence into two. Sometimes they substitute one word or phrase for another to make writing less abstract and more concrete. If you look at the characteristics of good media writing (discussed in Chapter 1), you typically can't tell the process behind the product. Maybe the writer wrote it that way in the first place, but it also might be the result of skillful copyediting. Remember, when you finish writing, you're not done. You have only completed the first step toward a reader-friendly piece of media writing. Now you move into revision to see how you can make it better.

Sometimes copy editors read aloud to get a sense of the flow of a piece. Anything hard to read aloud—any sentence you stumble over when you read—is going to present a problem for a reader. Any time you notice that verbs are too far from subjects or you have piled too many chunks of thought into a sentence, fix it. You are reading this piece because you wrote it and you want to improve it; readers won't be so understanding. Typically, when they find something difficult to read, they move on to something else. You may pore over your Byzantine history text because you have a test tomorrow and you have to get ready for it, but if you're scanning a news article and get bogged down, you bail.

The second part of editing is fixing. That includes grammar, spelling, punctuation, AP style and word usage (affect or effect? insure or ensure?). Fixing also includes editing for accuracy. Writers always double-check names, addresses, titles, ages and the like. Even on a university campus, readers lose respect for a college publication because they see too many grammar errors or they know people whose names have been spelled wrong or who have been identified as a biology major when they are really a chemistry major. Your parents probably told you that you get only one chance to make a first impression; that applies equally to your writing. A reader can look over eight pages of newspaper copy and come away remembering only the misspelled name in a lead on the sports page.

One of the best ways to develop a copy editor's mindset as a writer is to look at your writing from a professional copy editor's point of view. Here is a column by copy editor Pam Nelson (2012) written for other copy editors who are members of the American Copy Editors Society.

Check the Facts: 10 Tips for Copy Editors

~ Pam Nelson

Checking facts is part of some copy editors' jobs. When I have trained copy editors on newspaper desks, I tell them that the main fact-checkers are the writers, followed by the line editors. But I also tell copy editors that inaccuracy in a published piece hurts everyone's credibility.

I did not learn to check facts in my first few years as a copy editor. I was more focused on correcting grammar, usage and style and on writing a good headline. But when I began working at *The News & Observer* in 1987, the point of fact-checking was driven home. We copy editors were held responsible for mistakes that slipped through. I also developed a healthy skepticism about writers and line editors. As I have noticed errors slip through the editing at our central publishing center, I am reminded once again that copy editors can't trust everything they read.

Today's time-strapped newspaper desks have precious little time for fact-checking. Perhaps your job (as a freelancer or in another publishing field) allows you more time if fact-checking is a part of your duties.

Here are 10 basic fact-checking tips. By no means is my list definitive. Editors have many more things to be aware of—fairness, balance and internal consistency among them.

1. If a date is mentioned in the story, either recent or historical, check it. Nothing will undermine credibility like misstating the date of a historic event. Even if you are almost certain that Pearl Harbor was attacked on Dec. 7, 1941, check it. If a writer refers to the Enlightenment being a part of the 17th and 18th century, check it. (I just did.)

2. If the name of a well-known person appears in a story and you have any hesitation about it at all, check it. I can't even count the number of times I have corrected the spelling of actor Dan Aykroyd's name. You should also check the spelling of lesser-known people if you have time or doubts.

3. If a writer uses a place name that you are unfamiliar with or that is often misspelled, check it. The copy that I read most often has North Carolina names that need to be checked. (Alleghany, not Allegheny, is one.)

4. If there is arithmetic in a story, check it. Keep a calculator handy. If a writer says that the Declaration of Independence was signed 235 years ago, check it ($2011 - 1776 = 235$). If a percentage change is mentioned, check it. If a person's age appears in a story and you can check it, do. Check the birth date of well-known people and do the math.

5. If the story refers to a number of items within the story (15 steps to better health, 10 reasons to use an iPad), count the items. Make sure a well-known list (12 zodiac signs, 50 states) is complete if it is meant to be.

6. If a story refers to someone as "the late," make sure the person is dead. Also, if a story refers to someone you remember as having died, check it. I once caught a reference to Howard Jarvis, the California property tax protest leader, as scheduled to appear at a local anti-tax rally. Jarvis had died a few years earlier.

7. If a story uses a quote that seems off (a teacher misusing grammar, a politician or a law enforcement officer seeming to say the opposite of what you'd expect), check the quote with the writer. Sometimes a writer drops the "not" in a quote.

8. If a story refers to a direction, check it. That may mean getting out a map and looking at the direction. I recently read a published story that referred to Morganton, N.C., as a two-hour drive east of Charlotte, N.C. Having grown up near both Morganton and Charlotte, I was 99.9 percent sure that Morganton was northwest of Charlotte, but I pulled out my North Carolina map to check. (I was correct. I'd also question whether it was a two-hour drive and would have checked that if I had been the copy editor on the story.)

9. If a story refers to a recent event (a crime, the passage of legislation), check a previous story to see whether the facts mesh. If they don't, though, don't assume that one story is right and the other is wrong. You have to do more checking.

10. If something seems odd to you, check it. This is a lesson I've had to learn over and over. Don't risk letting a mistake slip through.

Reprinted by permission of Pamela B. Nelson.

Those tips reflect a copy editor's mindset. Wherever you eventually work, you will deal with people who edit your writing. But editing is also a part of writing, so we shouldn't leave it all to those whose title includes the word *editor*. If you think like an editor before you submit your writing, you will submit better-written, cleaner copy. Media writers who take time to edit carefully can eliminate wordiness, substitute concrete words for vague ones, find factual errors, eliminate jargon and edit for AP style and grammar mistakes.

For a look at how news used to be edited and produced, scan the QR code or visit: http://bit.ly/zc2YMs

Up until the last decade, most copy editing was done on printed copy. Copy editors took typed-out stories and marked them up to correct errors before the stories went on to typesetting. After the story was set in type, another layer of editing—proof editing—corrected errors that had been inserted in the typesetting process.

Today, media copy goes from the mind of the writer through to ultimate production without ever going into hard copy. Therefore, most editing occurs on a screen, not on a piece of paper.

So why are we including copy editing marks in this chapter? Aren't those relics of another era? Yes, they are. But there will still be times, especially if you intern or work in a small publication, when you may have to edit hard copy. And if you do, you need to know the common, traditional copy editing marks.

We're not talking about different rules of copy editing here. It's the same thing you do on a screen, but you do it by marking up a story, an ad or other copy on a printout. There may be a time when these marks will only be found in media museums, but for now, take a few minutes to familiarize yourself with them. If you ever need to edit hard copy—and chances are, you will—you'll be glad you did.

If you do a Web search for copy editing marks, you'll find that some authorities present different marks for the same editing function—like two ways to insert letters. But you will also notice that even the different marks have similarities. The following marks are fairly standard and will give you a solid foundation for editing copy on paper.

Copy Editing Marks

- Transpose words two like this
- Transpose letters like this
- Insert words like this
- Insert letters like this
- Separate words like this
- Join words like this
- Delete extra words words like this
- Abbreviate a word: 2805 South Parkmeadow Drive
- Spell out an abbreviation: 2805 S. Parkmeadow Dr.
- Spell out a numeral: 8 students
- Turn a word into a numeral: twelve students
- Begin a new graf. Your new graf would start at the beginning of this sentence.
- Capitalize a word: former president George Bush
- Lowercase a word: George Bush was elected President in 2000.
- Insert opening quotation marks: My opponent has misrepresented my record," the mayor said.
- Insert closing quotation marks: "My opponent has misrepresented my record, the mayor said.
- Insert an apostrophe: The mayor said Smiths poll numbers were inaccurate.
- Insert a comma: "My opponent has misrepresented my record" the mayor said.
- Insert a period: "My opponent has misrepresented my record," the mayor said
- Insert a hyphen: an 8-year old boy
- Insert a dash: The boy not his mother—was hospitalized.
- Insert a question mark: "What"
- Insert an exclamation point: "Stop"
- Insert a colon: The committee included the following faculty members
- Insert a semicolon: He refused she agreed.

Paula LaRocque

A VISIT WITH YOUR WRITING COACH
Avoid Vague Qualifiers

Avoiding vague qualifiers
http://snd.sc/LoVv7R

The Bottom Line

As media converge and old job descriptions are re-defined, copy editing has been one of the casualties. It's called in many quarters "the death of copy editing." Certainly there are fewer copy editors than in years past, with the responsibility for editing shifting more to media writers. Former copy editor Steve Yelvington (2008) made this observation in a blogpost:

> *If you're studying journalism, you'd better learn to rub your belly and pat your head at the same time, without making any mistakes, because there's not going to be anyone there to save you from your own shortcomings.*

> *Whether you or I like these changes isn't particularly meaningful. The forces acting on the business of journalism are going to rewrite job descriptions, and the luxury of specialization will continue to disappear. Sweetheart, rewrite don't work here anymore. [Editors' note: The "sweetheart" reference is an allusion to an old newspaper saying of a reporter calling the paper to ask for an editor specializing in rewrite, telling the person who answered the paper's phone, "Hello, sweetheart, get me rewrite."]. Some copy editors are going to lose their jobs. But so will some reporters. Because without copy editors, the reporters who are weakest at writing, at attention to detail, at stepping out of their own heads and critically examining their work, are going to be subjected to the harshest editors of all: a readership that today is empowered to talk back.*

Copyright © 2012 by Steve Yelvington. Reprinted by permission.

So consider editing one of the skills you must develop as a media writer. An editing mindset—taking the time to make editing a part of your writing process—can certainly set you apart from many other young writers who will be hitting the job market along with you.

References

Nelson, Pam. "Check the Facts: 10 Tips for Copy Editors." *American Copy Editors Society* (January 2, 2012). http://grammarguide.copydesk.org/2012/01/02/check-the-facts-10-tips-for-copy-editors/.

Yelvington, Steve. "Death of Copy Editing, or Death of Specialization?" *Steve Yelvington's Media Weblog*, July 8, 2008. http://www.yelvington.com/node/445.

Skills Development: Practice in Media Writing

Exercise 6.1

Practice inserting copyediting marks in the following. These are the same marks that appeared earlier in this chapter. To check your work, look back at that text.

1. Transpose words two like this
2. Transpose lettres like this
3. Insert words this
4. Insert lettrs like this
5. Separate words likethis
6. Join words li ke this
7. Delete extra words words like this
8. Delete extra letteers like this
9. A way to deletee extra letters at the end of a word
10. Abbreviate a word: 2805 South Parkmeadow Drive
11. Spell out an abbreviation: 2805 S. Parkmeadow Dr.
12. Spell out a numeral: 8 students
13. Turn a word into a numeral: twelve students
14. Begin a new graf. Your new graf would start at the beginning of this sentence.
15. Capitalize a word: former president George Bush
16. Lowercase a word: George Bush was elected President in 2000.
17. Insert opening quotation marks: My opponent has misrepresented my record," the mayor said.
18. Insert closing quotation marks: "My opponent has misrepresented my record, the mayor said.
19. Insert an apostrophe: The mayor said Smiths poll numbers were inaccurate.
20. Insert a comma: "My opponent has misrepresented my record" the mayor said.
21. Insert a period: "My opponent has misrepresented my record," the mayor said
22. Insert a hyphen: an 8-year old boy

23. Insert a dash: The boy not his mother—was hospitalized.

24. Insert a question mark: "What"

25. Insert an exclamation point: "Stop"

26. Insert a colon: The committee included the following faculty members

27. Insert a semicolon: He refused she agreed.

Exercise 6.2

More practice with copyediting marks.

1. president Obama
2. PResident Obama
3. PresidentObama
4. Presdient Obama
5. Obama President
6. Pres ident Obama
7. Pressident Obama
8. President Obamaa
9. President President Obama
10. President Obema
11. President Obma
12. "Did you vote for President Obama? she asked.
13. "Yes I did" he said.

Exercise 6.3

Use copyediting marks to edit the following story. Assume all names and facts are correct.

1. 2 teen-age brothers are being treated in a Ft. Worth hospital after a wreck Monday that killed two other youths and a young adult North of decatur.

2. Devin Ramey 16 and Dakota Ramey 15 of Newark were listed in serious condition Wednesday at John Peter Smith Hospital a hospital spokeswoman said.

3. The wreck happened about 7 pm Monday at a rest area on U.S. 287 when a Dodge Stratus carrying 5 people slid beneath the back end of a parked tractor-trailer, the Wise County Messenger reported. [Note: The Messenger is a local newspaper.]

4. The impact was so powerful that the car top was sheared off the newspaper reported.

Exercise 6.4

Use the correct copyediting marks to find and fix errors in Associated Press style. Names and facts are correct. *Do not rewrite the sentences.*

1. The nine-year-old girl was found in northern Oklahoma carrying 2 small boxes, five cents, and a bible.

2. Forecasters in N. Dakota said the temperature will fall from 0 to -15 by 12 midnight on Monday

3. During the eighteenth century, political leaders like Thomas Jefferson laid the foundation for what was to become today's democratic party in the US.

4. 'Pres. Obama does not realize how much opposition this will has among conservatives and republicans", Senator Mario Rubio said at the news conference.

5. The Federal govt. has spent 4,840,000 million dollars to protect wildlife in the Calif. Park.

6. Jason Hecht Jr. received his BA in the Spring of 84.

Chapter Seven

ORGANIZATION ISSUES: THE BODY OF THE STORY

Like most kinds of writing, news writing has a beginning and a middle and an end. We've already looked at the beginning, the lead. Now let's skip ahead to the end. The good news is that news stories typically don't have one. Remember that news readers seldom read all the way to the end. Stories written in the inverted pyramid give readers a chance to stop reading at any point, knowing there is nothing further down in the story more important than what they have already read. And why spend a lot of time crafting a great ending when it may be cut off in the editing process or never reached by readers who leave the story early? So basically, hard news stories written in the inverted pyramid don't have an end. They just stop.

One of the popular story forms we'll discuss in this chapter follows the contours of the hourglass. Unlike the inverted pyramid, the hourglass model allows writers to tell the story chronologically from the beginning, while still presenting the news early on for maximum impact.

> Remember, when we talk about the ending of a news story, we're referring to the inverted pyramid model. Later, we look at some soft news models, which—like feature stories—do have endings. As do broadcast and advertising copy and other types of media writing you may do. But when you're writing hard news in the inverted pyramid, you stop writing when you've covered everything you need to say about the news event you are writing about.

So there. We've covered the all-important lead and now the typically non-existent ending. But what about the middle, the body of the story? What comes after the lead?

The Inverted Pyramid

The most common organizational structure is to disregard chronology and traditional narrative style. Begin with the most important information and add information in order of progressively less importance. In the inverted pyramid, the lead contains more important information than graf two, and graf two more important information than graf three. And so on …

Obviously, the decision about what is most important is made by the writer. It sounds subjective, and it is. That's why you can compare three or four stories written by different journalists covering the same event and find that they have ordered information differently. Even their choice of leads might be different.

Let's look at an example of a political story (Rosen 2012) written in inverted pyramid style. This story covered one day in the primary season and combined two news events: a caucus vote in Maine and a vote of conservative political activists. Read the story before we analyze the organizational plan (grafs are numbered for easier analysis later):

1. WASHINGTON—Former Massachusetts Gov. Mitt Romney got a much-needed boost Saturday, winning a key symbolic vote over former Sen. Rick Santorum of Pennsylvania among some of the nation's most active Republican voters before besting the field in the Maine caucuses.

2. Romney's 38-31 percent defeat of Santorum in a straw presidential vote among thousands of activists at the annual convention of the Conservative Political Action Committee bolstered his claim that he can consolidate support among the Republican base.

3. "I think it will give people a little more feeling that in the upcoming primaries, Romney can appeal to the conservative wing of the Republican Party," said Michael McLaughlin, a retired foreign-service officer from McLean, Va., who attended the three-day conference in Washington.

4. In a separate nationwide survey of conservatives conducted by conference organizers, Romney bested Santorum by 27-25 percent.

5. The results were a setback for former House Speaker Newt Gingrich and provided fresh evidence that he's losing ground to Santorum as the strongest alternative to Romney in the GOP White House race.

6. Gingrich received 15 percent of the straw vote among 3,408 CPAC activists and 20 percent of the vote in the national survey of conservatives conducted by Republican pollster Tony Fabrizio, finishing third behind Romney and Santorum in both tallies.

7. "Santorum is the candidate who can best articulate and represent conservative values whether they be social or fiscal issues," said Wendell Walker of Lynchburg, Va., Republican Party chairman of the swing state's 6th Congressional District. "He's the candidate with the least baggage among the Republican field."

8. Paul won the CPAC vote in 2010 and 2011, but he finished fourth Saturday with 12 percent in a sign that Republicans are focused on electability this year in their quest to dislodge President Barack Obama.

9. Sarah Palin closed the conference with a populist rallying cry heavy with criticism not just of Obama but also of the "crony capitalism" that she says has infected Washington more broadly.

10. Too often, she said, those who decry Washington as a "cesspool" become comfortable in the "hot tub."

11. "The divide between Washington and the rest of the country has never been greater and never been more dangerous," Palin said.

12. "It is time that we drain the Jacuzzi and we throw the bums out with the bathwater."

13. Palin said the Republican Party would benefit from an extended primary battle.

14. "In America, we believe that competition strengthens us," she said. "Competition relates to victory in 2012."

From the *Fort Worth Star-Telegram*, 2012. Reprinted by permission.

Notice what the news writer had to work with:

- News event #1: Romney wins in Maine.
- News event #2: Romney wins CPAC straw poll.

- News event #3: Romney wins nationwide survey of conservatives.
- News event #4: Gingrich's finish and the effects on his campaign.
- News event #5: Paul's finish.
- News event #6: Sarah Palin's speech at the CPAC campaign.

Remember that when the reporter looked at those news events at first, he or she had no such neat order as we have in the list above. The reporter's task was to cover a day in the primary season: a day in which Romney won a caucus, a straw poll and a survey, Santorum finished second in the straw poll and survey, Gingrich took a political hit from his finishes and Paul failed to make up any ground. On top of all that, Sarah Palin gave a speech at the same conference where Romney won the straw poll. In other words, the reporter had to cover six discrete news events in one story.

The writer had to first determine which news event was more important, the Maine caucus win or the CPAC straw poll win. The choice was the caucus win because it reflected the vote of the party of a state, rather than a vote of meeting attendees. But the Conservative Political Action Committee is an influential group, so that came second. Then came the other candidates and finally the speech by Palin.

Transitions. There are many types of transitions in writing. The ones you may be the most familiar with are the obvious transitions: *however, therefore, also, and, but, or, next, finally, for example*, etc. Transitions are the glue that holds writing together, the ways writers signal relationships between ideas and events. News typically has different types of transitions.

Quotations are transitional because they often amplify the statement just before the quote. Note the statement in graf 2 about Romney uniting the party; the quote in graf 3 amplifies that statement and therefore is transitional. The quotes in grafs 7 and 14 amplify the ideas in the respective previous grafs. Also, sometimes quotations carry over partial quotes in the previous grafs and thus continue the speaker's train of thought.

Even when that does not happen, we know that readers who plan to stop reading a story will often continue for another graf when they see a direct quote coming up; so quotes can pull a reader one graf farther into the story—that's a transition.

There are other types of transitions common in news that are found in the Romney story:

- **Repeated words are transitional**. Since the lead was about Romney, every mention of his name in the subsequent few grafs is transitional, signaling more information about the topic already being explained. You will see the same transition as other names are repeated.
- **Pronouns are transitional by definition**. Every pronoun refers back to a noun, called its antecedent (with which it must agree). In referring back to a previous name, pronouns are gentle transitions. This story has a few pronouns, but not many. Why? Too many people are being mentioned: Romney, Santorum, Gingrich and Paul, plus the others being quoted. A pronoun like "he" might have an unclear antecedent.
- **One overtly transitional phrase is used in graf 4:** "In a separate nationwide survey of conservatives…"

Judgment calls? New writers always ask how the reporter knew how to organize the information. There are no easy answers. In this case, some knowledge of politics is helpful. Arranging an inverted pyramid story is often a dicey proposition, but the more you know about previous news stories on the same or similar topics, the better you will be able to make those decisions.

The best way to make good decisions is to be a news consumer. A math teacher can explain why you should put 6 after 5, and a history teacher can explain why Herbert Hoover came after Calvin Coolidge, but it's not always easy to explain why the Sarah Palin speech wouldn't have fit higher into the story. That comes down to news judgment, and news judgment is built by news exposure.

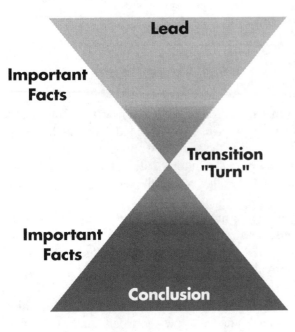

The Hourglass

Some news stories don't fit the inverted pyramid model, especially stories with a strong chronology. These are the stories where the news is the culmination of a long or complicated series of events that need to be recounted. The hourglass model provides media writers an organizational strategy that presents the news early in the story and then lets the writer tell the story chronologically from the beginning.

Here's how it works: You begin by summarizing the story in a short inverted pyramid, often called *the top* of the hourglass. Pretend you were going to write only a short inverted pyramid story and reduce the entire piece to the main facts in an inverted pyramid. You tell the reader that you are going to begin from the beginning and tell the story as a narrative. That sentence is called *the turn*, typically a transitional phrase that contains attribution for the chronological narrative to follow. It may be something like this:

- Police and witnesses gave the following account ...
- Eyewitnesses described the event in this way ...
- Firefighters said the rescue unfolded this way ...

Then, tell the story chronologically, from a starting point that will make sense to the reader.

Here's an example of an hourglass story. The *lightest gray* is the opening inverted pyramid section that presents a summary of the news. The *darker gray* is the transition. The *darkest gray* is the narrative.

A South Fort Worth convenience store clerk shot an armed robber who was attempting to hold up the store Tuesday night, police said.

The suspect, who was apparently shot in the shoulder, turned and ran out of the store after he had been shot. The man got into the passenger side of a late model black SUV in the parking lot and was driven away from the store, police said.

Robby Ricketts, 24, who has been working at the AAA Convenience Store, 244 W. Third St., for six months, said he pulled a pistol from under the counter when the man demanded that he hand over all the money in his cash drawer.

"He was acting really erratic, like he was high on drugs, and I was afraid he would shoot me after I gave him the money," Ricketts said. "So I decided to take a chance and pull my own gun. I must have surprised him because I got off a shot before he could react."

Police said the suspect is about 6 feet tall, weighs 180 pounds and has a heavily tattooed left arm and neck.

"We don't think the suspect could have made it far given his injury," said Sgt. Dave Malone, a police spokesman. "We're checking local hospitals and we're confident we'll have him in custody shortly."

Ricketts gave this account of the robbery:

The suspect entered the store about 11 p.m. and appeared to shop for a few minutes before he approached the clerk. The suspect asked Ricketts for a package of cigarettes. When Rickets reached to get the cigarettes, the man pulled a gun from his pocket and demanded money.

"I got his cigarettes and as I put the package on the counter I noticed that he was holding a gun on me," Ricketts said. "His hands were shaking and he seemed really nervous. He told me that if I didn't give him everything in the cash register and my own wallet that he would shoot me right there."

Ricketts said he opened the cash drawer as the man instructed and began to pull out the money. Ricketts said he noticed that the robber kept looking toward the front of the store, presumably to make sure that nobody else was about to come in. Ricketts took the opportunity to pull his own gun from the shelf just under cash drawer.

"I just acted on reflex," Ricketts said. "I've been shooting guns since I was a kid and I'm really comfortable handling them. I just pulled out my pistol and put a bullet in his right shoulder. He dropped his gun but he picked it up with his left hand and hit the door running."

Police said that no money was taken in the attempted robbery.

New writers always want to know how long each section should be. The answer: It depends. You take into account how much information you need to include, the amount of space you have to work with and what your editor wants from the story. Remember that the first section of the story, the inverted pyramid, can be easily trimmed because you have written it in descending order of importance. The last section is more difficult to cut because it is written as a narrative.

The Bottom Line

Organization is what carries the reader through the story. Most news readers want to know the most important information first. The implicit contract we have with readers is that if they read only the headline and the lead, there is nothing more important in the second or third graf than what they have already read. If they read five grafs, they don't have to worry that more important information was in the eighth graf. That puts readers in charge of obtaining as much or as little information as they want. We further help readers by providing transitional devices that make it easy for them to keep track of the flow of the story. The hourglass is the ultimate in reader friendliness. There, we tell readers that we will summarize the entire news event at the top of the story, and then allow them to bail out of the story or—if they are really interested—begin at the beginning and put everything into chronological context.

References

Rosen, James. "Elections & Politics." *Fort Worth Star-Telegram*, February 11, 2012. http://www.star-telegram.com/2012/02/11/3728176/romney-wins-straw-vote-at-conservative.html#storylink=cpy.

Skills Development: Practice in Media Writing

Exercise 7.1

Note: These exercises may contain errors in grammar, spelling, punctuation or AP style. Assume the names and story facts are correct, but fix any other errors you see when you write the story.

Write this for Sunday publication.

It's about bad weather coming up tomorrow (Monday). Your source for everything to follow is Nick Hampshire, a meteorologist with the National Weather Service in Fort Worth. Everybody had better watch out, because this weather could get rough. Here's what could happen. On Sunday, temperatures will be in the upper 70s, just like it has been for several days now. It will be cloudy and breezy. Winds will come out of the south. There may well be an afternoon thunderstorm on Sunday—a 20% chance. On Monday evening, some heavy rain will move in. The worst, most severe weather could be Monday afternoon into Monday evening. The storm, if indeed there is a storm, may bring winds of 60 to 70 m.p.h. Plus, there may be golf ball-sized hail. And maybe even isolated tornadoes. Areas to the south and east of the DFW area should receive more rain than the DFW area. Temperatures on Tuesday and Wednesday should be cooler, with highs in the seventies. Here is a quote from Hampshire: "We are not anticipating a widespread threat of tornadoes, after the severe weather rolls through, the area can expect the heavy rainfall through Tuesday morning, with one to three inches expected in the DFW area. Rain chances will end by Tuesday afternoon as the front moves east."

Exercise 7.2

Write this for Saturday publication.

A woman and a man were traveling down Texas 121 on Friday night about 9 p.m. She was driving. When she was in the 1900 block of 121, something bad happened. She was trying to make a lane change. Then she over-corrected so she wouldn't hit another car. She lost control of the car. She hit a construction barricade. No other cars were involved in this tragic accident. She was killed; the man was injured critically. You talked with Lt. Kirk Roberts, Bedford Police Department. He said he could not identify the woman yet, pending notification of her next of kin. Roberts said she lived in Bedford. The man was taken to a local hospital. He is expected to survive. The case is still under investigation.

Exercise 7.3

The grafs in the following inverted pyramid story are out of order. Starting with No. 1 for the lead, number each paragraph in such a way the story makes sense for you.

City spokesman Bill Begley said city election rules provide no avenue for appeal. Begley said the city secretary has five days to review the sworn application, but if that review period comes after the filing deadline, there is no recourse for the candidate to correct errors.

"The information on the candidate's application for a place on the ballot indicates that he is ineligible for the office due to length of residency in the district as required by the city charter," said City Secretary Mary J. Kayser. "The city charter requires that a candidate continuously reside in the council district for which he or she seeks election for a six full months before the first allowed filing date for the election."

Hobbs said Wednesday morning that he signed a lease for his residence on Oakland Boulevard on July 1, more than six months before the filing period began. He said he filled out the forms earlier and waited to see whether District 8 Councilwoman Kathleen Hicks would file for re-election. When Hicks, who is running for Congressional District 33, did not run again for her council seat, Hobbs filed the paperwork shortly before the 5 p.m. Monday deadline.

"I have lived in the district the proper amount of time," he said. "I think it's an atrocity that you can have one individual in the bureaucracy that can arbitrarily decide someone is off the ballot."

On his application filed Monday, Marshall Hobbs, 46, said he had lived in the district for six months, or since September. But the city charter requires a candidate to live in the district six months from the start of filing period, which began Feb. 13.

"I know district courts err on the side of the person participating, not erring on the side of preventing from participating," said Hobbs, a professor and pastor.

But Hobbs, who called the ruling "an administrative technicality," was meeting with lawyers late Wednesday afternoon and hinting at a legal challenge.

After the city secretary's ruling, Hobbs said he had heard from many of his supporters who were upset that he had been disqualified.

A candidate for the District 8 City Council seat was kicked off the May 12 special election ballot after the city secretary ruled that he did not meet residency requirements.

Without Hobbs, the special election has two candidates—business owner Ramon Romero Jr. and Kelly Allen Gray, executive director of the United Riverside Rebuilding Corp.

From the *Fort Worth Star-Telegram*, 2012. Reprinted by permission.

Exercise 7.4

This bank robbery story lends itself to an hourglass style:

On Tuesday afternoon, a man walked into First National Bank, 320 Main Street, in your city. The man was wearing a black hooded jacket and had a red bandana over his face. He was brandishing what appeared to be a handgun.

As soon as the guy got into the lobby, he yelled out: "This is a holdup. Everybody down." He told people to lie face-down on the floor. He went to a teller and ordered her to give him all of her money. She did. He then went to a second teller and told her the same thing. She was opening her cash drawer when the man sprinted out of the bank. He got into what witnesses described as a late-model white Chevrolet sedan.

A man was walking down the sidewalk and saw the masked man run to his car and get in. The man ran after the car to try to write down a license number.

One block from the bank, at the corner of Main and Thorndyke streets, the robber ran a stop sign and collided with another vehicle.

The man who had been following the car on foot ran up to the robber's car, opened the driver's-side door and pulled him out. He forced him down onto the street and held him until police arrived.

The man who captured the bank robber was Roy Bradford, owner of Central City Karate Studios, 360 Main Street. Bradford is a 5th degree black belt in Tae Kwon Do. He is 44 years old.

The bank robber is Lester Nurlmann, 1634 Runnymede Drive in your city. He is 23 years old and unemployed.

Cops found more than $3,000 in a bag in Nurlmann's car.

The FBI is investigating the robbery.

Exercise 7.5

The robbery suspect in 7.4 has now been indicted. Write the indictment story, using facts from 7.4 as background.

Yesterday, Nurlmann was indicted in federal court. If he is convicted, he could face 20 years in jail and a fine of $250,000.

Exercise 7.6

Write the following story about an award given to the man who apprehended the robber in Exercise 7.4. Use information from 7.4 and 7.5 as background.

The Downtown Rotary Club of your city has announced that Roy Bradford is being awarded its Citizen of the Year honor. It will be presented in a meeting of the club next Wednesday.

The citation reads: Roy Bradford has demonstrated the type of selflessness that makes for a great city. His bravery helped to apprehend a robber who had engendered the lives of citizens. We honor him as a man who put the public good and the public safety over personal considerations, and risked his own life so that our city could be a safer place.

References

for Chapter 7 exercises

Skills development stories for Chapter 7 were adapted from the following articles that appeared in the Fort Worth Star-Telegram:

Hanna, Bill. "Fort Worth Council Candidate Booted from Ballot." *Fort Worth Star-Telegram*, March 15, 2012. http://www.star-telegram.com/2012/03/14/3810509/fort-worth-council-candidate-booted.html.

McFarland, Susan. "Bedford Woman Killed in Construction Zone Crash." *Fort Worth Star-Telegram*, March 7, 2012. http://www.star-telegram.com/2012/03/17/3817123/bedford-woman-killed-in-construction.html.

———. "Severe Weather May Be on the Way to North Texas." *Fort Worth Star-Telegram*, March 17, 2012. http://www.star-telegram.com/2012/03/17/3817023/severe-weather-may-be-on-the-way.html.

Chapter Eight

USING QUOTES: ENLIVENING AND HUMANIZING THE NEWS

A great quotation can make a story. In this chapter, we explain how to identify the best quotations and how to use them for maximum impact.

Quotations add life to a news story. They let our readers meet newsmakers and hear them speak in their own words. Media writers use quotations to hold the reader's attention and to advance the story. Direct quotations provide credibility by sharing the exact words of a speaker or a document.

Media writers use quotations judiciously. Just because a news source says something does not mean it should be quoted. Quotations, besides being accurate, should be well stated. A good quotation is something interesting, said in an interesting way.

Here's an example. Let's assume the mayor says this during his re-election campaign:

"My opponent has misrepresented my record and I take exception to these mischaracterizations," the mayor said.

That quotation may be accurate—the mayor really did say those words—but it makes for a bad quotation because it's boring and certainly not uniquely stated. It would have been better to use it as an indirect quotation, like this: *The mayor said his opponent had misrepresented his record.*

But let's say he had said this:

"My opponent has lied about my record and I'm fighting mad about it," the mayor said.

That's uniquely stated and colorful and gives the reader a sense of the emotion behind the statement. It's a good quote. Writing coach Paula LaRocque (2000) notes that it's a media writer's job not only to select accurate quotes, but *the best* quotes:

Good journalism thrives on good quotations. The right quotes, carefully selected and presented, enliven and humanize a story and help make it clear, credible, immediate and dramatic.

Yet many quotations in journalism are dull, repetitive, ill-phrased, ungrammatical, nonsensical, self-serving or just plain dumb. We try to buttress stories with a source's exact words even when those words are weak rather than strong (p. 143).

You've heard them called *quotes* and *quotations*. Are those words interchangeable?

In media writing, we do frequently use them to mean the same thing: The speaker's words can be called a quote *or* a quotation. Actually, though, *quote* is a verb that means to repeat what someone has said or written. The noun for what we are quoting is a *quotation*. But in popular usage, *quotation* often sounds pretentious: *"Jeff, did you get some good quotations from the governor tonight?"* So in this book, we stick with the popular usage in mass communications and treat *quote* as a noun as well as a verb. If that bothers you, go complain to your English prof.

Types of Quotes

There are two ways to quote someone: as a direct quote, using that person's exact words or as a paraphrase, putting the source's thoughts into your own words while accurately representing what he or she said.

When you quote someone directly, you take the person's actual words and put them inside quotation marks. Then you add what media writers call a *speech tag* or an *attribution*, a phrase like *Jones said* that tells the reader who said the words inside the quotes. It looks like this:

"The president's proposed tax increase would further cripple small business and make it even more difficult to turn this economy around," Jones said.

Note the three parts of any quote:

1. A statement made by a news source;

2. An attribution, such has *Jones said*, that tells you who made the statement;

3. Quotation marks to cite the exact words of the speaker and a comma to separate the quote from the attribution.

As a writer, you have some options about how to format the quote, and we look at those options in the next section of this chapter. You also have an option on how you will report the statements of the source: as a direct quote or as an indirect quote (paraphrase).

You paraphrase all the time.

Let's say Steve meets a friend, Megan, on campus, and she tells him this: *"Well, I finally did it. I broke up with Colin. I told you last week that I've been thinking about this for some time. This morning I did it. Told him we just weren't going to work out. Broke it off completely. And I'm glad I did."*

The statements in the quotation marks above are the actual words Megan spoke to Steve. After Steve leaves Megan, let's say he runs into a mutual friend, Lois. Steve says this to Lois: *"Guess what! I just saw Megan and she said she broke up with Colin today. She said she told him that things weren't going to work out. She said they're finished."*

Notice that Steve, in referring to his conversation with Megan, used the word "said" three times. And yet he used hardly any of Megan's exact words. He put what Megan told him into his own words, but he still said she "said" that to him. Was he accurate? If Megan had heard what Steve said, would she have agreed that he had accurately related their conversation? Of course. Steve had paraphrased Megan in an indirect quote. It's how we report most conversations, and it is effective in media writing. The words Steve used were different from Megan's, but the thoughts were the same, only reworded.

That's the definition of an indirect quote, or paraphrase. Look back at the direct quotation used above:

"The president's proposed tax increase would further cripple small business and make it even more difficult to turn this economy around," Jones said.

You could have made it an indirect quote, like this:

Jones said the president's tax increase would be bad for small business and slow the nation's economic recovery. Different words, but the same idea, just paraphrased.

A writer might justifiably criticize the paraphrase because it is not quite as strong as the original statement. Jones said the tax increase would "cripple" small business. Was the paraphrase "would be bad for small business" an adequate paraphrase? These are the issues writers have to consider when they paraphrase quotes. You can use your own words and still use said as an attribution word, but you must be sure you have accurately paraphrased the speaker in both content and nuance. That's not as easy as it might look.

Sometimes media writers paraphrase a statement but still put strong wording in quotes within the paraphrase, reasoning that you cannot always paraphrase every word. For the quote above, this might give you something like: *Jones said the president's tax increase would "cripple" small business and slow the nation's economic recovery.*

Media writers try to avoid the use of these fragmentary quotes whenever possible, using them only in a paraphrase that contains words that are especially controversial, inflammatory or provocative or sometimes figures of speech or slang. In other words, indirect quotes, or indirects, paraphrase a speaker's words; however, some words cannot be accurately paraphrased or they lose the flavor of speech when you do. In those cases, use those words in quotes within the paraphrase.

Quote Forms

Let's say you have a quote and a source, and you are looking for options on how to handle it. Let's take this quote from the provost: *"The college newspaper is full of rabble-rousing hotheads, and I plan to seek support for shutting it down permanently."* Not a quote you're likely to hear, but probably a sentiment many provosts have secretly expressed. Here are ways you can arrange that statement and its attribution:

Attribution plus statement *The provost said, "The newspaper is full of rabble-rousing hotheads, and I plan to seek support for shutting it down permanently."*

> Note: This quote form is correct but is rarely used as a direct-quote form because it puts the attribution, the dullest part, up front in the sentence. One time you might find it used is when you have multiple sources in the story and you are transitioning from one source/speaker to another, so it has to be obvious to whom this particular quote belongs.

The provost said: "The newspaper is full of rabble-rousing hotheads, and I plan to seek support for shutting it down permanently. Shutting down the newspaper is what I want to be remembered for." [We used a colon after the attribution because the quote had two sentences. When you have an attribution followed by one sentence, use a comma. When it is two or more, use a colon.]

The provost said the newspaper is "full of rabble-rousing hotheads" and he plans to ask other administrators about the possibilities of suspending publication. [This is a good example of a paraphrase where you need the direct-quote inserts. How would you ever paraphrase "full of rabble-rousing hotheads"?]

Statement plus attribution *"The newspaper is full of rabble-rousing hotheads, and I plan to seek support for shutting it down permanently," the provost said.*

Attribution in the middle *"The newspaper is full of rabble-rousing hotheads," the provost said, "and I plan to seek support for shutting it down permanently."*

Statement plus attribution, with another sentence riding off the same attribution *"You can't believe half of what you read in the newspaper," the provost said. "You'd almost think they just sit around and make the news up."*

Note that in the sentence above, the second sentence is a direct quotation and therefore was obviously related to the attribution just before it. If the second sentence in the quote, the sentence following the attribution, had been an indirect quote, this would not have worked. Indirects do not ride off the attribution in the first sentence. Note this example:

Some people get carried away with quote marks. For a humorous look at the results, go to http://www.unnecessaryquotes.com/

"You can't believe half of what you read in the newspaper," the provost said. The staff apparently fabricates much of its news. This quote works down through the attribution. But what about the second sentence? Did the provost say it? Is this an editorial insertion by the writer? Note the two ways this could have been handled, either by adding a second attribution or by combining sentences:

"You can't believe half of what you read in the newspaper," the provost said. The staff apparently fabricates much of its news, he said.

The provost said that the newspaper lacks credibility because "the staff apparently fabricates much of its news."

Placing the attribution in quotes containing several sentences Let's say you have a two- or three-sentence quote. Where do you put the attribution? Typically it would go at the end of the first sentence, so you let the reader know immediately who the speaker is.

"The newspaper is full of rabble-rousing hotheads, and I plan to seek support for shutting it down permanently," the provost said. *"This kind of blatant disregard for accuracy and good taste cannot be allowed to continue on a university campus."*

Word order in attributions English speakers prefer a subject + verb word order. Do it the same way in your quotations. Make it *the provost said*, not *said the provost*.

Make an exception when there is an appositive for the speaker; then it would be *said Donovan*, not *Donovan, provost and vice chancellor for academic affairs, said*.

Other Guidelines for Quotes

There are other important guidelines for using quotes in mass media copy. These guidelines will help you use quotes consistently. If you're glancing ahead a couple of pages, you probably think there are a lot of these guidelines. That's probably true, but when you have these mastered, you're good to go. These guidelines are the same ones used by veteran media writers. If you end up writing for The New York Times or your university's media relations office or Edelman PR, you will still use the same quotation forms and guidelines you're studying in this chapter. Here are some more guidelines to add to your writing toolbox.

Going from a partial quote to a full quote You cannot go from a partial quote to a full quote in the same set of marks. You have to close out the partial quote and open a new set of quote marks for the full quote:

Do not: *The provost said the newspaper is full of "rabble-rousing hotheads. I plan to seek support for shutting it down permanently."*

Instead: *The provost said the newspaper staff is full of "rabble-rousing hotheads."*

"I plan to seek support for shutting it down permanently," he said.

Prefer *said* to all other forms of attribution Said means said. It means someone opened his/her mouth and words issued forth. *Explained, stated* or *commented* have different shades of meaning. *Claimed* means you doubt the truth of what someone said; *admitted* means you think he or she may be guilty of something. You may have been told that *stated, explained, continued,* insisted, and the like are synonyms for said. Not so. Each of them carries a little different shade of meaning.

Don't bury quotes When you start a new full sentence of quote, start a new graf. Example:

The provost said he planned to ask other administrators about the possibility of shutting down the newspaper. "This type of blatant journalistic irresponsibility should not be tolerated in a learning community," he said.

Begin a new graf with the second sentence, so it looks like this:

The provost said he planned to ask other administrators about the possibility of shutting down the newspaper.

"This type of blatant journalistic irresponsibility should not be tolerated in a learning community," he said.

Changing quotes Don't change what a speaker said. Put quotes around exact words uttered by a speaker. Never paraphrase a speaker and put quotes around your paraphrase. And never put two quotes together so that the quotes—even though they are accurate—make it appear the speaker is saying something he or she never meant to say. It is generally accepted that you can edit out fillers (uh, ah, um) that people use as verbal place-holders.

To read more about handling nonstandard English, visit: http://www.cjr.org/language_corner/gonna_wanna.php

But if the rule seems simple, just know that it really isn't. What about the politician or the quarterback who can't make a subject and verb agree? Should we fix that for them? And what about the senator who misstates the year the Vietnam War ended or misses the amount of the president's proposed budget by $1 trillion?

To read more about the issue of "fixing" or cleaning up quotes, visit: http://www.ajr.org/article.asp?id=1340

The simple rule on dealing with these issues is to ask your editor. That's not a cop-out. The way these issues are handled varies widely across media.

Quoting multiple speakers If you quote two or more people in the same story, you must be careful to let the reader know who is speaking. You can't quote Source A and go directly into another quote, leading readers to think it is a continuation of Source A's quote, only to discover that they have really been reading the thoughts of Source B. Here's an example of the wrong way to do it:

"I thought the senator gave some compelling reasons for intervening in the Libyan conflict on the side of the rebels," said Frank Moses, a sophomore environmental science major.

"I think the U.S. needs to stay out of Middle Eastern wars that don't concern our vital national interests," said Louise Morgan, a freshman art major.

Note that it looks like Moses is immediately contradicting himself until you get to the attribution. This slows down the reader. In stories like this, transition between the speakers:

"I thought the senator gave some compelling reasons for intervening in the Libyan conflict on the side of the rebels," said Frank Moses, a sophomore environmental science major.

Louise Morgan, a freshman art major, said she opposes U.S. involvement.

"I think the U.S. needs to stay out of Middle Eastern wars that don't concern our vital national interests," Morgan said.

Clarifying quotes Sometimes media writers have to insert a word in a quote in the interest of clarity. We do that when a source mentions a name, for instance, that the reader might not know—a name that was not mentioned earlier in the story. The writer may insert an identifier in front of that name. Or you may quote someone who uses a pronoun that is obvious in the context of the quotation but not obvious when you use the quote in the story. Instead of saying "he" in the quote, you can insert the pronoun reference in brackets: *"We are going to suspend [Smith] pending the outcome of his trial," Jones said.*

Now that you know how to use brackets, try not to. They're clunky. Sometimes they are necessary, but when you can, reword the sentence so you do not have to use them: *Jones said he would suspend Smith pending the outcome of his trial.*

Identifying speakers Always identify a speaker the first time his or her name is used. On first mention of the speaker, use first and last name (and middle initial if the speaker uses it) and some type of identifier, like a job title. After that, use only the last name. Do not use any other title on subsequent identifications. If the speaker is Mayor John Q. Smith, give the identification the first time you mention him in the story. On all subsequent mentions, it's just *Smith*, not *Mayor Smith*.

Avoid echo quotes An echo quote is when you paraphrase a statement, and then use a direct quote to say the same thing again in a direct quote in the next graf. For example:

The congressman said he was pleased with the primary results because they indicated that Democrat voters in the district agree with his pro-life positions.

"I am pleased with tonight's results," he said. "They certainly show that many Democrats agree with my pro-life positions."

Groupspeak? Attribute quotations to one person only, never a group of any size. Groups do not speak in unison unless they are part of a chorus in a play. This means you can never use phrases like *John Franklin and Chris Yarbrough said they thought the stadium implosion was "a sight no student should have missed."*

Here is writing coach Chip Scanlan's take on the *said* vs. *says* issue: http://bit.ly/oIwqVW

Says* or *said*? What tense do you use in attribution? Says? Said? Again, you're asking tough questions when it comes to media writing. The "safe" thing is probably to use *said*. Typically, *said* is used in news stories and *says* in feature stories or soft news stories (see chapter 13). If you're writing ad copy or many types of PR copy, you're likely to use *says*. Best bet: Ask somebody. It's not a stupid question.

Ellipses An ellipsis is three dots that indicate something has been left out. (Note: In broadcast writing, an ellipsis can be used to indicate a pause. More on that in chapter 14.) An ellipsis is an acceptable mark for many kinds of writing, but typically not for media writing and especially not for quotes. Many new media writers want to uses ellipses to select certain relevant parts of quotes to use in their stories. The problem is that readers don't always understand this mark, and they frequently think that writers have used it to leave out information to slant the story. So it's best not to use it. Instead, if the quotation has elements you do not want to use, paraphrase the whole thing or quote only part of it.

Rules for Punctuating Quotes

Unlike what probably seems like a lot of rules for how to use quotes, there are only a few rules for punctuating them. Here you go.

Rule 1: Keep all commas and periods inside quotation marks. Always. No matter what the context.
"The president is out of touch with working people," Jones said.
Jones said Obama is "out of touch with working people."
He said he was surprised when the Best Picture Oscar went to "The Artist." (Note: AP style mandates quotation marks around movie titles.)

Rule 2: Place question marks and exclamation points according to usage. If the quote itself asks a question or is an exclamation, put the mark inside the quote marks. Colons and semicolons always go *outside* the quotation marks.
"Who said that?" she asked.
"I didn't!" he said.
Who watches "Survivor"? (Note: AP style mandates quotation marks around TV show titles.)

Rule 3: For quotes inside quotations, go to single quote marks. If you have a quote within a quote within a quote, go back to double quotes.
"Who watches 'Survivor'?" she asked.
"He saved my life when he called out, 'Watch out for the shark!'" Jones said.

Rule 4: If a question mark or an exclamation point occurs where a comma should be used to set off the attribution, omit the comma and use the question mark or exclamation point to separate the quoted material.
"Who's ready?" she asked.
"I am!" he answered.

Rules 5: When you use an attribution between two chunks of quoted matter (splitting a quote in the middle), put a period after the attribution if the second part of the quote forms an independent clause (begins a new sentence). Put a comma after the attribution if the whole quote is one long sentence.
"I will never again run for elective office," Jones said. "I plan to devote my energies now to supporting those candidates who stand for the same ideals I always stood for."
"I will never again run for elective office," Jones said, "because I don't have the emotional energy it takes to spend months on the campaign trail."

Rule 6: When using a partial quote, do not capitalize the first word of the quote unless it begins a complete sentence of quoted matter.
Obama said House Republicans "are playing obstructionist politics."

The Bottom Line

Quoted speech is a common part of a media writer's toolkit of techniques that draw readers into the copy. Quotes can bring a story to life and make it real for readers. Quotes also add authenticity and credibility to a story. When we use quoted speech, we get out of the way and let readers encounter the subject of our stories. That's why it's so important that we understand how to use quotes effectively and how to punctuate them correctly. Remember, we don't quote someone just because they opened their mouth and words came out. Direct quotes are lively, interesting, sometimes colorful and always well stated. Otherwise, summarize and paraphrase in an indirect.

References

LaRocque, Paula. 2000. *Championship Writing: 50 Ways to Improve Your Writing.* Oak Park, IL: Marion Street Press.

Skills Development: Practice in Media Writing

Exercise 8.1

Put in periods, question marks, exclamation points, etc. If something is in italics, assume it is a direct quote. These are difficult, because they contain a number of quotes within quotes, and even quotes within quotes within quotes. But if you can punctuate the following sentences, you can punctuate anything you might ever have to work with as a media writer.

1. *Politicians pay more attention to poll numbers than to their convictions* George Smith said.

2. Smith said *Politicians pay more attention to poll numbers than to their convictions.*

3. Today's *politicians pay more attention to poll numbers* Smith said *than they do to their convictions*

4. *What can voters do* a student asked.

5. J.K. Rowling will sign her book Harry Potter and the Prisoner of Azkaban. [This is a book title.]

6. *Have you read J.K. Rowling's Harry Potter and the Prisoner of Azkaban* she asked.

7. *Yes, I read Harry Potter and the Prisoner of Azkaban* he said.

8. *I couldn't believe it* Susan Allen said. *She actually asked me, Have you read J.K. Rowling's Harry Potter and the Prisoner of Azkaban* [This has a quote inside a quote.]

9. *Shut up* she screamed. [Use an exclamation point.]

10. *I thought the book was slow* the reviewer said *I'm surprised it sold so many copies.*

Exercise 8.2

Put in periods, question marks, exclamation points, etc. If something is in italics, assume it is a direct quote. These are difficult, because they contain a number of quotes within quotes, and even quotes within quotes within quotes. But if you can punctuate the following sentences, you can punctuate anything you might ever have to work with as a media writer.

Put the book title, "Roots," in quotation marks wherever you find it, as mandated by AP style. Note that No. 8 uses a quote from No. 7, so punctuate accordingly. Just punctate sentences—do not rewrite them.

1 | Alex Haley is the author of Roots

2 | Did *Alex Haley write Roots* the professor asked his class.

3 | *Indeed he did answered* the freshman. *The book was turned into a multi-part TV series.*

4 | *You're right* the professor said [use an exclamation mark after the quote]

5 | *My fondest hope is that Roots may start black, white, brown, red and yellow people digging back for their own roots* Haley said *man, that would make me feel 90 feet tall*

6 | *Roots is the book I was always meant to write* Haley said *it is the symbolic saga of a people*

7 | *I look at my books* Haley said *the way parents look at their children – and my favorite child is Roots.*

8 | The professor asked *Did Alex Haley say I look at my books the way parents look at their children*

9 | *Haley's book is a masterpiece the reviewer said it should be required reading for every young American*

10 | The reviewer said This book can give us real insight into our history. I can still remember my favorite professor asking Why don't we require every college student to read Roots

Exercise 8.3

Write the following story for your campus newspaper or news site.

Your university has a problem with tailgating at football games. It seems a lot of fans just show up to tailgate. They don't go to the game—they don't even have tickets. On game day, they just show up at the stadium, park in the lot, and hang out at their tailgate during games.

Problem is, there is no parking for paying fans.

Joe Schultz, ticket manager at the university, said this: "We typically have around 50,000 people at games. Our parking lots are designed to accommodate that number. But we have another 10,000 people who just come to party. They don't buy a ticket or go to the game. They just pay to park and hang out. And they show up early to get a head start on that partying. That means that paying fans sometimes can't find a place to park. We're excited that they want to be here, and they even add to the game-day atmosphere, but they are keeping paying fans from parking."

Schultz said that beginning next season, fans who do not have a ticket to the game will not be able to park in the stadium parking lot.

Ralph Rasco, who lives two blocks from the stadium, predicted that the new rule would create more problems than it solves: "It'll just be impossible on game days. Checking everyone's game ticket at the entrance to the parking lot will back up traffic for miles. People still won't be able to park because they can't get into the parking lots. It'll be gridlock. And pity the poor homeowners who live in this area!"

Martha Radmore, who said she is a football fans and typically attends three or four home games every year, said this: "I'm not a season ticket holder. When I can attend games, I just drive to the stadium and park and pick up my ticket at Will Call. I won't have my ticket when I drive up, so am I not going to be able to park?"

Schultz told you the new tailgating rules go into effect at the first game next season, when the team plays Podunk State at a night game starting at 7:30 p.m.

(Your instructor may choose to play Joe Schultz to let you ask whatever additional questions you may have about the new rules.)

Exercise 8.4

Write the following story for a newspaper in your city.

Your city has an arts funding task force. The task force was created by the City Council one year ago. The function of the task force was to generate proposals to help fund the arts in your city.

Well, just last night they reported to the City Council.

The report contained several important points:

- It was recommended that the city return to previous levels of funding for the arts. During the economic downturn of two years ago, the Council cut back arts funding by 50%.
- It was recommended that the city increase arts funding by 10% every year, beginning in the next fiscal year, until arts funding was at its previous levels.
- It was recommended that the city make an immediate transfer of $450,000 to the Arts Council, to come from the city's rainy day fund. The Arts Council distributes grants to local artists and art organizations.

The report was endorsed by the Council by a vote of 8-1. Only Aaron Horchwitz voted against it.

Quotes:

Wanda Garner, member of the task force: "We understand the city has a couple more years of tight funding. As the projections move to surplus, we certainly look forward to a return to historic funding [levels] for the arts."

Mayor Harriet Harris: "Our budgets are still tight, but this is an investment we cannot afford to ignore. Every time we fund the arts and the arts grow, it brings in more money to the city."

City Council member Laura Seeley: "The task force worked really hard and found a lot of creative solutions. It's time we adopted this plan to get arts funding back on track."

City Council member Aaron Horchwitz: "Everyone loves the arts and we all support the arts. But this proposal could be an economic disaster for the city. We have to make a big lump-sum payment now and commit to annual payments. We can't afford to commit money we do not know we'll have."

Chapter Nine
ATTRIBUTION: SHOWING READERS WHERE WE GOT OUR INFORMATION

BY GEOFF CAMPBELL

In the previous chapter, we saw how using quotes can enliven and enrich our stories, press releases and advertisements. Or make them dull and pedestrian. Choosing the best quotations is an art, and fortunately for us, it's something we can all master.

Attributing quotes is less an art than a skill. And we can develop and nurture our skills with thought and diligent practice.

In this chapter, you'll learn when you need to attribute the information you use, an essential skill for anyone hoping for a career in mass media writing.

In general, media writers are not experts in much more than gathering relevant information and writing about it in a way the average reader can understand. Of course the field is filled with exceptions. An advertising copywriter for Halliburton, for example, is by necessity going to become something of an expert on extracting energy from oil sands or shale. A Federal Reserve Board beat writer for The Wall Street Journal needs to become an expert on the implications of a change in the discount rate or in reserve requirements for banks. And so on. And yet, even with this specialized knowledge, these writers depend on experts for information and analysis when they write their copy.

Even op-ed writers (those who write personal opinion pieces) seek out experts as they marshal support for their favored positions.

Attribution allows our readers to know who our sources are. It's a measure of transparency. It helps readers judge the credibility of our sources. Remember: In the journalistic world, our job is to provide readers with facts so they can form their own opinions. Obviously, public relations professionals and advertising copywriters try to sway readers to embrace certain opinions or take a specific action. But even they need to attribute information.

Consider this advertising copy for a fictitious brand of bath soap:

"Sparrow soap leaves no residue and gives users a youthful glow while providing skin with eight essential vitamins."

Without attribution, the statement sounds like just another come-on. But look what happens when we attribute the information: *"Sparrow soap leaves no residue and gives users a youthful glow while providing skin with eight essential vitamins, according to a double-blind study by a leading research university."* Provided the product was subject to such a study at a leading university, we've just made the information more credible.

In other words, it doesn't really matter what branch of the media writing art you hope to work in. Attribution is important.

Before we dive headlong into more rules (sorry, we have rules for attribution), let's look at instances in which we don't have to attribute information.

We don't have to attribute statements that reveal undisputed facts. Let's say we are, for reasons known only to our editors, writing a story about how the sun rises at a different time each day. We include the statement, *"The sun rose at 7:11 a.m. in New York City on March 12."*

Do we need to attribute that? Should we say the information came from the National Weather Service? Should we say we got the information from meteorologist Joe Momma?

No. It's an undisputed fact.

When people pick up a newspaper in the morning, why do they believe what they read? Attribution, among other things. News sources gain their credibility largely from the sources they attribute information to, which is why good attribution is so important.

Likewise, we wouldn't write a sentence like this:

"*The St. Louis Cardinals won the 2011 World Series, Major League Baseball spokesman Joe Momma said.*"

This, too, is an undisputed fact (except in some Texas backwaters).

We also don't need to attribute things we ourselves witnessed. Let's say you're sitting in front of a local frozen yogurt shop. As you're enjoying your treat and no doubt engaging in a bit of people watching, you see a man with a sledgehammer smash the windshield of a parked car. Even though it's your day off, you consider yourself a diligent reporter and you jump on the story.

As you describe the incident, do you need to say "police said" a man smashed the windshield of a parked car? No. You saw it happen. There will, however, be plenty of other things in that story you'll have to attribute.

As a rule, always attribute direct quotations, indirect quotations, partial quotations, expressions of opinion and analysis. Attribute also facts that are not common knowledge or statements that make an accusation.

In some respects, this rule represents nothing more than common sense, and there's nothing wrong with that. Media writing is important, but it's not brain surgery.

Let's say you're writing a story about how a local sushi eatery attempts to cater to customers who don't like sashimi.

You write, "*Tempura rolls provide an alternative for diners who do not like raw fish.*" At this juncture, it appears this statement is your opinion. Someone else might suggest that a juicy hamburger likewise provides a viable alternative. So let's attribute this statement. "*Sushimania owner Joe Momma said tempura rolls provide an alternative for diners who do not like raw fish.*"

We also need to be careful when writing about accusations. Consider the following sentence:

"*The mayor's policies represent 'a power grab unseen since the days of robber barons and whale-bone corsets,' and voters should express their displeasure at the ballot box.*"

Here we have two statements of opinion, a partial quote and an accusation. To say we need attribution is an understatement. Readers need to know where this statement came from. Otherwise, it sounds like an expression of opinion from the writer. And as we know, journalists should remain objective and impartial.

Attribution in such cases is important for another, more personal reason.

Imagine the mayor sitting down to breakfast. She's enjoying her scrambled eggs and toast while reading the paper. She just finished reading a story about a county roadside beautification project, and now comes to your story about her policies. She reads the unattributed diatribe and calls her lawyer. You're going to get sued. The fact that she's a public figure works in your favor; it's a lot harder to prove libel when you're a public figure. (The burden of proof rests with the accuser, and the accuser must prove that you acted with actual malice, that you knew the information was untrue or you showed a complete lack of interest in whether the information was true. This statement is not provided as legal advice. If you find yourself being sued, consult a qualified attorney.)

But do you really want to go through the hassle of a lawsuit? Regardless of your feelings, know that your publisher doesn't want to incur the expense of defending you in such a case, especially because you could have avoided the whole thing by attributing your information.

So attribute. Readers need to know whether the statement came from a disgruntled employee who lost his job because of the mayor's policies or from a nonpartisan watchdog who considers it her mission to protect the public interest or from a candidate trying to unseat the incumbent.

You see, attribution does more than let readers know who said what. It also provides context.

Let's say you're following a local election for the county sewer board, and it is getting nasty and silly at the same time. Candidates are attacking each other without even waiting to see if their previous accusations stick. (If this sounds familiar, you've followed the 2012 presidential election. Or the 2008 election. Or the...)

You're faithfully covering the melee for the local newspaper or online news site. One day you learn that candidate Joe Momma wears combat boots. Leaving aside the important threshold question of whether this fact is newsworthy (spoiler alert: absent background or contextual information to the contrary, it's not), it will matter to readers where this information came from.

Maybe it came from Bill Ding, a candidate for the same seat who served three tours of duty in Iraq, who said he thinks that Momma is trying to cash in on voters' sympathy for veterans. Maybe it came from failed chef Barry Compote, a candidate who said he believes combat boots on a sewer board member is one step removed from martial law. Or maybe it came from Momma's mother, Yolanda "Yo" Momma, who revealed that she and her son wear the boots because they're "*comfortable.*"

Context is everything, and attribution helps to provide it.

In the previous chapter, you learned acceptable methods of attribution, so there's no need to plow through that again here. With one exception.

You can't overuse *said*. Maybe it's hardwired into the human psyche, but for reasons known only to the Great Editor in the Sky, aspiring practitioners of the media writing art seem to have a fetish for finding what they hope are synonyms for *said*. Otherwise bright students who eat Lucky Charms and one boiled egg for breakfast every day nevertheless believe it's important to provide variety in their copy.

There are a couple of problems with this approach. For one thing, because it is a widespread convention among professional media writers to rely primarily on *said*, readers find it jarring when writers trot out alternatives like *stated*. Readers start thinking about why you used *stated* instead of thinking about the substance of the quote.

Another problem is that a lot of the words students substitute for *said* are value laden. Let's say we write, "*The new structure was built to survive a Category 4 hurricane, Joe Momma claimed.*" By using *claimed*, we are casting doubt on Momma's remarks.

Said is neutral. So stick with *said* and stop annoying your media writing instructor.

According to...

What about *according to*? Is that a good attribution phrase? In some cases, yes. If you are attributing information to a person, use *said*. But if you are telling readers that you got your information from a printed or online source, use *according to*. You will find it in attributions like this:

... according to Dallas County voter registration records.

... according to Census records.

... according to the university catalog.

... according to red light camera records maintained by the Department of Transportation.

You will occasionally see *according to* used as an attribution word in news, but reserve it for records and information, not people.

The Bottom Line

Here are some guidelines that review the principles for when you attribute information in news articles or PR news releases. You attribute information:

- When it's an opinion.
- When it's a criticism.
- When it's a fact in dispute—perhaps a judgment call about which some but not all people would agree. For example: *"TCU has made significant progress in making the campus more handicapped accessible in the last decade, Don Mills said." Attribute if any reasonable person might dispute the accuracy of the statement. You need not attribute a statement like: "Gary Patterson has coached the Horned Frogs since Dennis Franchione left to take the head coaching job at Alabama."*
- When it might damage someone's reputation.
- When you did not see it and cannot verify that it is true. Let's say Hector Blodgett, a professor of psychology, announces findings of his research that 42 percent of freshmen indulge in binge drinking during their first year of college. He goes on to give the reasons found by his research for their drinking behavior. You would need to attribute both the fact that 42 percent binge drink and then attribute all his reasons. It's his research, not yours. You don't know that 42 percent of freshmen do binge drink. All you know is that Blodgett said they do. You don't know that they feel overwhelmed by the pressures of college life. All you know is that Blodgett *says* that is one of the reasons they drink.

Skills Development: Practice in Media Writing

Exercise 9.1

Pick up a newspaper and skim through 10 news stories. Underline every attribution word you find, whether for a direct quote, an indirect, or an information source. Note what kinds of information are attributed and how attribution is handled. Are all the attribution words in past tense?

Exercise 9.2

Read the following sentences. If they appeared in a news story you wrote, would they need attribution?

1. Baton Rouge is the capital of Louisiana.

2. The university has raised more than $200 million in its capital fund campaign.

3. The university's journalism school offers one of the most innovative strategic communication curricula in the nation.

4. The Olive Garden restaurant was destroyed by fire Tuesday night.

5. The restaurant and its contents are valued at $1.2 million.

6. Arson was the probable cause of the fire.

7. The plus-minus grading system was adopted by the university in 2006.

8. The plus-minus grading system is used by 48 percent of American universities.

9. The plus-minus grading system can be unfair to students who are trying to achieve 4.0 grade point averages.

10. The proposed health care plan will help the homeless get preventative care.

11. The Supreme Court's decision in Roe v. Wade overturned laws outlawing abortion.

12. The Supreme Court's Roe v. Wade decision caused many Americans to believe that their federal government had turned its back on a basic Judeo-Christian principle.

Chapter Ten

The Speech Story: A Media Writing Basic

Speech stories are one of the most common news types for journalists and public relations practitioners. They are as basic for media writers as blocking and tackling are for football players. That's because speech stories contain some of the most common types of writing: They present the news and they do it using quotes and paraphrases of speakers and the audience or knowledgeable experts who heard the speech. Besides being a common story type, they help new media writers prepare to do interviews and feature stories, both of which use a lot of quoted information. Even if you never cover a speech as a journalist, learning to write a speech story can give you valuable skills that you will use in other types of media writing.

Writing speech stories is a pretty common first assignment for both journalists and public relations practitioners. Lucky for you, we're giving you a framework in this chapter that'll help you get started on just about any speech story you encounter.

Many news stories are about events. Speech stories are about ideas and opinions. But you still handle the speech story much as you would any other type of news story. You begin with the most important elements and arrange the story in descending order of importance. If you have taken a basic speech class in college you know that speeches often begin with attention-getting or introductory material, then move on to several salient points the speaker wants to make. Most often, the primary point is the last one. No speaker wants to do what news writers do, that is, begin with the most important stuff and gradually work down to less important information. Speakers want to end with a bang—something memorable to leave the audience with.

News writers cannot structure their stories in the same way the speechwriter did. That doesn't necessarily mean that we start at the end, because the most important point might have been three-quarters of the way through the speech. We handle speech writing the same way we would tell anybody about a speech we just heard, even if we were not covering it. If you listen to a speech as an audience member, not as a journalist, and someone asks you what the speaker said, you don't start with, "Well, she spoke about foreign policy and she outlined what she thinks we should do to support pro-democracy groups in the Middle East." Instead, you say, "She said we should bomb military bases of repressive regimes to support pro-democracy groups."

That's how you approach speech stories. But let's be more specific and look at how speech stories are structured, from the beginning.

Step 1: Before You Write

Begin with your notes. Occasionally, you may have a speech text given to you by the speaker. Even if you have a text, be sure to follow it throughout the speech. Some speakers do a lot of freelancing with the text, and sometimes their best or most newsworthy quotes aren't on the printed text. Once you have the notes or the text-plus-notes, go through and mark the most important ideas. Then rank them, beginning with No. 1 for the idea or quote you will want to put in your lead. You may find it helpful to strike through information you know you will exclude from the story, like opening jokes or acknowledging guests. Look at additional information you may want to include, for example quotes from people who heard the speech or the organizers, biographical background on the speaker, additional quotes you got at a post-speech interview or press conference or any news events or other information you want to mention to give the speech context. These need to be ranked along with the speech. If the speaker said something in response to an audience question that is more important than anything he or she said in the speech itself, you can lead with that.

Lead with the biggest news of the speech event, not necessarily a point made by the speaker in the speech. If the speaker is drowned out with boos during a part of the speech and argues with hecklers, that may be your lead, not something said during the speech.

Step 2: The Lead

Now you have marked out what you will exclude, highlighted or checked what you do want to put into the story and ranked those items you want to include. In other words, you have a rough outline of the story. Time to write the lead.

What will your lead be about? You will want to tell your reader the most important point the speaker made.

Lead-killers

There are some things you can do in a speech lead that will kill it. They basically involve leaving the news out of the lead. Remember, the big news won't be that a person spoke or what he or she spoke about, but rather about the most important thing he or she said.

Let's assume, for instance, that CBS newsman Bob Schieffer speaks on campus. Here are three ways *not* to write the lead:

- CBS newsman Bob Schieffer spoke on campus Tuesday night about covering political campaigns. (Only his speech topic—no news.)
- CBS newsman Bob Schieffer addressed a group of journalism students on campus Tuesday night, speaking about covering political campaigns. (We know who spoke; we know to whom he spoke; we know when he spoke; we know what he spoke about. But we *don't* know what he said.)
- "We're in danger in America because political coverage is more about covering the political horserace than it is about covering what candidates say about the issues," CBS newsman Bob Schieffer said on campus Tuesday night. (Quote leads should be avoided. When you begin to read, you don't know who's talking. You don't even know who the "we" refers to.)

There are three primary ways that news writers approach speech leads. You'll find a lot of variations on these, but these three lead patterns cover most well-written leads: the speaker/news lead, the news/speaker lead, and the speaker/audience/news lead. Let's look at them.

The speaker/news lead. In this lead, you tell who said something and what was the most important thing said. You also typically throw in a time element. Like this:

CBS newsman Bob Schieffer said Tuesday night that news coverage of elections focuses too much on the election contest itself and not enough on the candidates' stand on the issues.

In the case above, the speaker is well known, so his name needs to appear in the lead. What if you considered the speech worth covering but nobody would recognize the name of the speaker? You handle it like you would any other type of news story where the name is not instantly recognizable; you give a general description of the speaker and move on to the news itself. Let's say the speech alluded to above was given not by Bob Schieffer but by Joe Blow, news director of WXYZ-TV. The lead would look like this:

> *The news director of WXYZ-TV in Burleson said Tuesday night that news coverage of elections focuses too much on the election contest itself and not enough on the candidates' stand on the issues.*

Then you name the news director in the second graf (more on what else to put in the second graf later in this chapter).

The news/speaker lead. Sometimes you write a speech story where the speaker is not well known but what the speaker says is important or interesting. That's the time for the news/speaker lead, where you lead off with the news and mention the speaker later in the lead, typically by description rather than by name. An example:

> *News coverage of elections focuses too much on the election contest itself and not enough on the candidates' stand on the issues, the news director of WXYZ-TV in Burleson said Tuesday night.*

The speaker/audience/statement lead. If the audience is important, that is, if readers would benefit from knowing whom the speaker was addressing, work that element into the lead. You should use the verb told instead of said to accommodate the audience element, like this:

> *CBS newsman Bob Schieffer told TCU journalism majors Tuesday night that news coverage of elections focuses too much on the election contest itself and not enough on the candidates' stand on the issues.*

Step 3: The Second Graf

Once you have written your lead, it's time to craft the second graf. Remember, in an inverted pyramid story, the second graf should contain the second-most-important facts in the story. Usually, you follow up on the lead, expanding the idea you put in the lead and telling the reader more about it. You also fill readers in on anything they need to know about the speech—what was the occasion, how many attended or other important information to put the speaker's words into context. Here's an example of a second graf, following a speaker/news lead we looked at above:

> *CBS newsman Bob Schieffer said Tuesday night that news coverage of elections focuses too much on the election contest itself and not enough on the candidates' stand on the issues.*
>
> *Schieffer, speaking at a meeting of the Fort Worth Society of Professional Journalists, <u>said the emphasis on polling and campaign strategy stories meant that issues like the economy and peace in the Middle East were ignored by the media.</u>*

In the story above, note how the second graf follows up on the lead, telling more about information introduced in the lead. It also gives some background on the occasion of the speech. Note that the news is included in the independent clause (underlined), and the background information ("speaking at a meeting …") is in a participle phrase that modifies the subject (Schieffer) of the independent clause.

There are three important keys to writing a good second graf:

1. Make sure the second graf contains the second-most-important information in the story, after the lead.

2. In most cases, the second graf should extend the lead; in other words, elaborate on the lead's news element.

3. If you need to give additional information about the occasion of the speech, do that in the second graf. If your lead identified the speaker without naming him or her, the second graf should name the speaker.

Step 4: The Third Graf

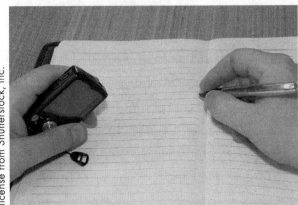

When it's time to include exact quotes in your story, having a recording of the speech can be helpful. Be sure to take notes that can help you find important quotes, though, so you're not listening to the whole speech again while up against a deadline.

The speech story's third graf is often a direct quote, but not just any direct quote from the speaker. It must be a direct quote that elaborates on the lead and the second graf. Let's look one more time at the story we've been building on the Schieffer speech. Look first at the lead and second graf, then read the third, which further elaborates but in a direct quote.

CBS newsman Bob Schieffer said Tuesday night that news coverage of elections focuses too much on the election contest itself and not enough on the candidates' stand on the issues.

Schieffer, speaking at a meeting of the Fort Worth Society of Professional Journalists, said the emphasis on polling and campaign strategy stories meant that issues like the economy and peace in the Middle East were ignored by the media.

"We've watched the level of national political discourse disintegrate," Schieffer said. "Presidential campaigns are now covered like horse races, with the press limited to telling who's ahead, who's coming up from behind and how the crowd is reacting to the race."

This may seem like a formula to you. It's not. You will see many speech stories that are not structured in the format we have just outlined. But it's a good way to get started until you have written enough of these types of stories to be comfortable structuring your story to fit the speech.

Step 5: The Rest of the Story

The rest of the story follows the inverted pyramid. Remember Step 1? You chose the key points in the speech and ranked them. You took the most important of those key points and put it in the lead. Then you followed up with more information on that point in the second graf and gave a direct quote elaborating on that point in the third graf.

Now you have a choice: Let's say the speaker made four key points and you have just talked about Point #1 in the first three grafs. Now you must decide if the less important aspects of Point #1 are more important than Point #2. If they are, stay with Point #1 for a few more grafs, continuing to give additional information until you think you need to go on to Point #2. You move on to #2, giving the most important ideas on that point. And then on to the other points in descending order of importance.

Your organizational plan for the rest of the story is the inverted pyramid. If it is a pretty simple story, you may be able to follow the rough outline you made when you decided on the order of presentation of the speaker's main points. But here's what can complicate that: When the *most important facts* of Point #3, for instance, outweigh the *least important facts* of Point #2. Confused yet? Here's a diagram of how a story like that may look, assuming you have four key points from the speech. Each box represents a paragraph. Words in quotes represent a paragraph or direct quote.

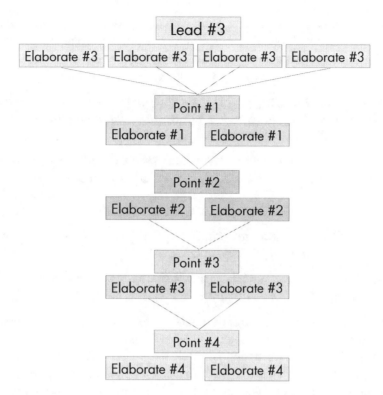

Other than the main points made by the speaker, what else might you expect to find in a speech story? These elements are common:

- The crowd's reaction
- Reaction to the speech by event organizers or those in attendance
- The speaker's statements given in a question-and-answer session following the speech or a press conference before or after the speech
- An estimated number of those in attendance
- Speaker's biographical or background information
- News events that give context to the speech (if a speaker reacts to recent news, for instance, don't assume your readers are familiar with the details of the events to which your speaker is responding)

Your obvious question at this point is "Where does all that stuff go?" The answer: in the inverted pyramid. A crowd estimate might not even be included in the speech. But if the crowd is especially large or especially small, it may be important and even included high in the story. Should it go in the lead? That depends. Is it as important as or more important than what the speaker said? The organization of a speech story is much simpler when you realize that your readers want the most important information, and they will read until they are bored or think they have enough. Just make sure that whenever they quit reading—the lead, the third graf, the eighth graf, the 12th graf—there is nothing deeper in the story that is more important than what they have already read.

Other Guidelines for Speech Stories

The speech story format ideas above will help you put together a story that accurately reflects the ideas of the speaker and presents them in the style used by the mass media. But there are other guidelines that you need to be aware of:

Avoid the quote lead. Writing an all-direct quote lead is a temptation for many writers. Resist it. Pulling a direct quote from a speech and leading with it confuses the reader. Since the first thing they see is a quote mark, they are unaware of who is speaking. They begin with an out-of-context statement made by the speaker. Instead, paraphrase an idea (use direct quotes for especially colorful or strong phrases if you need to) and tell the reader in the lead who said it. Below are two leads: The first is a direct quote lead and a second graf, and the next is a rewrite of that lead in a way that helps the reader put it into context.

"Our young people are out of control, and this town desperately needs a teen curfew to control crime and vandalism—indeed, to do as a community what many parents seem unable to do, to control their own children."

That statement was made by Centerville Mayor Tom Olsen when he spoke to the Rotary Club Tuesday about his proposal to the City Council to enact an 11 p.m. curfew on school nights.

Centerville Mayor Tom Olsen said Tuesday that he is proposing an 11 p.m. curfew for teenagers to control crime and vandalism in the city.

Olsen, speaking to the Rotary Club, said the city needs "to do as a community what many parents seem unable to do, to control their own children."

Notice how the second lead puts the mayor's proposal into context. Readers know the essence of the proposal, who made it and when he made it. Quote leads never give that sense of context to readers.

Avoid "creative" attribution words. Your job is to tell the reader what the speaker said. Focus on those direct and indirect quotes that convey that message. Journalism students often get frustrated because their profs urge them to use *said* rather than *thinks* or *believes* or *feels* or even *stressed* or *insisted* or *admitted*. In many cases, that is because the students still remember high school English classes where their teachers encouraged them to use variety in their speech tags.

If you want to add life to a speech story, you don't do it with speech tags. Ever seen anyone read a novel and remark, "I loved the book! The speech tags were gripping!" Of course not. Novelists know they hold readers with great dialogue, not creative attributions.

If you watch the Food Network, think of the plates used by the chefs. Ever see any really "creative" plates with hand-painted scenes on them, or even in bold colors? No. All the plates are white. It almost looks like they are trying to use the most boring plates possible. But what they are doing is emphasizing the food and the plating. The plates are boring on purpose because their only function is to frame the food. So look at the attributions as the plates and the quotations as the food. If you find yourself thinking, "I'm tired of these boring always-use-said attributions," then congratulations! You're writing your speech story in a way that emphasizes the quotations, not the attributions.

Use paragraph variety. Most paragraphs in a speech story are either direct or indirect quotes (the exceptions are background grafs on the speaker or the issue, information about the event where the speaker was speaking, crowd reaction and the like). In your paragraphs of quotes, keep them varied between directs and indirects. Not necessarily direct, then indirect, then direct, then indirect, but that's the principle. Don't have long stretches of directs with no indirects or indirects with no directs.

Avoid "stage directions." The speaker you are covering has a plan for the speech. Perhaps the speaker started with thank-yous for organizers, then moved on to some warm-up humor, then main point 1, then main point 2, then main point 3, then a conclusion. That's pretty typical of speeches, but not of speech stories. The speaker knew she had her audience for about half an hour and was able to build her case slowly and end with a stirring conclusion. You do not have that luxury. You must begin with the most important information.

There's no need for you to include "stage directions," information that tells the reader what the speaker *started with* or *ended with* or *said in conclusion*. Your lead might even start with the conclusion. Readers only want to know what the speaker said, not what relative point in the speech that statement came from.

The Bottom Line

Speech stories are one of the most valuable story types for media writing students to learn. That's partly because these stories are among the most common for news writers in journalism or PR. Remember, if you are a PR student working for a hospital and you have a ribbon-cutting where the board chair makes a few remarks, the story form you will use to report those remarks in news releases and on your website is the speech story. What you learn in doing speech stories will prepare you to do interview stories and even features, because both rely heavily on reported speech in quotations. So learning to write a good speech story gives you skills that have many applications for media writers.

A Checklist for Your Speeches

1. Does your lead have only one sentence? ____yes ____no

2. Any buried quotes? ____ yes ____ no

3. Do any of these words appear in your story?
   - *believes* as an attribution? ____ yes ____ no
   - *stated* as an attribution? ____ yes ____ no
   - *thinks* as an attribution? ____ yes ____ no
   - *feels* as an attribution ____ yes ____ no

4. Have you run spellcheck? ____yes ____ no

5. Is there any place in the story where you have a direct quote, with an attribution, and then an indirect following in the same graf with no attribution? ____yes ____ no

6. Do your attributions say "X said" rather than "said X"? (The exception, of course, is when you have an appositive for X.) ____ yes ____ no

7. Are your attributions past-tense? ____ yes ____no

8. Do you avoid *according to* except when referring to written sources? ____ yes ____ no

9. Have you included any "stage directions," like *began by, ended by, concluded, opened with, closed with*, etc.? ____yes ____ no

10. Have you varied your use of direct quotes and paraphrases, so that you do not have long stretches of directs or long stretches of indirects throughout the speech? ____ yes ____no

Skills Development: Practice in Media Writing

Exercise 10.1

Lincoln's Gettysburg Address

Speaker: Abraham Lincoln
Occasion: dedication of the Soldier's National Cemetery at Gettysburg, Pa.
Time: Thursday afternoon
Situation: Assume you are a reporter for The New York Sun. Write this story to appear in the Sun on Friday morning. If you need more information on the occasion, you can find it easily on the Internet.

Fourscore and seven years ago our fathers brought forth on this continent a new nation, conceived in liberty and dedicated to the proposition that all men are created equal.

Now we are engaged in a great civil war, testing whether that nation or any nation so conceived and so dedicated can long endure. We are met on a great battlefield of that war.

We have come to dedicate a portion of that field as a final resting-place for those who here gave their lives that that nation might live. It is altogether fitting and proper that we should do this.

But in a larger sense, we cannot dedicate, we cannot consecrate, we cannot hallow this ground. The brave men, living and dead who struggled here have consecrated it far above our poor power to add or detract.

The world will little note nor long remember what we say here, but it can never forget what they did here. It is for us the living rather to be dedicated here to the unfinished work which they who fought here have thus far so nobly advanced.

It is rather for us to be here dedicated to the great task remaining before us—that from these honored dead we take increased devotion to that cause for which they gave the last full measure of devotion—that we here highly resolve that these dead shall not have died in vain, that this nation under God shall have a new birth of freedom, and that government of the people, by the people, for the people shall not perish from the earth.

Exercise 10.2

Presidential Radio Address

Speaker: President Barack Obama
Occasion: Weekly presidential radio address
Time: Saturday
Situation: Every week the president gives a short radio address. Write a speech story that covers the address below.

Hi, everybody. I'm speaking to you this week from a factory in Petersburg, Virginia, where they're bringing on more than 100 new workers to build parts for the next generation of jet engines.

It's a story that's happening more frequently across the country. Our businesses just added 233,000 jobs last month—for a total of nearly four million new jobs over the last two years. More companies are choosing to bring jobs back and invest in America. Manufacturing is adding jobs for the first time since the 1990s, and we're building more things to sell to the rest of the world stamped with three proud words: Made in America.

And it's not just that we're building stuff. We're building better stuff. The engine parts manufactured here in Petersburg will go into next-generation planes that are lighter, faster, and more fuel-efficient.

That last part is important. Because whether you're paying for a plane ticket, or filling up your gas tank, technology that helps us get more miles to the gallon is one of the easiest ways to save money and reduce our dependence on foreign oil.

The recent spike in gas prices has been another painful reminder of why we have to invest in this technology. As usual, politicians have been rolling out their three-point plans for two-dollar gas: drill, drill, and drill some more. Well, my response is, we have been drilling. Under my Administration, oil production in America is at an eight-year high. We've quadrupled the number of operating oil rigs, and opened up millions of acres for drilling.

But you and I both know that with only 2% of the world's oil reserves, we can't just drill our way to lower gas prices—not when we consume 20 percent of the world's oil. We need an all-of-the-above strategy that relies less on foreign oil and more on American-made energy—solar, wind, natural gas, biofuels, and more.

That's the strategy we're pursuing. It's why I went to a plant in North Carolina earlier this week, where they're making trucks that run on natural gas, and hybrid trucks that go farther on a single tank.

And it's why I've been focused on fuel-efficient cars since the day I took office. Over the last few years, the annual number of miles driven by Americans has stayed roughly the same, but the total amount of gas we use has been going down. In other words, we're getting more bang for our buck.

If we accelerate that trend, we can help drivers save a significant amount of money. That's why, after 30 years of inaction, we finally put in place new standards that will make sure our cars average nearly 55 miles per gallon by the middle of the next decade—nearly double what they get today. This wasn't easy: we had to bring together auto companies, and unions, and folks who don't ordinarily see eye to eye. But it was worth it.

Because these cars aren't some pie in the sky solution that's years away. They're being built right now—by American workers, in factories right here in the U.S.A. Every year, our cars and trucks will be able to go farther and use less fuel, and pretty soon, you'll be able to fill up every two weeks instead of every week—something that, over time, will save the typical family more than $8,000 at the pump. We'll reduce our oil consumption by more than 12 billion barrels. That's a future worth investing in.

So we have a choice. Right now, some folks in Washington would rather spend another $4 billion on subsidies to oil companies each year. Well you know what? We've been handing out these kinds of taxpayer giveaways for nearly a century. And outside of Congress, does anyone really think that's still a good idea? I want this Congress to stop the giveaways to an oil industry that's never been more profitable, and invest in a clean energy industry that's never been more promising. We should be investing in the technology that's building the cars and trucks and jets that will prevent us from dealing with these high gas prices year after year after year.

Ending this cycle of rising gas prices won't be easy, and it won't happen overnight. But that's why you sent us to Washington—to solve tough problems like this one. So I'm going to keep doing everything I can to help you save money on gas, both right now and in the future. I hope politicians from both sides of the aisle join me. Let's put aside the bumper-sticker slogans, remember why we're here, and get things done for the American people.

Thank you, God bless you, and have a great weekend.

Exercise 10.3

The weekly presidential radio addresses like the one you wrote in Exercise 10.2 provide great practice for beginning media writers. Visit the White House website and go to the Briefing Room, then the "Your Weekly Address" tab. You will find the president's short weekly radio addresses—both text and video, if you want to practice taking notes. If you would like to write a longer speech story, go to the Briefing Room and then click on Speeches and Remarks. If you would like to write a speech from a former president, go to the Wayback Machine, an Internet archive (http://bit.ly/9xcLSW). Type in whitehouse.gov into The Wayback Machine and it will show you what dates are available to pull up. Only President George W. Bush pages are available. You can also find many speeches by political leaders and corporate executives on their Web pages.

Exercise 10.4

Speaker John Boehner's address on the economy, debt limit and American jobs

Speaker: John Boehner, speaker of the U.S. House of Representatives
Occasion: Peter G. Peterson Foundation Fiscal Summit
Place: Washington, D.C.
Time: Tuesday
Situation: You are covering this Tuesday event for a newspaper to be published Wednesday. For more information on Boehner or any issue referred to in the speech, do some background research on the Internet.

Assignment: This is a 2,500-word speech. You should write a 500-word news story. Obviously, you will have to make some decisions about what is most important in the speech and what your story should focus on.

It's truly an honor to be with you in the historic Mellon Auditorium. It was here in the spring of 1949 that the United States and our closest allies gathered to sign the North Atlantic Treaty, giving birth to NATO.

On that occasion, President Truman declared that people "with courage and vision can still determine their own destiny. They can choose freedom or slavery."

In our time, all of these great nations face a grave threat to freedom, one from within, and that is debt. It is shackling our economies and smothering the opportunities that have blessed us with so much.

Once again the world looks to the United States for what it always has: an example. It is the example of a free people whose hard work and sacrifice make up the sum total of thriving towns and a vibrant economy. It's a humble government that lives within its means and unleashes the potential of first-rate ideas and world-class products. It's a nation never content with the status quo and always on the make.

I got a glimpse of this example growing up working at my dad's tavern just outside Cincinnati, and then lived a piece of it running my own small business.

Instead of this shining example, what does the world now see?

A president on whose watch the United States lost its gold-plated triple-A rating for the first time in our history;

A Senate, controlled by the president's party, that has not passed a budget in more than three years;

And, earlier this month, another unemployment report showing that the world's greatest economy remains unable to generate enough jobs to spur strong and lasting growth.

If you should know one thing about me, it's that I'm an optimist.

Yes, times are tough, but our future doesn't need to be dark. We don't have to accept a new normal where the workplace looks more like a battlefield and families have to endure flat incomes, weak job prospects, and higher prices in their daily lives.

We have every reason to believe we can come out of this freer and more prosperous than ever. And we will, if we confront our challenges now while we still have the ability to do so.

For the solution to what ails our economy is not government—it's the American people.

The failure of "stimulus"—a word people in Washington won't even use anymore—has sparked a rebellion against overspending, overtaxation, and overregulation.

Americans, who take pride in living on a budget, recognize we can't go on spending money we don't have, and that our economy is stuck in large part because it's stuck with debt.

Nationwide, we're seeing a groundswell of support for bold ideas that reject small politics, cast off big government, and return us to common sense and first principles—the kind of ideas that will restore prosperity and substantially improve the trajectory of our economy.

In March, as part of our Plan for America's Job Creators, the House passed an honest budget with real spending cuts, pro-growth tax reform, and serious entitlement reform. It's a far-reaching effort to control government's worst habits and capitalize on the American people's best. This budget gets our fiscal house in order

AND promotes long-term growth. Far from settling for stability, it offers a true path to prosperity.

Various bipartisan commissions and coalitions have devised ambitious plans as well. The math and the mix are different, but the goals are mainly the same.

And of course, there are summits like these that bring together people who just get it. Of course, while I'm happy to be here and I'm sure we all enjoy each other's company, we can also agree that we've talked this problem to death.

It's about time we roll up our sleeves and get to work.

For all the focus on Election Day, another date looms large for every household and every business, and that's January 1, 2013.

On that day, without action by Congress, a sudden and massive tax increase will be imposed on every American—by an average of $3,000 per household. Rates go up, the child tax credit is cut in half, the AMT patches end, the estate tax returns to 2001 levels, and so on.

Now, it gets a little more complicated than that. What will expire on January 1 is cause for concern—as is what will take effect. That includes:

Indiscriminate spending cuts of $1.2 trillion—half of which would devastate our men and women in uniform and send a signal of weakness;

Several tax increases from the health care law that is making it harder to hire new workers;

As well as a slate of energy and banking rules and regulations that will also increase the strain on the private sector.

But ... it gets even more complicated than that.

Sometime after the election, the federal government will near the statutory debt limit.

This end-of-the-year pileup, commonly called the "fiscal cliff," is a chance for us to bid farewell—permanently—to the era of so-called "timely, temporary, and targeted" short-term government intervention.

For years, Washington has force-fed our economy with a constant diet of meddling, micromanagement, and manipulation. None of it has been a substitute for long-term economic investment, private initiative, and freedom.

Previous Congresses have encountered lesser precipices with lower stakes, and made a beeline for the closest lame-duck escape hatch.

Let me put your mind at ease. This Congress will not follow that path, not if I have anything to do with it.

Having run a business, I know that failing to plan is planning to fail. The real pain comes from doing nothing ... "austerity" is what will become necessary if we do nothing now. We'll wake up one day without a choice in the matter.

There's also no salvation to be found in doing anything just to get by, just to get through this year.

"Nothing" is not an option, and "anything" is not a plan. To get on the path to prosperity, we have to avoid the fiscal cliff, but we need to start today.

To show my intentions are sincere, I'll start with the stickiest issue, and that of course is the debt limit.

On several occasions in the past, the debt limit has been the catalyst for budget agreements. Last year, however, the president requested a quote-unquote "clean" debt limit increase—business as usual.

Well I've run a business, and that's no way to do it. It's certainly no way to run a government either, especially one that has run up a debt bigger than the entire economy. Business as usual will no longer do.

So last year around this time, I accepted an invitation to address the Economic Club of New York. I went up there and said that in my view, the debt limit exists in statute precisely so that government is forced to address its fiscal issues.

Yes, allowing America to default would be irresponsible. But it would be more irresponsible to raise the debt ceiling without taking dramatic steps to reduce spending and reform the budget process.

We shouldn't dread the debt limit. We should welcome it. It's an action-forcing event in a town that has become infamous for inaction.

That night in New York City, I put forth the principle that we should not raise the debt ceiling without real spending cuts and reforms that exceed the amount of the debt limit increase.

From all the way up in Midtown Manhattan, I could hear a great wailing and gnashing of teeth. Over the next couple of months, I was asked again and again if I would yield on my "position," what it would take, if I would budge ...

Each and every time, I said "no" ... because it isn't a "position"—it's a principle. Not just that—it's the right thing to do.

When the time comes, I will again insist on my simple principle of cuts and reforms greater than the debt limit increase. This is the only avenue I see right now to force the elected leadership of this country to solve our structural fiscal imbalance.

If that means we have to do a series of stop-gap measures, so be it—but that's not the ideal. Let's start solving the problem. We can make the bold cuts and reforms necessary to meet this principle, and we must.

Just so we're clear, I'm talking about REAL cuts and reforms—not these tricks and gimmicks that have given Washington a pass on grappling with its spending problem.

Last year, in our negotiations with the White House, the president and his team put a number of gimmicks on the table. Plenty of thought and creativity went into them—things like counting money that was never going to be spent as savings.

Maybe in another time, with another Speaker, gimmicks like these would be acceptable.

But, as a matter of simple arithmetic, they won't work.

They won't work, and as I told the president, we're not doing things that way anymore.

What also doesn't count as "cuts and reforms" are tax increases. Tax hikes destroy jobs—especially an increase on the magnitude set for January 1st. Small businesses need to plan. We shouldn't wait until New Year's Eve to give American job creators the confidence that they aren't going to get hit with a tax hike on New Year's Day.

Any sudden tax hike would hurt our economy, so this fall—before the election—the House of Representatives will vote to stop the largest tax increase in American history.

This will give Congress time to work on broad-based tax reform that lowers rates for individuals and businesses while closing deductions, credits, and special carve-outs.

Eyebrows go up all over town whenever I talk about this, but when I say "broad-based" tax reform, I mean it. We need to do it all ... deal with the whole code, personal and corporate, it's fairer and more productive for everyone.

That's why our bill to stop the New Year's Day tax increase will also establish an expedited process by which Congress would enact real tax reform in 2013. This process would look something like how we handle Trade Promotion Authority, where you put in place a timeline for both houses to act.

The Ways & Means Committee will work out the details, but the bottom line is: if we do this right, we will never again have to deal with the uncertainty of expiring tax rates.

We'll have replaced the broken status quo with a tax code that maintains progressivity, taxes income once, and creates a fairer, simpler code.

And if we do THAT right, we will see increased revenue from more economic growth.

Again, change doesn't need to be sudden or painful.

Last fall, when I addressed the Economic Club of Washington, I said that making relatively small changes now can lead to huge dividends down the road in terms of debt reduction. As we approach the issue of the debt limit again, we need to continue to bear this in mind.

As you know, we could eliminate all of the unfunded liabilities in Social Security, Medicare and Medicaid tomorrow, and the effect within the Congressional Budget Office 10-year window could be minimal.

That's because changes to these programs take time and are phased in slowly.

For example, when Congress last increased the retirement age for Social Security, the increase—a mere two years—was scheduled to fully take effect 40 years after the law was enacted.

Another example: take the House Budget Resolution and its assumptions for Medicare reform. Those would not even begin until after 2022.

Smart and modest changes today mean huge dividends down the line.

Now, I can already hear the grumbles ... partisans getting all worked up or people saying, eh, let's wait until after the election.

We can't wait. Employers large and small are already bracing for the coming tax hikes and regulations, which freeze their plans. The markets aren't going to wait forever; eventually they're going to start reacting.

We now know that we ignore these warnings at our own peril.

That's why the House will do its part to ease the uncertainty surrounding the fiscal cliff. And I hope the president will step up, bring his party's Senate leaders along, and work with us.

Because if there's one action-forcing event that trumps all the rest—even the debt limit—it's presidential leadership.

Ladies and gentlemen, I believe President Obama cares about this country and knows what the right thing to do is. But knowing what's right and doing what's right are different things.

The difference between knowing what's right and doing what's right is courage, and the president, I'm sorry to say, lost his.

He was willing to talk about the tough choices needed to preserve and strengthen our entitlement programs, but he wasn't ready to take action.

As it turned out, he wouldn't agree to even the most basic entitlement reform unless it was accompanied by tax increases on small business job creators.

We were on the verge of an agreement that would have reduced the deficit by trillions, by strengthening entitlement programs and reforming the tax code with permanently lower rates for all, laying the foundation for lasting growth.

But when the president saw his former colleagues in the Senate getting ready to press for tax hikes, he lost his nerve. The political temptation was too great. He moved the goalposts, changed his stance, and demanded tax hikes.

We ended up enacting a package with cuts and reforms larger than the hike. But it could have been so much more.

The letdown was considerable. And, in turn, our nation's credit rating was downgraded for the first time.

Well it should also be the last time that happens, which is why I came here today.

If the president continues to put politics before principle—or party before country, as he often accuses others of doing—our economy will suffer and we may well miss our last chance to solve this crisis on our own terms.

But if we have leaders who will lead … if we have leaders with the courage to make tough choices and the vision to pursue a future paved with growth, then we can heal our economy and again be the example for all to follow.

I'm ready, and I've been ready. I'm not angling for higher office. This is the last position in government I will hold. I haven't come this far to walk away.

All my life, I've operated by a simple code: if you do the right thing for the right reasons, good things will happen.

Well, NOW is the time to do the right thing.

Let's do it for the right reasons—we don't need to be dragged kicking and screaming. That's not the American way. Let's summon the courage and vision to choose freedom, to choose prosperity, and to determine our destiny.

Then we'll not only have succeeded in solving this crisis—we'll be worthy of that success.

Thank you all. (Boehner 2012)

Exercise 10.5

Statement by Gary Patterson
Speaker: Gary Patterson, TCU head football coach
Time: Wednesday
Occasion: 17 TCU students have been arrested in connection with a drug investigation, including four football players. Head football coach Gary Patterson appears before a press conference, at which he reads the following statement and then refuses to take questions.

Assignment: Cover this short statement for your Thursday campus newspaper

"There are days people want to be a head football coach, but today is not one of those days. As I heard the news this morning, I was first shocked, then hurt and now I'm mad.

"Under my watch, drugs and drug use by TCU's student-athletes will not be tolerated by me or any member of my coaching staff. Period. Our program is respected nationally for its strong ethics and for that reason the players arrested today were separated from TCU by the University. I believe strongly that young people's lives are more important than wins or losses.

"This situation isn't unique to TCU—it is a global issue that we all have to address. This isn't just about bad decisions made by a small percentage of my team. It is about a bigger issue across this country and world.

"As a coach, I do the best I can to educate members of my team. We have programs in place that teach student-athletes about what they should and shouldn't do and how to be successful in life. I talk to them about how to be students and upstanding men that uphold the TCU name and its traditions.

"At the end of the day, though, sometimes young people make poor choices. The Horned Frogs are bigger and stronger than those involved." (Osborne 2012)*

---

* From TCU360, 2012. Reprinted by permission.

References

for Chapter 10 exercises

Osborne, Ryan. "Patterson, Del Conte release statements about recent drug arrests." *TCU 360*, February 15, 2012. http://www.tcu360.com/football/2012/02/14526.patterson-del-conte-release-statements-about-recent-drug-arrests.

Boehner, John. "Speaker Boehner's Address on the Economy, Debt Limit, and American Jobs." John Boehner website, May 15, 2012. http://boehner.house.gov/News/DocumentSingle.aspx?DocumentID=295546.

Chapter Eleven

More Common News Story Types: Localization, Advances, Follow Stories

There are many types of news writing that media writers do in print and online for journalism and public relations, obviously as varied as the types of news itself. But in this introductory course, we want to look at several types of writing you may have to do in internships, in student media and in part-time media work. You are likely to have to localize a news story, to write an advance story on an upcoming event, and to write a second-day story to follow up on a news story that's big enough to extend coverage over several days or weeks. So let's look at how you would approach each type of story.

Localization

We saw in chapter 2 that one of the key definitions of news is proximity. We are more interested in what happens close to home or in an area we are familiar with. Some stories don't need localization because they are already local. If you are covering the story of a fraternity hazing on your campus, or a national award given to a prof in the business school or a faculty senate recommendation on tenure policy, you don't have to be concerned with localization. It's local already. It happened on your campus, to people associated with your university. It deals with local issues. The people affected are local. And the interest is local.

But let's assume a national magazine announces its list of the top 100 business schools, and the b-school on your campus is named to the list. Or perhaps a student film wins a Hollywood award and a film major from your university was the special-effects director. Or the NCAA announces a new policy for drug testing athletes that will obviously affect athletes on teams at your school.

Writing those essentially national stories with a local angle you want to feature—that's a technique we call *localization*. You localize a story by featuring the local angle in what might otherwise be a state or regional or national or international story.

If you come from a small town or you are the only student from your community at your university, you may find yourself the subject of a localization when you graduate. Would your hometown newspaper likely run a story that says X number of students graduated from your university? Probably not. There is no local interest. But when *you* graduate, your hometown newspaper may well run a story that begins like this:

"Ian Jacobs of Smithville was awarded a Bachelor of Science degree in public relations by Texas Christian University in graduation ceremonies in Fort Worth on Friday."

The news service at your university will begin with a list of graduates and hometowns, then match those graduates with local media and send individual news stories to those media highlighting their local graduates. Some of the story will be what media writers call boilerplate: the standard information on the graduation ceremony and the speaker and the total number of graduates that will go into each news story. You may have several grafs of boilerplate that will be pasted into each story after the information on the local graduate. If there are five graduates from Smithville, the lead will say, *"Five graduates of Smithville High School were awarded degrees ..."* and then list the names in the second graf.

Your first internship or job may be at an Internet news site that specializes in covering one local area. The new buzzword that describes the coverage philosophy of these websites is *hyperlocal* (Miller and Stone 2009). These sites cover the news of interest only to a particular neighborhood or section of the city. Will these journalists cover City Council? They will, but they are interested only in Council decisions affecting the area they cover. Let's say the city votes to build three new swimming pools. Will that story be on the hyperlocal site? Only if one of the pools is in that area. And if one is, the story will feature the pool to be built in the site's coverage area, mentioning only in passing that it is one of three scheduled for construction next year.

If you work in public relations, much of your writing will be localizations, as you write news releases for local media highlighting what your company is doing in a specific local area. You localize the story to increase your chances that media will use it.

Often, localization is just rewriting. Let's say you are working for your college newspaper and you get a news release saying that a national business organization has named the Top 10 Business Profs in America. The story goes on to list the winners, and a professor from your campus is one of the 10. To localize that story, you will rewrite it to feature the professor on your campus. Later on, you will mention the other nine winners, probably far down in the story. If the story did not give biographical information on each of the winners, you will need to get that. And you will need to call the professor and probably the dean of the business school for reaction to the award. That's localization.

Advances

Most news stories are about things that have already happened. But a common story type is the advance, a story about coming events: meetings, speeches, athletic events, special programs, exhibitions, elections and the like.

News stories about past events typically emphasize either the *who* or the *what*. News stories about coming events focus on the *where* and the *when* in addition to the *what*. These stories tell readers what they want to know about upcoming events:

- What exactly is happening?
- Where will it occur?
- When will it occur?
- Who can attend?
- What is the cost, if any?
- Where can I get tickets?

Here is a news release written by a community journalism center on a university campus, announcing an upcoming event:

> The Texas Center for Community Journalism will hold a Design Boot Camp for Community Newspapers on March 14 through 16 on the TCU campus in Fort Worth, led by the Center's design specialist, Broc Sears.
>
> Sears said the workshop is oriented toward meeting the following needs:
>
> - People new to the world of community newspaper design and visual journalism;
> - Those who have migrated to the news design field and are a little bewildered as to how the technology, tools and tensions combine to produce crisp, clean, creative and striking presentations;
> - Those whose responsibilities have been expanded to include design and visual presentation or supervision of those who do.

> The workshop will cover the fundamentals of design, layout, typography, ideation, information graphics, software strategies and online resources. Participants will have opportunities for hands-on sessions with Photoshop, Flash and InDesign.
>
> Sears said that applicants should have at least a basic working knowledge of InDesign and Photoshop.
>
> "This is an ideal workshop for those with only one or two years in the profession," he said. "We've tried to make this experience an intense and inspirational design boot camp."
>
> Because of the hands-on nature of the workshop, only 15 applicants will be accepted. The workshop is free, including meals and a hotel room for two nights while in Fort Worth.
>
> The workshop begins at 6 p.m. Wednesday, March 14, and concludes at noon on Friday, March 16. Tommy Thomason, TCCJ director, said that only applicants who can attend the entire workshop will be considered.
>
> The workshop is funded under a grant from the Texas Newspaper Foundation.
>
> Reprinted by permission of Texas Center for Community Journalism.

As you look over the news release (an example of PR writing), note several things:

- The lead tells readers who is doing something, what is being done, when and where it will be done and who is leading the workshop. (The name was used because in the world of design, the writer thought that this name would be recognizable to many in the primary audience for the news release.)
- The story is written throughout in inverted pyramid form.
- A bulleted-list device is used in the second graf to summarize several points in a readable way.

If the story is about an upcoming speech or program, readers want to know who the speaker or performer will be, what the speech or program will be about and when and where it will be held. Sometimes writers organize on what they call a STOP formula:

- The **s**peaker;
- The **t**opic;
- The **o**rganization to be addressed or the sponsoring organization;
- The **p**lace, day and hour of the event (Some media writers arrange these as time/date/place—7 p.m. July 15 at the County Civic Center.)

After you have written a few advances, you will develop your own approach and variations on the STOP formula. But that will give you a good place to start.

Follow Stories

Some news events rate a single story. But others take several days to report. Let's say a tornado hits your city. There will obviously be a big story that summarizes the damage. But the tornado will generate stories for days or weeks afterward: stories on the cleanup, stories on insurance coverage, stories on damage to individual neighborhoods and businesses. If there is a major drug bust on campus, there will be a story breaking that news, but there will be weeks of follow stories as the investigation continues, people are arrested and charged, trials begin and the campus copes with fallout from the arrests.

Following is part of a news story from the Fort Worth Star-Telegram on City Council approval of a zoning variance to allow a Walmart store to be built. Look it over, and then move on to the second-day story, which appeared one day later. This is a typical second-day piece, shedding more light on the original story by giving background on the vote. Note that the writer briefly summarized the original story for readers who hadn't read the original piece.

> *FORT WORTH—In a decision that divided residents of several south-side neighborhoods and upset at least one council member, the Fort Worth City Council voted 7–2 Tuesday night to approve zoning variances for a Wal-Mart Neighborhood Market but included restrictions that prohibit fuel sales and leave a parcel along West Berry Street undeveloped for now.*
>
> *The vote came on a substitute motion by Councilman Sal Espino that included last-minute compromises suggested by Wal-Mart.*
>
> *Councilman Joel Burns, who represents the neighborhoods the store would serve, had offered his own motion for approval. His motion would have prevented Wal-Mart from paving 14 parking spaces until development took place on a parcel of the lot that fronts West Berry. During discussion, council members initially signaled support for Burns' recommendation but changed their minds after hearing from Wal-Mart (Hanna 2012a).**

> *FORT WORTH—In the end, the debate about zoning variances for a Wal-Mart Neighborhood Market came down to 14 parking spaces.*
>
> *At Tuesday night's City Council meeting, Councilman Joel Burns, whose district includes the proposed store at Hemphill and West Berry streets, was willing to recommend approving the variances as long as 14 parking spaces were held back as an incentive for Wal-Mart to develop a parcel fronting West Berry to help conform with the urban village concept outlined for the area.*
>
> *But the council voted 7–2 in favor of a substitute recommendation by Councilman Sal Espino to approve the variances with a restriction on fuel sales but without prohibitions on paving those 14 parking spaces.*
>
> *The vote came after a Wal-Mart representative said that stipulation was unworkable and would actually take 25 spaces away from the store (Hanna 2012b).**

When you write a second-day story, you cannot assume the reader is familiar enough with the original story to pick up on the narrative and make sense of the story you are writing unless you give background on that original story. Therefore, you include what media writers call a *tie-back*, a sentence or graf or perhaps several grafs that give readers the background they need on the original story.

The following story covered the first charges following a campus drug bust one month previously. The story below is about the first formal charges following the earlier arrests. The writer had to present the "new news," but also put it into context of the previous news stories.

The tiebacks have been italicized:

The Tarrant County District Attorney's Office formally charged three people Wednesday in connection with the TCU drug investigation.

During the investigation, Fort Worth Police <u>arrested 24 people</u>, including 16 students, in February based on information gathered during a <u>six-month investigation</u> of drug sales near TCU's campus, according to the arrest warrants and police reports.

Of those arrested, William Joseph Hoffman, 20, Katherine Petrie, 20, and Jordan Sherman, 22, are the first *of the 24* **to be charged. Sherman was arrested on March 2, according to police records.**

Melody McDonald, public information officer for the district attorney's office, wrote in an email that more charges could be filed Thursday (Muller 2012).†

---

* From the *Fort Worth Star-Telegram*, 2012. Reprinted by permission.

† From TCU360, 2012. Reprinted by permission.

This news story appeared online, so note the underlined phrases—those are hypertext, a special type of tieback. Print writers have to supply all the background information in the story itself. But when you're writing online, you can hypertext words and phrases that supply the tiebacks in previously published stories. More on that in chapter 17.

The Bottom Line

In terms of writing, we have presented nothing new in this chapter. We're still talking about presenting news events in an inverted pyramid format. The most important news still goes in the lead. What we have done in this chapter, though, is to show you three types of news that are somewhat different from what you have looked at before. Localization involves extracting news of local interest from a larger, more generalized news event. Writing advances involves telling people about news that hasn't happened yet—the news is that it *will* happen. And follows involve news that presents new developments or insights on an older story.

References

Hanna, Bill. "Fort Worth Council Approves Zoning for Wal-Mart Market." *Fort Worth Star-Telegram*, March 6, 2012a. http://www.star-telegram.com/2012/03/06/3790035/fort-worth-council-approves-zoning.html#storylink=cpy.

———. "Wal-Mart Dispute Hinged on Parking." *Fort Worth Star-Telegram*, March 7, 2012b. http://www.star-telegram.com/2012/03/07/3793227/wal-mart-dispute-hinged-on-parking.html#storylink=cpy.

Miller, Claire Cain and Stone, Brad. "'Hyperlocal' Web Sites Deliver News Without Newspapers." *The New York Times*, April 12, 2009.

Muller, Mary. "Three People in Relation to Drug Sweep Formally Charged." *TCU360.com*, March 7, 2012. http://www.tcu360.com/campus/2012/03/14782.three-people-relation-drug-sweep-formally-charged.

Skills Development: Practice in Media Writing

Exercise 11.1

Based on the information below, write a story that can be posted to your news organization's website on Thursday morning (the day after the shooting described below).

This happened Wednesday night. Your source for everything is Lt. Jacob Salter, Fort Worth police. There was a shooting at Froggie's Sports Bar, 423 Lamar St. Two men in the bar got into an argument. When the two started shoving each other, the bartender threw them out. For several minutes, people in the bar said they could hear the men still arguing on the street outside. Then there was the sound of a shot being fired. A few patrons rushed outside to see what had happened, and one of the men who had been arguing lay on the ground in a pool of blood. He'd been shot in the forehead. The shooter was nowhere to be seen. The shooting occurred around 11:45 p.m. The man was rushed to John Peter Smith Hospital but was DOA. Salter says detectives don't yet have a motive for the shooting, but he speculated that the two might have been arguing over a drug deal. The dead guy is Joseph O'Keefe, 34, of 676 Oakmont Terrace.

Exercise 11.2

Assume you are sitting by your phone Thursday afternoon when Lt. Jacob Salter of the Fort Worth Police Department calls with the below update about the shooting you wrote about earlier in the day. Write a story that can be posted to your news organization's website Thursday evening as a follow-up.

Lt. Jacob Salter, FWPD, tells you Thursday afternoon—the day after the shooting—that Fort Worth cops arrested an ex-con named Harold Merrick, 47, in connection with the shooting. Turns out a patron at the bar knew Merrick and identified him as the shooter for detectives. Police arrested Merrick at his house at 3447 Mulberry Drive. Salter said Merrick was arrested without incident. Salter says Merrick confessed to detectives that he was selling cocaine to the victim when the shooting occurred. Merrick said the shooting was an accident; he says he and O'Keefe were arguing over money and got into a shoving match. Merrick says he pulled out the gun just to scare O'Keefe, but O'Keefe grabbed the gun and it went off accidentally as they struggled. O'Keefe was hit in the head. Salter says Merrick is due to be arraigned later on Thursday.

Chapter Twelve

Writing Headlines: Hooking Readers, Summarizing Stories

Headline writing is more important now than it has ever been. In this chapter, we teach you some best practices to get you started writing headlines.

We said a few chapters ago that the easiest way to write a lead is to think about a news story and figure out what you'd tell your mom about the story when you walked in the front door. Taking that analogy further, headlines are what you'd tell her if you had to yell to her from across the street. That's essentially what headlines do for readers of your stories. Headlines yell out and draw readers to your copy.

We usually think of headlines as the giant bold type that titles a newspaper story. But headlines are more than that. Headlines go on blog posts and are used as the link text on most websites where your content will appear someday. When press releases are distributed, headlines are often the subject line. And when your story is passed around the Internet, there's a good chance that a savvy social media user will use your well-crafted headline as the text of a tweet. Needless to say, as the way we distribute content has changed over the past few years, the headline has grown in importance.

When headlines were only used to title newspaper stories, the average newspaper reporter didn't need to know how to write them. And if we were writing this book a few decades ago, we probably wouldn't have included headline-writing in an introductory writing text for advertising, public relations and news writers. It's not 30 years ago, though, and there are two big reasons why today's media writers need to know how to write headlines.

First and foremost, it's a fantastic way to coach yourself toward a better-pegged news story. We want you to understand how writing a headline for your own story, even if the public will never see it, can help you write a better story. Second and more practically, few of you will go into an environment where someone else will write your headlines. So over the next few years of your mass comm education, it's important that you hone your headline-writing skills because good headlines are more important now than they've ever been.

The good news is that if you get to be a master headline writer, the benefits are big. The bad news is that often headline writing is more art than science. The best headline writers get a great deal of practice. At newspapers, the copy editors who write the headlines have decades of experience doing so. They write dozens a week and all that practice goes a long way. That's another good reason for you to learn how to write headlines now. You'll need the next few years of your education to practice if you want to write headlines like a pro.

Headline-Writing Conventions

You need to understand the conventions and style of headlines before you can dive in and start practicing. Here are the main conventions:

Tense

Getting headline tenses right is one of the biggest challenges for new headline writers. Most headlines are written in present tense:

Man breaks marathon record

Grand jury indicts local politician

Local man sets world record

The above headlines refer to events that happened in the past, but the headlines are still written in present tense. There are exceptions to this rule. For example, items that would normally be in past perfect tense (using "had") are often written in past tense:

Report: Police were informed of suspect's past

Students were expecting tuition increase, study finds

Attribution

Just like in the body of a story, unattributed words in a headline are viewed as claims of the writer. If it's a claim that needs attribution in the story, it probably needs attribution in the headline. There are two conventions for attribution in headlines, one of which is unique to headlines. Just as in a news story, you can attribute using *said*—or, because it's a headline—*says*. For example:

Chancellor says tuition will be frozen

Tuition won't increase this year, chancellor says

Alternatively, you can set the attribution off with a colon. For example:

Chancellor: No tuition hikes this year

Tuition to remain the same: chancellor

Headlines vs. hammers

Often when learning to write headlines for the first time your first instinct will be to try to write in "headlinese." You'll attempt to imitate the conventions from headlines you've read before, which isn't an all-bad approach.

Before you set out, though, it's important to understand that not everything you see in large type above a story in newspapers or on online news sites is a headline. To allow for extra points of entry into stories and get more information on the surface, page designers use *overlines, hammers, decks* and all sorts of other design tools.

The point of entry most easily confused with the headline, however, is the hammer. Hammers are distinct from the headlines we're teaching you to write in this chapter in a couple of ways. Typically, hammers don't have a verb and are one to three words. In newspapers, they're usually splashed across the front page in huge type.

Hammers are important tools for newspapers. Their short length allows them to be blown up on a front page to a font size large enough to draw readers in. But their length and lack of a verb rarely allow for much detail.

So while you're still learning to write headlines, even if your headline sounds like it's written in perfect "headlinese," ask yourself whether it has a verb. If the answer is no, then you've got a hammer and it's time to rewrite. It's one of the most common mistakes young media writers make and it may take some practice before you break the habit of writing hammers instead of headlines.

The second treatment, with the attribution set off by a colon at the end of the headline, is used less frequently because it's a bit awkward. It's an important technique to have in your back pocket, though, in case you really want the attribution to be secondary to what's being said in the headline.

Quotes

It is possible to use quotes in headlines and a great quote can make for a truly great headline. A so-so quote can make for a dull headline, though, so this is a technique best saved for those times when you've got a really great quote to work with—or if you have a quote that is news in itself.

Quotes in headlines are set off with single quotes rather than double quotes. The quotes still have attribution, but unlike in a news story, they might not be attributed by name. Often in a headline a job title or other descriptive term is used in place of the name. That's OK because if the quote is a big enough deal to make it into the headline, it will (and should) also be in the story, attributed by name to the person who said it.

Capitalization

Headlines are written in sentence case, meaning that the capitalization is basically the same that it would be if you were writing a sentence. The first word gets capitalized and so do proper nouns. The first word after a colon also usually gets capitalized. Some newspapers, such as The New York Times, write their headlines in title case, capitalizing every word. That's a pretty uncommon approach, though.

Numbers

Numbers are important elements of headlines. They can provide scale to a story and succinctly provide concrete information. Unlike in the body of the story, numbers don't have to abide by AP style. In headlines, numbers under 10 can be written as numerals—even if they are the first item in a headline.

Replacing 'and' with a comma

Words are precious in headlines, which is why some of these conventions, such as colon attribution, help eliminate words. Another word we rarely use in headlines is *and*. Usually *and* is replaced with a comma:

Peas and carrots are good for you, your mom says

becomes

Peas, carrots good for you, your mom says

This replacement is most common when you're using *and* to join a pair of nouns, and most often when those nouns are the subject of your headline. Often when you're joining two clauses it's more common to use a semicolon.

Mayor demands tax hike and City Council isn't happy

becomes

Mayor demands tax hike; City Council isn't happy

No more 'to be'

Forms of the word *to be*—am, are, is, was, were, been, being, etc., are typically omitted when writing headlines. Sometimes omitting one of these words means a headline no longer makes sense. In those cases, it's best to leave it in. When possible, this is another valuable way to trim a few words from your headline.

City council is planning tax hike becomes *City council planning tax hike*

Students are upset about new fees becomes *Students upset about new fees*

Omit articles

In addition to omitting *to be*, common articles *a* and *the* are also unnecessary.

Abbreviations

Common abbreviations that you may not usually get away with in a story are OK in headlines, as long as the person reading your headline will understand the abbreviation. This is a judgment call on your part. A headline that reads *FW mayor won't support new highway*, to residents of Fort Worth, Texas, is clearly about the Fort Worth mayor. To residents of Fort Wayne, Ind., it may have a different meaning. Abbreviations that are approved for second reference by the AP Stylebook are almost always OK for a headline.

Length

Headline length is something you won't hear talked about much in some circles, because for most newspaper headline writers the length of the headline isn't determined by the headline writer. Typically the person who lays out the page puts a headline in that's just dummy text—essentially prescribing for the headline writer the length of the headline. The headline writer replaces those "spec headlines" with actual headlines. In those cases the length of the headline is driven by the design, rather than by the amount of space the headline writer wants.

You're not writing newspaper headlines, though, so you get to choose the length of your headline and don't have to worry about how it fits onto a page. Even though you don't have space constraints to be concerned with, you should still keep your headlines on the short side. When readers scan headlines on a page they tend to skim. Sometimes they're looking for "trigger words" that draw them into a specific item. Other times they may be perusing the page, looking for something that piques their interest. Either way, the more unnecessary words you put in a headline, the more you obscure those important trigger words. That means you want to get through to the reader in as few words as possible, while still getting across the important stuff.

How long is the perfect headline? That answer is ... it depends. Most weigh in at about seven words, although, again, there isn't a hard rule. If you have to make a choice between adding an eighth word and having a hard-to-understand headline, it's worth adding the extra word.

Finding your words

Many of these things probably seem like common sense if you're an avid news reader. Eventually, you'll learn to write in what many call "headlinese," the sometimes awkward but effective language of headlines. Understanding the convention and style is only half the battle, though. Now you have to actually write a headline.

The content of your headline is closely tied to what you learned in the chapter about lead writing. Figuring out what to headline your story requires that you understand what the most newsworthy thing is about your story. Once you've figured out that hook, you've got a topic for your headline.

What if you don't have a hook, though? What if your story has several equally prominent topics in it that need to be addressed in the headline? Well that's a problem. It's one thing for it to be difficult to find the right words to fill out your headline. It's a whole other thing to not be able to find the hook in your story, and that's sometimes a sign that you don't have one or that you haven't successfully drawn it out.

This is where headline-writing becomes a helpful tool in writing your story. Sometimes when you have to boil a story down to eight words, you realize things that you couldn't see when you had 400 words to work with. It may even be that you understand the hook for your story when you're trying to write the headline and realize that you don't articulate that hook anywhere in the story. Again, that means it's time to revisit your story before writing the headline.

Your headline should always play off something that's in the story. Your headline should complement your story, but it can't replace a good lead.

Sometimes even if your story is well pegged and has a defined hook, it *still* can be difficult to figure out what to highlight. And sometimes this is when it's time to sit down and start writing. Just like with lead writing, it can be painful to sit there staring at a blank page.

Great headlines often don't flow off the fingertips of even the best headline writers. Rather, a writer is likely to put a few words on the page and tweak and tweak and tweak until he or she is looking at the perfect headline. That same writer may throw the entire headline out many times before arriving at the final one.

There are a few steps you can take to get yourself on the right track when a blank page is staring you down:

1. All headlines have nouns and verbs, and sometime it helps to figure out what the *action* is that you're trying to get across in the headline. Think of the action that's the real hook.

2. Once you've figured out what your action is, pick your noun. This should be easy. Who did it? What words can you use to describe this person? Let's say it's the mayor. You only have a few options: the mayor's last name, *mayor*, etc. Because most headlines are written in active voice, you've likely found your first word.

3. Now that you have the headline subject, what's your verb? Headlines revolve around really good verbs. Did the basketball team *beat* its cross-town rival? Or did they *dominate*, *rout*, *shut down* or even *pummel* them? Each one of those verbs has a different connotation. It's important that you add some color without getting so creative that you unintentionally convey something because you got a little crazy with the thesaurus.

4. Does your headline have an object? In our above example about a basketball game, who did your team beat? Just like in step 2, you only have a few options here. You now have the start of a headline: Someone (step 2) did something (step 3) to someone (step 4). That's the format for almost every headline.

5. Do you need attribution for the action in your headline? If you do, now's the time to add it.

6. You probably have a few extra words to play with now. This is where you add important adjectives, adverbs and other descriptors. It may even be a short prepositional phrase at the end. Building on our earlier example, we may choose to add something like "in cross-town rivalry" or the score of the game:

Dogs shut out Cats 67-0 in annual rivalry game

This method will get you the simplest of headlines and doesn't apply to every situation, but it gives you an idea of how to write the most basic headline. Often, just like when writing a story, you'll find that it's best to work through the headline piece by piece.

Now that you've written your headline, it's time to do a bit of self-editing on it to make sure you've avoided the common headline traps. Here are a few questions to ask yourself:

- Does your headline have a noun and a verb? If it doesn't, it's not a headline. You may be chuckling at this question now, but you'd be surprised how often this rule is broken in student newspapers.
- Is your headline in active voice? If your headline is about an action, actions always come through stronger in active voice. So it's probably time to reorganize your headline.
- If someone read nothing but this headline would they understand the most important thing about your story? Would they at least understand the *who* and the *what*, even if the *why* is too complicated to fit in a headline? On the flip side, does your story make sense without your headline? It should.
- Does your headline closely resemble the lead? That's called "parroting," and it's time to rephrase.
- Read your headline aloud. Is it awkward? Does it have good rhythm, or do you stumble over it when you're reading it? Headlines should flow. So if you, as the writer, can't easily get through it, you probably need to change it.
- Are there excess words? Are there words in your headline that you could drop without harming it? If so, then do it and don't look back.
- Could someone read a double meaning into your headline? Read it with your mind in the gutter and with your sixth grade boy glasses on. The last thing you want is for your headline to become the next Internet meme. Here are some examples of a few headlines that can be read with a double meaning. Often one word with a double meaning can create this problem, such as the words in bold below:
    - Juvenile court to **try** shooting defendant
    - NJ judge to **rule** on nude beach
    - **Bar** trying to help alcoholic lawyers
    - Prostitutes **appeal** to pope
    - Defendant's speech ends in long **sentence**

Other times, words that can act as both nouns and verbs cause confusion. Note how plans, when used as a verb, creates a much different headline than its intended use as a noun:

*Large church **plans** collapse*

And were police chasing winds or did the chase wind through three towns:

*Police chase **winds** across three towns*

The Bottom Line

All the tests above don't mean anything even if your headline is written in perfect headlinese and doesn't accomplish one important goal. The best headlines should always make you answer *yes* to one important question: After reading this headline, do you want to read this story? If the answer is *no*, then you either have a boring story or an ineffective headline. In either case, you've got work to do.

Headlines, as we said in the introduction to this chapter, should scream out at you, drawing you into the story. If you don't accomplish that central goal, then your headline isn't working, regardless of how witty it is or the great verb you found to anchor it. In a world where the headline not only titles the page, but also often serves as a hyperlink through a website or acts as the link that surfaced in the search results of our favorite search engine, a great headline can draw users in as well as a great photo. Unlike a photo, though, you can rewrite a headline until its perfect, and that's the beauty of headline writing.

The Doo-Dah Rule

Here's another way to check your headlines—sing them. Like poetry, heads should have a rhythm about them. Old-timers said you should be able to sing a head to the tune of "Camptown Races," adding the *doo-dah* twice at the end of the head. Try it—after, of course, you look around to make sure nobody's listening. Here are some examples:

- Three rescued in Bedford fire, doo-dah, doo-dah
- Germans hunt for terrorists, doo-dah, doo-dah
- College bills are on the rise, doo-dah, doo-dah
- Marijuana crackdown launched, doo-dah, doo-dah

Now that's not saying that all heads should be doo-dah heads, just that this seven-syllable rhythm is pleasing to readers. It's an old cadence (London Bridge is falling down, doo-dah, doo-dah, and Mary had a little lamb, doo-dah, doo-dah), and when you write one it's somehow internally satisfying to readers.

And now that you know that, don't tell anyone where you got it. We do have an academic reputation to protect …

Skills Development: Practice in Media Writing

Let's practice by writing headlines for some of the stories used earlier in the book. Try writing headlines for the following stories.

Follow the steps outlined in this chapter for how to write headlines. Show your work by answering every applicable question for each story.

Think of several verbs and several words you can use for your subject. That'll get you the best results for your final headline. Make sure your headline is written as concisely as possible.

Exercise 12.1

- The Randy Travis story, pages 53-54 (chapter 3)

    What is the action or hook?

    Your subject?

    Your verb?

    Object?

    Do you need attribution? If so, to whom do you need to attribute this information?

    The completed headline:

Exercise 12.2

- The golf course brawl story, page 49 (chapter 3)

    What is the action or hook?

    Your subject?

    Your verb?

    Object?

    Do you need attribution? If so, to whom do you need to attribute this information?

    The completed headline:

Exercise 12.3

- The campaign fundraising story, page 83 (chapter 5), Exercise 5.2

    What is the action or hook?

    _____

    Your subject?

    _____

    Your verb?

    _____

    Object?

    _____

    Do you need attribution? If so, to whom do you need to attribute this information?

    _____

    The completed headline:

    _____

Exercise 12.4

- The Froggie Sports Bar shooting story, page 193 (end of chapter 11), Exercise 11.1

    What is the action or hook?

    _____

    Your subject?

    _____

    Your verb?

    _____

    Object?

    _____

    Do you need attribution? If so, to whom do you need to attribute this information?

    _____

    The completed headline:

    _____

Chapter Thirteen

Another Approach to News: The What, When and How of the Alternative Lead

By Robert Bohler

Editors' note: This chapter explains those leads you see that seem to violate everything we've already said about approaching a news lead (see chapter 5). The author advises a student newspaper, so some of the illustrations are from student media writers on a university publication.

The hard news, or summary, lead doesn't work for every news story you write in journalism or for PR news releases. The hard news lead is largely unadorned because the media writer wants to pack the critical elements objectively and tightly into a single sentence to give readers a clear and quick understanding of what has happened.

Let's say you discover a compelling aspect of a story that characterizes the focus of the story. You may want to use an alternative approach to building the lead (sometimes called a "soft news lead"). If your publication is producing a multistory package, an editor may want to complement a hard news story and a summary lead with a complementary story that takes an alternative, soft news approach and focuses on single aspect of the major story.

The hard news lead may address the *who, what, when, where, why* and *how* of the story. Alternative leads often emphasize the *who* and the *what*. If you're writing a sidebar, you'll probably want to expand on some facet of the story—maybe an explanation of how or why someone did something or a look at how a series of events occurred. That alternative approach to that angle of a story generally calls for an alternative lead.

Here are some keys to decide which lead to use: the traditional hard news or the alternative lead:

1. Which of the two, the hard news lead or the alternative lead, will result in the greatest reader impact?

2. Which approach, the hard or the alternative lead, will best highlight the story's news angle?

3. Is the news more interesting than it is important? If so, you may want to use an alternative lead.

4. Is there a good chance the reader may have already heard about the news on radio or TV? When readers are already familiar with the news angle, we frequently choose alternative leads.

5. Is this a second-day or follow story (see chapter 11)? When we look at continuing implications of previous news stories, typically we take alternative approaches.

One important note as you read this chapter: You'll notice that we're not using the word *lead* exactly as it has been used before in the book. That's because media writers use that word to mean two different—but still similar—things, and only by looking at the context can you determine the meaning. The simplest meaning of *lead* is the way it has always been used in this book: the first graf of a news story, typically one sentence. But you can also use *lead* to mean *the first several grafs* of a story—in effect a *lead element*, not just the one-graf lead.

Let's say you use an anecdotal alternative lead, a lead that tells a story in a few grafs. You can look at those few grafs and call them the lead of the story. Or maybe you write a descriptive alternative lead, and the description is the first three grafs of the story. You can call those three grafs the story's lead, or you can call only the first graf of the story the lead. Confused yet? Once you become more familiar with alternative approaches, you'll be able to tell which is being described.

Alternative Leads Add Appeal to 'Routine' News Coverage

If you work for campus media and your news beat is student government or Greek organizations, your leads are going to become stale if they always start with "The Student Senate voted to …" or "The Kappa Delta sorority will sponsor a talent show Saturday to raise funds for …"

That's when you need to find the angle to write the alternative lead. Sometimes it's called the "feature lead," because it's more standard in feature stories than in news stories.

After reporter Michael Gutierrez interviewed students and staff associated with the campus Interfaith group about its upcoming service trip to San Francisco during spring break, he could have written the following summary lead:

> *Students with Interfaith will learn about non-Christian faiths, deliver meals to elderly members of a Jewish congregation and work with other religious groups in rehabilitating homes for the needy, Religion and Spiritual Life Associate Chaplain Todd Boling said.*

That lead would have satisfactorily addressed what the students would be doing, but it wouldn't reflect the overall purpose of their trip. So here's the lead Gutierrez fashioned (Gutierrez 2012), with the *hook* in the first paragraph (underlined) and *idea* in italics:

> <u>Explore, serve, pray and learn. These are the four objectives of this year's Interfaith spring break trip to San Francisco.</u>
>
> Todd Boling, associate chaplain for Religious and Spiritual Life, organized activities designed to expose students to faiths and cultures that might be unfamiliar to students.
>
> Boling said, "College is an opportunity to figure what you stand for and what you want to do personally."
>
> Interfaith, an initiative of the Office of Religious and Spiritual Life, commits to providing students with opportunities to connect with people of all faiths, Boling said.
>
> *Students on the trip would understand more about Buddhist, Islamic and Hindu worship practices, he said. Service activities would include delivering meals to the elderly with a Jewish congregation and habitat rehabilitation with other faith communities, he said.**

The lead now captures the overall objectives of the spring trip, placing them in a larger perspective for the reader, and gets to the basic idea in what would otherwise be an accurate but less engaging news lead.

Likewise, when reporter Emily Atteberry wrote about an alumnus' efforts with a service fraternity to boost the college enrollment of low-income high school students, she could have written the following satisfactory summary lead:

> *Fort Worth Polytechnic High School students are applying to college in record numbers, says a TCU alumnus who works as their adviser.*

She didn't, though. In looking at the scope of her research, she decided the lead should reflect the degree to which the enrollment had improved. Here's her alternative lead (Atteberry 2012):

> *Staying in high school was a feat in and of itself. Going to college? Not even a consideration.*
>
> *But now Fort Worth Polytechnic High School students are applying to college at record numbers with the help of alumnus Geovanny Bonilla and Phi Kappa Sigma.**

---

* From TCU360, 2012. Reprinted by permission.

In depicting this contrast, Atteberry adopted a conversational style for the first three sentences to constitute her *hook*, used the oppositional coordinating conjunction *but* to establish the conflict that was to be overcome, "now" to establish the present situation, and concluded with the *idea* that captures the change.

It's important to note that in both Gutierrez's and Atteberry's leads, the writers crafted alternate leads after looking at the greater picture of the situation they were reporting and not limiting their consideration for their leads to the "who/what/when" formulaic pattern.

Are These Feature Leads?

Alternative news leads can be confusing, because they look like leads for feature stories. They start with an attention-getting statement whose only focus is to draw you into the second and subsequent grafs, or they start with an anecdote or perhaps a descriptive passage. Their similarity to feature stories is no accident. That's where those techniques came from.

As newspapers lost their breaking-news franchise to radio, TV and then the Internet, they turned more to alternative lead approaches, because the traditional hard news lead was only telling readers what they already knew.

News writers took the news peg of the story, dropped it to the second or third graf, and "topped" the story with an anecdote or some other device designed to pull in the reader.

This technique had been used before on feature stories or what was called "soft news"—news that was more interesting and entertaining than it was important. But now, writers often borrow the soft news approach for all kinds of other stories, like the ones mentioned in this chapter.

Remember that there are two types of alternative, or soft news, approaches:

1 | Soft news leads on soft news stories (features and stories with more entertainment value than news value) and

2 | Soft news leads on hard news stories where you use a feature-type lead and delay the hard news angle until later in the story.

Alternative Leads for PR Practitioners

Alternative leads are as useful for PR practitioners as for journalists. PR writers use alternative approaches for many of their writing tasks, from direct mail pieces to newsletters to websites. The lead may be an attention-getting statement, or an anecdote, or a description of a place or person; the goal is the same—to draw the reader into the story.

A media writer for Meals on Wheels in State College, Penn., was doing a story on the 40th anniversary of the organization. Obviously, the writer could have crafted a traditional hard-news lead, something like this:

> *State College Meals on Wheels is celebrating its 40th anniversary after delivering 1.25 million meals to seniors in the State College Area School District.*

Instead, the writer took this approach (Buffington 2011):

> *In August 1971, six vehicles left the parking lot of Grace Lutheran Church to deliver 26 prepared meals to clients who were homebound and unable to cook for themselves.*
>
> *Since that time, Meals on Wheels has continued to feed those who need the agency's service regardless of age or the ability to pay.**

When PR professionals write news for release to the media, they generally write hard-news-type leads and inverted pyramid stories. But news releases are only one type of writing that PR writers are responsible for. And when they write for their organization's magazines or newsletters or blogs, they often turn to alternative approaches.

---

* Reprinted by permission of Anna Carol Buffington.

Alternative Leads Can Bring Sports Coverage to Life

Alternative leads are great for the sports writing toolkit, allowing you to craft information gathered for a game story into an entertaining lead for an advance story. Sports coverage will probably go online almost immediately, but print stories sometimes appear several days after a weekend game. One tactic used by the sports reporters is to repackage the information they've gathered—whether it was reported in the game story or not—into fresh copy with new angles. Most of the time, that's done with alternative leads.

For his coverage of the TCU-Colorado State men's basketball game for the website, Ryan Osborne had to post the game story quickly following the game, and to do so he turned to the tried-and-true staple of the summary lead. Here are the first three graphs of the story:

> *Craig Williams had a team-high of 20 points on 7-of-11 shooting, including 4-of-5 from three-point range leading his team to victory.*
>
> *The TCU men's basketball team beat Colorado State 75-71 Saturday night at Daniel-Meyer Coliseum.*
>
> *TCU, 14-10 overall, 4-4 MW, held a 71-69 lead going into the final 20 seconds of play when point guard Kyan Anderson was fouled and sent to the line for two shots. (Osborne 2012a)**

Those first two grafs—which might have been better crafted into one sentence—capture the results of the game and put the victory in context for the reader, a satisfactory execution of the summary lead.

By Tuesday morning, however, that Saturday night story is going to be dated; almost anyone who is, or was, interested in the results of the TCU-Colorado State game will already know the outcome. So, what are the newspaper's options when it comes to maintaining its coverage? The route Osborne takes for Tuesday's print coverage is also a reporting staple: revising the content to analyze the game's outcome or to point ahead as an advance story for the upcoming contest, in this case a matchup with 11th-ranked University of Nevada-Las Vegas or a combination of the two.

So Osborne, whose post-game interviews with players and the head coach are included in the game story, chose to craft an alternative lead, in this case employing a descriptive *hook*, one that depicts the exhaustion felt by head coach Jim Christian following the close game on Friday. Here's the story (Osborne 2012b), with the information that constituted the game story's summary lead now forming (in italics below) the idea that rounds out the alternative lead.

> **TCU head coach Jim Christian trudged out of the home team locker room late Saturday night, making his way down the hallway leading to the corps of reporters huddled in the open area under the north end of Daniel-Meyer Coliseum.**
>
> **Christian looked drained—physically, emotionally, mentally.**
>
> **"We've played 24 games," Christian said. "I feel like 19 of them have come down to the last possession."**
>
> **This time, Christian's squad came out on the high end.**
>
> *The TCU men's basketball team beat Colorado State 75-71 over the weekend, improving to 14-10 on the season and 4-4 in Mountain West Conference play.**

The story addresses the details of the game, with information already obtained from post-game interviews, looks at the ebb and flow of the Horned Frogs' efforts in the three previous games, and looks ahead—again with quotes from a post-game interview with Christian—to the upcoming UNLV game.

The beauty of the strategy is that it works for follow coverage regardless of the publication schedule, daily, weekly or semiweekly, or the print or web platform most available to you.

---

* From TCU360, 2012. Reprinted by permission.

Alternative Leads Highlight Enterprise Reporting

Some of your writing will center on breaking news or sporting events, of course. But the bulk of it will address the events and issues that develop from the multitude of interactions within your communities. The alternative lead approach, when it presents itself, will enable you to better characterize the particularities and significance of these events and to provide a better showcase for your readers.

One of the more difficult tasks for reporters who cover events that occur on a regular or frequent basis is finding new angles for their stories. If the local Chamber of Commerce quarterly or annually recognizes business leaders in your community, it can be hard not fall into a template manner of reporting where only the names and the dates change in the lead. Or if your community hosts an annual fall or spring festival, you'll want to avoid writing the announcement lead that never changes except for the dates or year.

In Fort Worth, Texas, which has a heavy military and military contract presence, it has become a customary practice, as in many other cities, for volunteers to welcome armed forces members as they return from combat deployments. So the problem facing reporters who cover those events from time to time is how to bring a fresh approach to readers.

In March 2012, reporter Terry Evans' task was aided somewhat by the fact that this would be the last welcome home provided by a local volunteer group. And Evans' lead might have read in summary form:

> *The local volunteer group that has been greeting soldiers, Marines and pilots at the Dallas/Fort Worth Airport for eight years welcomed its final group of returning troops Wednesday.*

That summary lead works, and it is distinguished by the mention that it is the final event for the group. But Evans used interviews with the returning troops to capture the emotion of the event, fashioning an anecdotal lead, in which a short account is typical of the overall scenario, with the idea coming in the fifth paragraph (Evans 2012):

> *DFW AIRPORT—Army Maj. Clydellia Prichard-Allen cried when people hugged her and gave her flowers, water and goodies.*
>
> *"I didn't expect this," the 82nd Airborne Aviation Combat Brigade soldier said Wednesday. "They told us about what might happen, but we didn't expect this much."*
>
> *Prichard-Allen was among dozens of soldiers, Marines and airmen who were the last to be greeted by volunteers with the Welcome Home A Hero program.*
>
> *The volunteers have been there to cheer for returning troops with every R&R flight at Dallas/Fort Worth Airport for eight years.*
>
> *Wednesday marked the final arriving flight for the program, and hundreds of people showed up to welcome the troops, packing gate D-22 so thoroughly that it was impossible not to step on toes.**

Star-Telegram reporter Alex Branch encountered a similar issue in reporting on the latest round of graduations from the United Way's local Earn Well program that provides technical and financial training for low-income residents. Eleven of the 19 people who had graduated had landed jobs by the time Branch's story appeared a month later, a number significant enough to warrant the news angle for a summary lead. But Branch interviewed one of the graduates whose success pops out to readers in the following lead and shows, rather than merely tells, the reader about the Earn Well program. The *idea*, which might have served as the basis for a summary lead, is in the fourth paragraph and italicized (Branch 2012):

> **Robert Taylor went to school a few years ago and got a certificate to be a surgical technician, but all he could find was part-time work.**
>
> **For a man with a wife and two young children, part-time pay doesn't cover the bills, he said.**
>
> **Taylor, 31, of Arlington, found his way into United Way of Tarrant County's Earn Well program, intended to help the underemployed become financially stable. Ten weeks later, he has a new job as an oil and gas production technician that he is told will pay around $60,000 a year, including overtime.**

---

*From the *Fort Worth Star-Telegram*, 2012. Reprinted by permission.

In fact, of the 19 people who graduated Feb. 24 from Taylor's class, 11 already had jobs waiting, officials said.

"It was great for us and a big relief for me and my wife," Taylor said.

"It's going to be a relief paying the bills and getting caught up."*

The Bottom Line

The alternative lead is a valuable asset for the reporter when the opportunity presents itself as a way to improve storytelling. It's certainly not the only way, but it offers reporters the opportunity to be more creative with their writing, and it's a way to pull the readers—who may be only casually interested—more deeply into the story through the use of appropriate story-telling techniques.

Three tips to remember:

1. Your news judgment should be constant, regardless of the type of lead you select. The idea should be consistent with a summary lead for the same story.

2. Don't alter your story line only because you've got a great anecdote or quote; make sure your hook reflects the nature of the story.

3. The degree to which you have choices of alternative leads largely depends on your reporting ability. The media writer who is always eyeing the additional interview or asking the additional question is more likely to develop those choices than the reporter who only covers the bases. Sources often need to be prompted to offer up lively or colorful details, and the non-inquisitive reporter is less likely to prompt sources.

Paula LaRocque

A VISIT WITH YOUR WRITING COACH
Anecdotal Leads Don't Always Lead

The perils of the anecdotal lead

http://snd.sc/LoV9hv

---

* From the *Fort Worth Star-Telegram*, 2012. Reprinted by permission.

References

Atteberry, Emily. "Alumnus Helps High School Students Get Computers, Apply to College." *TCU360*, February 21, 2012. http://www.tcu360.com/campus/2012/02/14604.alumnus-helps-high-school-students-get-computers-apply-college.

Branch, Alex. "United Way Program Trains Workers for Jobs That Need Them." *Fort Worth Star-Telegram*, March 15, 2012. http://www.star-telegram.com/2012/03/14/3810476/united-way-program-trains-workers.html.

Buffington, Anna Carol. "Updates Will Improve Meals on Wheels Services." *centredaily.com*, October 5, 2011. http://www.centredaily.com/2011/10/05/2938647/updates-will-improve-meals-on.html.

Evans, Terry. "DFW Volunteers Welcome Home Final Flight of Troops." *Fort Worth Star-Telegram,* March 14, 2012. http://www.star-telegram.com/2012/03/14/v-touch/3810512/dfw-welcomes-final-flight-of-troops.html.

Gutierrez, Michael. "Chaplain Offers Interfaith Service Trip to San Francisco." *TCU360*, February 9, 2012. http://www.tcu360.com/campus/2012/02/14456.chaplain-offers-interfaith-service-trip-san-francisco.

Osborne, Ryan. "Slideshow: Men's Basketball Team Conquers Colorado State." *TCU360*, February 12, 2012a. http://www.tcu360.com/mens-basketball/2012/02/14483.slideshow-mens-basketball-team-conquers-colorado-state.

———. "Frogs Beat Colorado State, Turn Attention Toward No. 11 UNLV." *TCU360*, February 14, 2012b. http://www.tcu360.com/mens-basketball/2012/02/14497.frogs-beat-colorado-state-turn-attention-toward-no-11-unlv.

Skills Development: Practice in Media Writing

Exercise 13.1

Let's do a scavenger hunt for alternative lead structures. First, remember the two definitions of leads mentioned in the chapter: Although a lead is most often the first graf of a news story, we can also use *lead* to refer to the opening section of the story. Look online and in print for news leads that fall into the following categories:

- **Anecdotal leads.** These are leads that tell a story to draw in the reader.
- **Descriptive leads.** These leads describe a person or place or something else from the story.
- **Zinger lead.** This is one sentence designed to grab the reader. Standing alone, they don't tell you much, because their function is to draw you deeper into the story.
- **Question lead.** The lead consists of a question, which the article goes on to answer in subsequent grafs.
- **Quote lead.** This is rare. It's just a direct quotation. The article goes on to identify the speaker and supply the context.

This isn't an exhaustive list of alternative lead possibilities. Perhaps you can find others. For each story you clip out of a print publication or copy from the Internet, underline the news peg for the story.

Be sure to include some sports news among the alternative leads you clip.

Exercise 13.2

Review the stories you just clipped and rewrite several of the leads into traditional hard news leads. Remember that for every story, writers must decide whether to use a traditional hard news lead or an alternative lead. Often media writers take different approaches on the same story, with one writer crafting a hard news lead and another writing an alternative lead. Choose some of the alternative leads you copied, find the hard news element deeper in the story, and rewrite the lead to put the news element in the lead.

182 Writing for Media Audiences

Exercise 13.3

Write the following story as a traditional hard news story. Then rewrite with an alternative lead structure.

- This happened in Jonesville; write it for the Jonesville Daily Tribune.
- On Tuesday, seven-year-old Samantha Smith set up a lemonade stand at her house.
- She lives at 5005 Parkmeadow Court in Jonesville.
- She sold pink lemonade that her mother made for fifty cents a glass at a stand in her front yard.
- She looked so cute with her stand and a sign that said "Limmonade Stannd" that some people stopped to take her picture; of course, they also bought lemonade from her.
- She opened the stand at 11 a.m.
- At 12:45, the local cops showed up.
- They asked for her business permit, which costs $400 at City Hall.
- She ran in to get her mother, Suzanne.
- Suzanne argued with the cops, but they said she would have to shut down the stand.
- In Jonesville, the city council recently passed an ordinance preventing vendors from selling products without a business license, including kids who want to sell lemonade.
- Cops told mom Suzanne that if she did not shut down the stand immediately, they would have to issue a citation, which could cost $500.
- Suzanne said: "I can't believe that this city would shut down a kid's lemonade stand. How do I explain this to Samantha?"

Exercise 13.4

Some exercises that you have already written with hard-news leads could have been written with an alternative lead. Go back and rewrite Exercises 5.5, 5.8 and 5.9 with alternative leads.

Chapter Fourteen

Long Story Short: Writing News for Broadcast

By Suzanne Huffman

Broadcast writing is short. It's simple. It's conversational. It's written to be heard by the ear. It's not written to be read by the eye. That's why it's important to get to the point quickly and to say what you mean clearly. Those in the audience do not have a chance to go back and re-read a sentence to figure out what you meant by what you said.

When we first start writing "broadcast style" in class, I tell my students to "say it out loud in your own words and cadence" before you write anything down. We naturally talk "broadcast style." If you say the story out loud first, it will sound more like you're talking to your viewers when you deliver the script, and not like you're reading the newspaper out loud to them. Simply put, writing for broadcast is *not* the same as writing for newspapers.

Whether you're writing for television or radio, writing for broadcast is all about simple, conversational sentences.

© WithGod, 2013. Used under license from Shutterstock, inc.

Remember the example from chapter 5 about the Walmart rezoning story in Fort Worth?

Here's the newspaper lead the way it actually appeared in the Fort Worth Star-Telegram (Nishimura 2012) with the second and third grafs included to let you see how the writer continued to develop the story after the lead. The printed story is actually much longer than these three grafs and it is much more detailed.

> *The Fort Worth Zoning Commission voted 7–2 Wednesday morning to deny Walmart the rezoning of a site at Hemphill and Berry streets, where it wants to raze a church-owned community center and build a Walmart Neighborhood Market.*
>
> *Commissioners said they were troubled by the idea of setting a "precedent" in granting Walmart waivers it wants on the site, after neighborhood leaders said the company's overall plan would hurt the city's Hemphill/Berry Urban Village design for the area. Walmart is the first developer to seek waivers in the district since the city approved the urban village several years ago.*
>
> *Neighborhood leaders said they want the Walmart Neighborhood Market, but want it to better fit the urban village plan, which calls for Old-style buildings that hug street fronts and sport lots of windows that highlight activity inside and draw pedestrians in.**

Here's how you might write it for broadcast:

> *Fort Worth zoning commissioners say they do not want to set a precedent by granting Walmart waivers for a store on Berry Street at Hemphill. So the commissioners said "no" this morning to Walmart's request to re-zone the property, tear down a community center and build a neighborhood market there. Leaders in the neighborhood say they want a store on the corner of Berry Street at Hemphill ... but they want it to be a better fit for their urban village plan. That plan calls*

---

* From the *Fort Worth Star-Telegram*, 2012. Reprinted by permission.

for old-style buildings that sit close to the street and have lots of windows. Walmart planners and neighborhood leaders say they will continue to talk about how they might accomplish this.

Find a newspaper story and read several grafs aloud. See how far you get in 30 seconds. Chances are, you will only get to the second graf. An average broadcast story will run five sentences and take 30 seconds to deliver out loud. Some run only 15 or 20 seconds. While the content is similar, the delivery is different. A newspaper reader has the luxury of going back over a story and re-reading it. A broadcast viewer or listener does not get that chance. A broadcast story goes past once and there's only one chance to "get it."

Think about the Sound of the Words

In addition to writing short and simply, in broadcast you have to consider how the words will come out of your mouth. The following string of words looks fine on paper: *This is a story about a soldier who is having shoulder surgery Sunday.* But try saying it out loud. It doesn't come out of your mouth easily.

It's the same with proper names and places. Call him Coach K at Duke if you cannot properly pronounce Mike Krzyzewski and make us believe you know whom you're talking about. And say the plane went down near a city in Central Russia rather than saying it went down near Yaroslavl if you cannot say it convincingly. Saying "Central Russia" locates the site generally for most of your viewers and listeners. You want to sound professional and knowledgeable because you are the newscaster and expert. You do not want to stumble over and mispronounce words and you *never* want to guess.

Audience members are busy. They're pressed for time and may be multitasking. They'll switch to the next station in a heartbeat if they're bored or your story is "taking too long" or it's too hard to follow or understand. Broadcast writing is the ultimate "long story short." Just say it. Get to the point. And tell your audience the "main things" they need to know. Remember your history teacher—the one you liked—who told stories. The one you didn't like was all about memorizing names and dates and numbers and factoids—not about telling stories about what happened where and why it mattered.

There are no re-takes in a live newscast and sometimes little or no time to review the script in advance. As a result, numerous conventions in broadcast writing are designed to make it easy to deliver a script cleanly from the teleprompter on first sight. There are no abbreviations, symbols and long strings of zeros in broadcast writing because the newscaster has to be able to deliver the script accurately as it scrolls up and over the 'prompter screen in real time. For example:

- Write *Tennessee*, not *TN*.
- Write *doctor* or *drive*, not *Dr.*
- Write *street* or *saint*, not *St.*
- Write *amazon-dot-com*, not *amazon.com*.
- Write *46-million-dollars*, not *$46,000,000.00*.
- Write *three and a half billion* (because it's more conversational), not *3.5 billion* or even *three-point-five billion.*
- Letters said individually are hyphenated: F-B-I and N-B-A and N-F-L. That way it's clear the individual letters are to be said (and not a word to be pronounced).

You want to make sure the script can be delivered cleanly and clearly the first time—no matter who wrote it and even if the legendary anchor Ron Burgundy is delivering it.

Write to Avoid Mispronunciations

Broadcast writers will write a word phonetically if the pronunciation of a word is in doubt. Broadcasters need to know for sure how to say what they're writing about because mispronouncing a word calls their credibility into serious question. Mexia is a town in Texas. It's pronounced Ma-HAY-yah. Saying it incorrectly tells local listeners "you're not from around here and you don't know what you're talking about." Cairo can be pronounced KYE-row or KAY-row, depending on which city you're talking about. Sometimes you even need to misspell a word in a broadcast script. Do you mean a bass fiddle or a bass fish? Then write base fiddle or bass fish.

You want to be grammatically correct but not overly so. *Lie, lay, lain* is grammatically correct but few people talk that way. Same with *who* and *whom*.

You don't need long titles and everyone's name in a broadcast story. And you don't need long internal modifying phrases like those used in newspapers. The TCU chancellor is named Victor J. Boschini Jr. In a newspaper text story, he will be identified as Victor J. Boschini Jr., chancellor of Texas Christian University. In a broadcast story, we call him Chancellor Boschini or TCU's chancellor. And we say T-C-U. Because that's how we talk. And a broadcast story is delivered out loud as a "talk" story. You literally are "talking" to your viewers when you deliver the news to camera or microphone.

You can also start a sentence with a conjunction to emphasize it in the delivery. See the paragraph above as an example.

You usually do not need everyone's full name, age and address either. In a newspaper text story, a person may be identified by name, age and sometimes street address. For example, we might read, "Russell Brand, 36, was arrested in New Orleans this morning." In a broadcast story, we might say, "Comedian Russell Brand is under arrest in New Orleans this morning."

Numbers and math can be mind-numbing and hard to understand. They drive your audience away. If last's year's attendance was 958,649 and this year it was 41,351 more, just say a million people attended this year's fair. The audience cannot and will not "do the math" in their heads. Do it for them and make it easy. Same with gas prices, percentages, mortgage rates and all things math.

Use contractions because they're more conversational. Say "today" or "yesterday" to locate the story in time. Give the day of the week if you're writing for a 24-hour worldwide audience such as CNN's. Say Central Time or Eastern Time if it clarifies when the away game will begin for a local audience. Say "in Fort Worth" or "in Dallas" to locate the story in space.

It can be hard to follow a train of thought when a broadcaster uses several pronouns, so it's often better to repeat the noun. You want to be clear about who "he" or "she" is on second or third reference. For example, "Police say the neighborhood watch volunteer shot the young man. He's a former football star." We don't know if "he" is the shooter or the former football star.

It's also OK to be redundant. If you say a person's name in the first sentence or two of a story, repeat it in the last sentence or two. That way you reinforce for your viewers/listeners who you are really talking about. They may not have started to listen to you until the second or third sentence anyway. And now they want to know who you're talking about.

Attribution comes first in broadcast writing. Write, "Police say the woman is indeed the one they were looking for." Not, "The woman is the one they were looking for, police say."

Writing for Real-time Delivery

Many broadcast stories are written with a present-tense or a continuing-present-tense lead sentence because the audience is listening to the newscaster "right now" "in real time," and they want to know what's going on "right now." A newspaper story often starts with a past-tense lead sentence because it literally was written "last night" before the paper went to the printer. The "right now" broadcast lead may in fact be found near or at the end of a newspaper story.

Here is a story that appeared in the printed edition of the Fort Worth Star-Telegram (Mitchell 2012). It is followed by the same story written for broadcast.

> *ARLINGTON—A man was found dead outside a north Arlington apartment Thursday afternoon, and officers were looking for a man seen running from the complex, police reported.*
>
> *A woman called 911 shortly before 4 p.m. after finding the body in front of her unit at the Huntington Meadows Apartments in the 2200 block of Stratton Lane. Officers with dogs searched the area as other officers conducted interviews, according to a news release from Tiara Richard, a police spokeswoman.*

The man appeared to have been shot, she said.

School officials locked down nearby Nichols Junior High School for a short time.

Anyone with information is asked to call police Detective Lisa Wade, 817-459-5325, or Crime Stoppers at 817-469-8477. All tipsters may remain anonymous and are eligible for a reward up to $1,000.

Before you write your story, always call first to find out the latest information. But here's how the story might be rewritten for broadcast:

Arlington police are offering a reward for information about a man found dead outside an apartment there. Police say the man appeared to have been shot. His body was found outside the Huntington Meadows Apartments on Stratton Lane in Arlington. A woman called 9-1-1 shortly before four o'clock Thursday to report the death. Anyone with information is asked to call Crime Stoppers. Tipsters do not have to give their name and may be eligible for a one-thousand dollar reward.

You do not want to strain to put a sentence into an awkward, forced present tense. "The coach dies over the weekend" sounds weird. Try "The family of the coach is making arrangements for a memorial service to be held on campus."

Do not write double entendres (double meanings) unless you're writing for Weekend Update on "Saturday Night Live." If a quarterback connected with a receiver several times during the game, they did not "hook up a lot" because that has another meaning.

Broadcast is a different style of writing. And it can be fun. Think quick. Think easy. Say it out loud. Write it down.

The style can be applied to many story types in broadcast: readers, voiceovers, sound on tape, and packages.

A "reader" is when the newscaster simply reads the story aloud. There may be a simple over-the-shoulder graphic in a produced television broadcast.

A "voice over" adds video to the reader. The newscaster reads the story aloud while video of the event is rolling on the screen.

A "sound on tape," or "SOT," is where the newscaster reads a short introduction into a sound bite that's been recorded. There are variations of this: With a "VO/SOT" and "VO/SOT/VO" the newscaster reads the story out loud while video of the event is rolling, followed by a sound bite, and more video rolling.

A "package" is when the reporter has recorded video and sound in the field and edited them into a complete story for the audience. The broadcast narrative is written to the video and sound so that the picture and sound components of the story "match up" with the writing itself. All this is covered in detail in a book titled "Broadcast News Handbook" (Tuggle, Carr and Huffman 2014).

Remember to use non-sexist language and inclusive language. You are writing for a diverse audience and you want to keep them, not drive them away. Say firefighters and police officers, not firemen and policemen. Say faculty members attended with their guests; don't assume all guests are what would be legally defined as spouses. Say service members and congressional representatives, not servicemen or congressmen, because women do those jobs now in ever-growing numbers.

Call a thing what it is … in the best, clearest, most inclusive language.

Paraphrase quotes and tweets … so they don't sound like you're making the statement yourself. If Russell Brand tweets, "Since Steve Jobs died I cannot bear to see anyone use an iPhone irreverently, what I did was a tribute to his memory," you need to re-word that. Try "Russell Brand says in a tweet that he threw the phone through the window because he thought the photographer was using it irreverently." If the name is well known, it's OK to start with it. But don't start with an unknown name. Instead identify an unknown person as a college student from UNC or a resident of Chapel Hill or a basketball player from Duke or whatever is relevant in the first sentence. Put the detailed identification in the second or third sentence if it's important.

Put your story in language the average person can understand. If the governor's *clavicle* needs surgical repair, call it a collarbone. If the punter will undergo surgery to remove an *intramural ganglion cyst* from his kicking knee, call it a cyst. If someone is *agoraphobic*, just say they're afraid of crowded spaces.

The Bottom Line

You cannot put everything in a broadcast story ... only what's most important right now. Museums do not display all their paintings at the same time; they select a few at a time for display so those can truly be seen.

Broadcast writing is truly "long story short." These guidelines will help you get started. Make your story as simple as possible, as easy to understand as possible. Viewers and listeners have only one chance to understand you. If a person wants all the nitty-gritty details, facts, figures, names, ages, addresses, numbers, dates and percentages, they can go to a newspaper or website where they can read and re-read and contemplate the details at their own speed.

Paula LaRocque

A VISIT WITH YOUR WRITING COACH
Say It Right: Common Pronunciation Errors

The key to proper pronunciation

http://snd.sc/LoVFMs

References

Mitchell, Mitch. "Man Found Dead Outside Apartment." *Fort Worth Star-Telegram*, March 30, 2012: 4B.

Nishimura, Scott. "Fort Worth Zoning Commission Denies Walmart's Hemphill/Berry Rezoning." *Fort Worth Star-Telegram*, February 8, 2012. http://www.star-telegram.com/2012/02/08/3720448/fort-worth-zoning-commission-denies.html#storylink=cpy.

Tuggle, C. A., Carr, Forrest, and Huffman, Suzanne. 2014. *Broadcast News Handbook*. 5th ed. McGraw Hill Higher Education.

The Life of a Radio Reporter
'Seconds are precious, minutes are like hours'

~ Jim Ryan

It's 4:13 a.m. and I'm sipping on my second cup of coffee and sorting through the three dozen emails sent to my newsroom overnight. My first report is to air at 5 a.m. and I have no idea what it'll be about.

You can read this section, or to hear Jim Ryan reading it, scan this QR code or go to http://snd.sc/Oo4FX4.

For a radio reporter, seconds are precious and minutes are like hours. And so, with 47 minutes until my first deadline, it's way too early to worry that I won't find anything to write. Something always ... always ... materializes, whether it's breaking news or an interesting nugget buried in the emailed news releases.

At 4:16, the scanner crackles to life: "Battalion 8, Engine 34, Rescue 34, Boat 54: Car in the water ... LBJ Freeway at Dowdy Ferry. People trapped." I push down hard on the gas pedal and mentally begin to compose my 5 a.m. story: "Rescue workers in a boat and on the banks of the Trinity River are responding to a report that someone has driven into the water. WBAP's Jim Ryan is in southeast Dallas."

Jim Ryan covers news events ranging from the automobile accident mentioned here to national political events. Here Ryan is reporting from a political rally in Springfield, Mo., the day before the Super Tuesday primary.

I should probably define "newsroom," because the term still evokes images of chain-smoking men in white shirts huddled around a noisy teletype printer. My 21st-century newsroom has four doors and a V-6 engine and pulls slightly to the right at high speeds. The 2010 Toyota Camry with the WBAP logo on the sides is outfitted with a computer mount, a power inverter, a laptop and broadband card. My digital audio recorder, microphone and an HD still/video camera are within easy reach as I head east on I-20 toward Dowdy Ferry.

When I pull up behind the big red Dallas Fire-Rescue engine and open my door, the green digits of the dashboard clock advance to 4:39. I have 21 minutes to gather the facts, load audio into my laptop, write, edit, voice and produce the final story for the anchor to use at 5 a.m.

"We had a motorist call 911 and report seeing a sport utility vehicle eastbound on the freeway go over the bridge and into the water," says Dallas Fire Battalion Chief Don Murray over the roar of a fire engine. "Right now we've got rescue personnel in our boat and we're using utility lights on the truck to see if we can find it."

Satisfied that I have enough information to write my story, I'm walking back to the news car when I see a man on the riverbank watching the rescue workers doing their job. I smile at him as I approach: "Good morning," I offer as I glance down to make sure my recorder is running and to check my watch. It's 4:47 a.m.

"I'm with WBAP Radio," I tell the man. "Did you see what happened?"

"Yeah, I was headed home from work when this black Explorer went flying past me," the man says. "He started swerving toward the guardrail and I thought: 'He's gonna crash!' Sure enough, he slammed into railing and the whole truck flipped over the rail and fell over the side of the bridge."

"What were you thinking at the time?" I ask my witness.

"I just couldn't believe it! A couple of seconds earlier and he would have side-swiped my car and taken me into the water, too!"

I ask the man his name, thank him, hustle to the car, slide into the driver's seat, plug my audio recorder into the laptop and load both interviews—the battalion chief and the witness. Ten minutes to deadline and it's Crunch Time.

If one word describes the life of the radio reporter, it's "quick." Finding content, responding to changing stories, interviewing and writing must all be done against the backdrop of a looming deadline. At WBAP, I'm expected to have a fresh story set to go every half hour. That amounts to 13 stories on five or six different topics during my shift. And each of my pieces should be under 25 seconds. Actualities (the segments taken from within an interview) must be brief and descriptive.

For this story, I decide to use a very short cut from each interviewee.

Chief Don Murray: "Right now we've got rescue personnel in our boat and we're using utility lights on the truck to see if we can find it." (:05)

Witness Jerry Macon: "He started swerving toward the guardrail and I thought: 'He's gonna crash!'" (:04)

I already formulated a lead (the part the anchor will read to introduce my recorded piece) as I was driving to the story, and so now it's just a matter of filling in the blanks, incorporating the nine seconds worth of actualities.

A useful tool in telling almost any story is to tell the story of someone who was affected by the event. That's what I want to do with Jerry Macon, who should have been home an hour ago, but instead is standing on a dark riverbank alongside a freeway. Here's how the anchor lead and the copy will look:

(ANCHOR) RESCUE WORKERS IN A BOAT AND ON THE BANKS OF THE TRINITY RIVER ARE RESPONDING TO A REPORT THAT SOMEONE HAS DRIVEN INTO THE WATER. WBAP'S JIM RYAN IS IN SOUTHEAST DALLAS:

(RYAN) WHAT BEGAN AS AN UNEVENTFUL DRIVE HOME FROM WORK HAS ENDED AS ANYTHING BUT FOR JERRY MACON, WHO WATCHED A FORD EXPLORER BLAZE INTO HIS REAR-VIEW MIRROR: (MACON) "HE STARTED SWERVING TOWARD THE GUARDRAIL AND I THOUGHT: 'HE'S GONNA CRASH!'" (RYAN) THE TRUCK WENT OVER THE RAIL AND MACON CALLED 911: (MURRAY) "RIGHT NOW WE'VE GOT RESCUE PERSONNEL IN OUR BOAT AND WE'RE USING UTILITY LIGHTS ON THE TRUCK TO SEE IF WE CAN FIND IT." (RYAN) BUT SO FAR, SAYS BATTALION CHIEF DON MURRAY, WITHOUT SUCCESS. IN SOUTHEAST DALLAS, JIM RYAN, WBAP 24/7 NEWS.

The produced story comes in at precisely 25 seconds. Using remote-connectivity software, I upload the mp3 and the lead from my laptop into the newsroom computer back at WBAP, where it's available for the anchor to use in her 5 a.m. newscast. The dashboard clock shows 4:55 a.m.

About the author
Jim Ryan is a reporter for WBAP radio in Dallas and ABC News Radio. He is a two-time winner of the Radio Television News Directors Association's Edward R. Murrow Award.

Skills Development: Practice in Media Writing

Exercise 14.1

Record a radio news program, the type you typically find at the top of the hour on radio stations that carry news. Then play it back and time everything—anchor introductions to stories, the stories themselves and commercials. How long is the newscast? How much of that is commercials? How much time is devoted to news? How many stories are there?

Exercise 14.2

Get a copy of your college newspaper and a local professional newspaper. Choose five stories from each and rewrite them as 25-second radio news stories. Time yourself to make sure your stories time out correctly.

Exercise 14.3

Using your campus newspaper or news site, put together a three-minute newscast that could be broadcast on your campus radio station. Use only campus stories in the newscast. If you are an advertising major, you might want to add a couple of minutes of ads, too.

Exercise 14.4

Go back to the Chapter 5 exercises you wrote for a newspaper or website. Rewrite them for radio. Unless your instructor tells you differently, write each as a 25-second reader.

Chapter Fifteen

Writing and Fairness: Avoiding Bias When Writing about Minority Groups

Do stylebooks reflect current usage, or do they guide and influence it?

Obviously, both. The first "Associated Press Style Book" (it was two words in those days) in 1953 included instructions for capitalizing Oriental when referring to Asians and told journalists that military enlisted personnel were "enlisted men." Of 20 entries on religion, 16 dealt with Christianity and Islam; Buddhism and Hinduism were left out altogether.

The stylebook has become more enlightened as have mass communication practitioners, and now many groups publish their own stylebooks to help journalists, PR practitioners and others deal more sensitively and accurately with the language they use to describe groups ranging from gays to people in wheelchairs to faith groups.

Sometimes the language used by mass communicators in news stories, ads or PR copy reflects unconscious biases or stereotypes. News stories about women politicians frequently focus on the domestic aspects of the life of a politically active woman or her appearance. Could you imagine a 5-foot 5-inch male senator being called a slim, petite blond?

But in other situations, the language and even the rules of grammar can lead us into unconsciously biased written constructions.

Words change over time. *Gay* obviously doesn't mean the same thing today that it did 50 years ago. *Mistress* was once a title of honor and now refers to a man's illicit lover. We now know that we should avoid using words that stigmatize people who have a disability as being "stricken with," "suffering from" or "a victim of" some disease such as muscular dystrophy. And it's never OK to describe women by physical appearance in ways that we would never describe men.

Pronouns

Sometimes media writers think they must either be grammatically correct and sexist in their writing or grammatically incorrect but gender neutral. That's because until near the end of the 20th century, masculine pronouns were used to refer to humanity in general. So you ended up with sentences like these, which are correct in their grammar but incorrect in assigning masculine gender to groups that include women:

- A voter should keep his registration card and take it when he goes to vote.
- A reporter should not let his biases affect his writing.
- Everyone should lock his car to prevent auto theft.

The guideline on gender-neutral writing is simple: Don't use "his" to cover men and women. Years ago, many professions were not open to women—policemen and firemen were literally men, as were congressmen and city councilmen and mailmen and chairmen and businessmen. Thomas Jefferson can be forgiven for saying that "all men are created equal" and that "governments are instituted among men, deriving their just powers from the consent of the governed" in the Declaration of Independence. After all, women of that day could not vote. Jefferson's language reflected his world and his worldview. But today, the writing of mass communications professionals must reflect *our* world.

Writers have two choices when confronted with a sentence that is grammatically correct, but insensitive, like this one: "The winning contestant must claim his prize in person." Often, we end up with a sentence that trades grammatical incorrectness for sexism: "The winning contestant must claim their prize in person." The two solutions here are either to change the pronoun to include both genders or to change the noun to a plural: "The winning contestant must claim his or her prize in person," or "Winning contestants must claim their prize in person."

Writing that stereotypes women and minorities is typically not motivated by insensitivity or prejudice. Instead, it's the result of not recognizing unconscious if innocently motivated stereotypes. Here are some examples that illustrate some of these issues.

Writing about Women

In most stories, marital status is not relevant. Whether a person—man or woman—is single or married or divorced is most often not important to the piece. Writers are more likely to give a woman's marital status than a man's, even though neither relates directly to the story.

- Refer to a woman as Martha Jones, not Mrs. John Jones. On second reference, use only her last name, just as you would a man—unless your stylebook mandates the use of courtesy titles for both men and women.
- Do not describe a woman by physical characteristics such as hair or eye color or height, unless such descriptions are germane to the story.
- Avoid gender-specific designations for fields that include both men and women. For example: Make it *business professional* rather than *businessman*, *police officer* rather than *policeman*, *firefighter* rather than *fireman*, *mail carrier* rather than *mailman*, *flight attendant* rather than *stewardess*, *humans* or *humanity* rather than *mankind*, *spokesperson* rather than *spokesman* and *work-hours* rather than *man-hours*.
- Don't use gender when it's unnecessary. Make it *nurse* rather than *male nurse* and *jockey* rather than *female jockey*.

Writing about People with Disabilities

Don't refer to a disability unless it is relevant to the story. People are not defined by their disabilities. Make it "the coach, who has a disability" instead of "the disabled coach."

- Don't say someone is *afflicted with*, *stricken with* or *the victim of* some disability. Many of these people do not consider themselves afflicted or stricken or victimized. Those are stereotypes. Instead, say that "Jones has cerebral palsy."
- Don't refer to a person as handicapped, though you can use the word to describe places or regulations, like "handicapped parking."
- Don't use the term *able-bodied* to contrast people who do not have disabilities. It assumes that persons who have a disability lack "able bodies." Tell that to a wheelchair basketball athlete. Instead, call them *non-disabled* or say that they *do not have a disability*.
- Don't identify people with the name of their disease. If someone has cerebral palsy, say that *she has cerebral palsy*. Don't call her a *victim of cerebral palsy* or say she is *cerebral palsied* or worse yet, *spastic*.
- Don't say that someone is *confined to a wheelchair* or *wheelchair-bound*. Just say they *use a wheelchair*.
- There's no such thing as Down's syndrome. It's Down syndrome.

- Make it *mentally disabled*, not *mentally retarded*.
- Don't use terms like *dumb*, *mute* or *deaf-mute* to refer to people. Instead, say that someone is *deaf* or *hard of hearing*. You can see how much semantic baggage words like *mute* or *dumb* carry.
- Style guidelines to help writers avoid stereotyping people with handicaps can be found on the website of the National Center for Disability and Journalism at http://ncdj.org/styleguide.

Writing about the LGBT Community

If you are writing about people with Acquired Immune Deficiency Syndrome, don't use terms like "AIDS sufferer" or "AIDS victim." Call them "people with AIDS" or "AIDS patients" if you're writing about a medical situation. Avoid the phrase "full-blown AIDS."

- Sometimes you just have to ask when you're working on stories involving the LGBT community. Terms like *fag, faggot, queer* and *dyke* are pejorative, but have now been reclaimed by portions of the gay community. It is typically best to avoid these terms.
- Always ask people what terms they prefer to be applied to them. Typically, for instance, *gay* is a term applied to homosexual men and *lesbian* refers to women who are attracted to other women. But some lesbians prefer to be called gay, and typically the term *gay* can refer to all homosexuals.
- In obituaries or stories about the death of gay people, use the term *partner* and refer to them in the same way you would to the spouse of a heterosexual person.
- Use the term *sexual orientation* instead of *sexual preference*.
- Style guidelines to help writers avoid stereotyping people in the LGBT community can be found in the stylebook of the National Lesbian & Gay Journalists Association, http://www.nlgja.org/resources/2010stylebook.pdf.

Writing about Ethnic Minorities

- Use *Latino* or *Latina* when a person prefers that term. Sometimes *Hispanic* might be the preferred ethnic term. How do you know? Ask.
- *Chicano* is more localized to the Southwest. Use this only if the story's subject asks you to.
- Hispanics may be of any race, so do not write "Hispanics and whites." Instead, say "Hispanics and non-Hispanics."
- Never use racially derogatory terms unless they are a part of a quotation and they are essential to the story.
- Refer to someone's ethnicity only if it is relevant to the story. If you are unsure, ask subjects what ethic group they prefer to be classified as.
- Do not use the term *Oriental* in referring to people or regions. Use *Asian* or *Asian-American* instead. Some may prefer a term reflecting their country of origin, as in *Japanese-American*. The term *Asiatic* is considered offensive when it is applied to people.
- The terms *black* and *African-American* are both acceptable. When referring to groups, use *black people* and not just *blacks*—though that term is acceptable in headlines. The term *colored* is considered derogatory in the United States, but not in some other countries. The Associated Press Stylebook suggests the phrase *mixed racial ancestry* as a substitute.

- Do not identify by race in crime stories unless you are describing people being sought by police, and even then you should give physical characteristics other than skin color.
- When writing about visa violations, avoid the terms *illegal immigrant*, *illegal alien*, or *illegals*. Use *illegal* only to refer to an action, not an individual. So you can talk about *illegal immigration*, but not an *illegal immigrant*.

Writing about Religion

- Not all conservative Christians are fundamentalists. It has come to have a pejorative meaning and should be applied only when the group applies the term to itself.
- The term *Bible-believing Christian* is appropriate only when it is clear that people are using it to describe themselves.
- Be careful of religious labels, such as *born-again Christian*. Use it when people apply it to themselves, as in "Smith, who calls himself a born-again Christian …"
- For specific help in writing about religion, see the stylebook of the Religion Newswriters Association, http://religionstylebook.com/.

Looking at these issues may seem to be an accommodation of political correctness in language and writing. Not so. Paying attention to the words we use to describe people and events is an acknowledgment of the power of language.

General semanticists point out that "the word is not the thing." In other words, the symbol (word) is not the object or the event that is symbolized. On the other hand, we know that people frequently react to the word instead of the reality we are using that word to denote. Thus, politicians speak of "revenue enhancement" when they mean "taxes" or "collateral damage" when they mean "civilian casualties" or "downsizing" when they mean "layoffs" and "firings." That's because politicians realize that people frequently react to the word rather than the objective reality for which it stands. Writers must therefore choose words carefully so that readers can react authentically to the events about which we write—not to the language we use to tell our stories.

Paula LaRocque

A VISIT WITH YOUR WRITING COACH
Metaphors and Other Mangled Logic

Avoiding mangled metaphors

http://snd.sc/LoVlNM

AP Stylebook Updates Entry on Racial IDs in News Stories

By Mallary Jean Tenore

The AP Stylebook has updated its entry on when journalists should publish information about a person's race.

The update says that race is pertinent in stories about crime suspects who have been "sought by the police or missing person cases," so long as "police or other credible, detailed descriptions" are used. When the suspect is found or apprehended, the update says, the racial reference should be removed.

Some news organizations use racial identifiers in crime stories, as the AP suggests, despite criticism. There are many times, however, when a source's race is irrelevant and shouldn't be included.

One of the challenges, said AP Deputy Standards Editor David Minthorn, is determining whether descriptions of suspects are accurate.

"We have to use our news judgment on racial references, but if we have reason to believe that it's from a credible, reasonable source and appropriate for the story, we would include it," Minthorn said by phone.

But even when you do have an accurate description of a person's race, is that enough to make it relevant?

My former colleague Keith Woods wrote that racial identifiers are rarely relevant or revealing and can perpetuate stereotypes. While they carry information about heritage and geography, they don't describe much about a person's physical appearance.

"What, for example, does a Hispanic man look like? Is his skin dark brown? Reddish brown? Pale? Is his hair straight? Curly? Course? Fine? Does he have a flat, curved nose or is it narrow and straight?" Woods wrote. "Telling the public that he's 5-foot-8, 180 pounds, with a blue shirt and blue jeans says something about the person's appearance. But what do you add to that picture when you say Latino?"

He pointed out that journalists probably wouldn't say, "The suspect appeared to be Italian," or "Police are looking for a middle-aged man described as 'Jewish-looking.'"

"There are good reasons those descriptions never see the light of day. They generalize. They stereotype," Woods wrote. "And they require that everyone who hears the description has the same idea of what those folks look like. All Irish-Americans don't look alike. Why, then, accept a description that says a suspect was African-American?"

This isn't to say race is always irrelevant. In racially motivated crimes, such as the murder of James Byrd, race is an important element of the story. The AP Stylebook update explains other instances when it's relevant:

"In biographical and announcement stories that involve significant, groundbreaking or historic events, such as being elected U.S. president, named to the U.S. Supreme Court or other notable occurrences.

"When reporting a demonstration or disturbance involving race or such issues as civil rights or slavery."

Minthorn, who is one of the Stylebook editors, said the update was added for clarity's sake.

"What we're trying to do is formalize practices that we know to be reasonable," Minthorn said by phone. "I don't think we have a definition here that covers all instances, but we're trying to be fair and reasonable in our guidance." (Tenore 2012)

From Poynter.org by Mallary Jean Tenore. Copyright © 2012 The Poynter Institute. Reprinted by permission.

References

Tenore, Mallary Jean. "AP Stylebook Updates Entry on Racial IDs in News Stories." *Poynter*, March 14, 2012. http://www.poynter.org/how-tos/newsgathering-storytelling/diversity-at-work/166506/ap-stylebook-updates-entry-on-racial-ids-in-news-stories/.

Skills Development: Practice in Media Writing

Exercise 15.1

Revise the following sentences so that the language avoids gender bias and is grammatically correct.

1. Each public relations executive should schedule performance reviews so that he is done discussing them with members of his team by Dec. 15.

2. Checking the validity of all software licenses will take a significant number of man hours.

3. Everyone on the task force must report his progress monthly.

4. The advertising director will be responsible for hiring, training, and overseeing a staff of eight people under his charge.

5. The security office desk is manned 24 hours a day.

6. After determining his production goals for the quarter, each supervisor should report these targets to his division vice president.

7. Professors and their wives are invited to the graduation reception.

8. Each vice president should make sure that his secretary greets callers courteously.

9. Each writer is responsible for correcting all his grammar and style errors.

10. All clergymen are available for special hospital parking permits.

Exercise 15.2

Revise the following sentences so that the language avoids gender bias and is grammatically correct.

1. Do you believe that all men are created equal?

2. Entrepreneurship lets every man be his own boss.

3. You should hire the best man for the job.

4. The room is noisy, but boys will be boys.

5. In an emergency, it's every man for himself.

6. Everybody and his brother showed up for the store's giveaway promotion.

7. The government has no right to search without a warrant because a man's home is his castle.

8. He believes that John Q. Public will eventually support higher taxes.

9. Every schoolboy knows how solar eclipses work.

10. They came to a gentleman's agreement on how the transition would work.

Exercise 15.3

The following sentences contain biased language that includes stereotyping by race, religion, gender, handicaps and age. Edit them to avoid the stereotyping.

1. Any applicant for the position of fireman must submit a medical report signed by his physician.

2. Let's try harder to meet our older customers' demands for personalized service.

3. Despite her cerebral palsy, Cheryl Kama was promoted to office manager.

4. Each reporter should save his notes, even after his story is published.

5. During the 1800s, men by the thousands headed west.

6. The average American is proud of his heritage.

7. Frank Smith and his wife were killed when the tornado struck their home.

Exercise 15.4

The following sentences contain biased language that includes stereotyping by race, religion, gender, handicaps and age. Edit them to avoid the stereotyping.

1. Will housewives support the Republican candidate?

2. Jim Patterson and Mrs. Thomas Clark were named to the committee.

3. Will the pastor appoint laymen to the committee?

4. The director will form a new scholarship committee and name a chairman.

5. Every delegate hopes he will be named to the platform committee.

6. He does not like to talk with insurance salesmen.

7. He said that ladies could leave their purses in the room while the group is on break.

8. Would the Founding Fathers have agreed with universal health care?

9. After the layoffs, the office has a manpower shortage.

10. The common man is less concerned with foreign policy than with economic issues.

Exercise 15.5

Give better alternatives for each of these discriminatory terms. There is more than one acceptable alternative for many of the terms.

1. businessman _____
2. career girl, career woman _____
3. cleaning lady _____
4. delivery boy _____
5. foreman _____
6. girl Friday _____
7. insurance man _____
8. landlady, landlord _____
9. mailman _____
10. newsman _____
11. policeman _____
12. repairman _____
13. saleslady, salesman _____
14. serviceman _____
15. steward, stewardess _____
16. waitress _____
17. workman _____
18. corporate wife _____
19. freshman _____
20. front man _____
21. hostess _____
22. middleman _____
23. ombudsman _____
24. self-made man _____
25. spokesman _____

26. common man _____
27. fatherland _____
28. forefathers _____
29. fraternal _____
30. Frenchmen _____
31. mankind _____
32. mother tongue _____
33. thinking man _____
34. working man, working woman _____
35. ladylike _____
36. maiden name _____
37. man (verb) _____
38. manhood _____
39. statesman _____
40. workmanship _____

Chapter Sixteen

Public Relations Writing: A Different Approach to Media Writing

By Maggie Thomas

Imagine that you are at a party with some friends. As the group begins to gather, the conversation drifts from the usual, casual chatter to topics that are more important.

"What's your major?" someone asks you after being introduced.

"Public relations," you say.

"What's that?" she asks with a hint that she really is interested in your answer.

"That's simple," you think as you begin to reply. Simply much more than one thing is the next thought that shoots through your mind.

"What do you think it means?" you ask as you buy yourself some time to think about your answer.

Before she speaks, you think about students with majors that don't have to be explained—nursing, education, engineering, pre-med or pre-law. Friends don't have to ask those students what their majors involve because most of us have known a nurse, teacher, engineer, doctor or lawyer.

Before learning to write as a public relations practitioner, we first have to understand what public relations is.

But how many students have ever asked a public relations practitioner for help? Or, can you say you ever landed a summer job working in public relations? Do you know where the public relations agencies are in your town? Do you even recognize public relations when you see it?

As you gather your thoughts, the word writing crosses your mind, so you blurt it out.

"Writing?" the puzzled young woman asks. "What does writing have to do with public relations? She tells you she is more interested in event planning because she is a "people person."

Aha, you think, trying to stifle a chuckle as you remember one of your former professors. The curmudgeon told a prospective PR student who said she liked people that dogs like people, too. The writing professor was trying to tell the prospective student that there is much more to public relations than dealing with people, which can be challenging enough.

Thoughts are racing through your mind as you recall discussions from classes and online debates that included derogatory terms—*flack* and *spin doctors*—to describe PR professionals.

You try to sort through some negative opinions before you speak.

What Do PR Practitioners Do?

"If you're not in the public relations industry, it's likely your perception of PR professionals is that we plan parties, coerce journalists, and lie for a living," Gini Dietrich wrote in a blog April 10, 2012, about "PR's Perception Problem: Redefining Public Relations."

Dietrich wrote, "Like most industries, PR has been transformed by social media, but that doesn't mean people's perceptions of so-called 'spin doctors' have changed too" (Dietrich 2012).

You also debate whether to insert some reality into your conversation. You go ahead and mention the main points of a report you just found online including 20 Jobs That Are Worse Than You Thought (Editors 2012). Right in the middle of the list, compiled by human resources editors worldwide, at No. 5 is the public relations executive.

Lots of people think public relations practitioners have a cushy job going to fancy parties, spending time with movers and shakers in the community and schmoozing with the media. This perception is far from the reality of a day in the life of a public relations person. Although some public relations agencies focus on event planning, it is more likely that PR practitioners spend more time working to get a mention and a photo in a newspaper or magazine, writing speeches or editorials for clients, maintaining an effective social media presence and trying to keep everyone happy. The reward for juggling all these tasks while trying to satisfy all expectations? Their clients get the credit for their work if things go well, and the PR people get blamed if something fails.

After a few moments of stunned silence, the young woman continues the conversation by asking you what public relations practitioners write. First, you tell her about the wide variety of places PR majors can work.

Public relations majors, you tell her, hold a wide range of jobs with an even wider range of job titles: communications specialist, marketing coordinator, account executive, lobbyist, speechwriter, press agent—and the list goes on. You mention that PR majors also can get jobs in organizations varying from health care, public or private schools or universities, technology, sports, religion, fashion, theatre, business, art and other settings in the United States and internationally.*

Good Public Relations Doesn't Involve Shoulda, Woulda, Coulda

The best public relations practitioners can create stories that make target audiences want to take specific actions. That means good PR writing manages to persuade without being too pushy.

Successful public relations practitioners are effective communicators who work to persuade people to join an organization, attend an event, buy a product or answer the question, What's in it for me? That means PR involves explanations about the value or benefits being promoted, but does not try to boss you around.

Public relations messages are carefully crafted stories for target audiences that make people want to take specific actions. PR people are out of line if they try to tell you what you should do, think or feel. Avoid the temptation to insert your opinion into a news release, feature story or other PR materials.

Delete the opinion that weasels its way into statements such as "Old Town residents need to get ready to support the fund-raising bungee jump contest Thursday between professors and students. Don't miss the fun. This is a must-do for your spring entertainment."

If the benefits of your message are planned and written well, you are more likely to accomplish your goal by using quotes from others to express opinions in contrast to imposing your own views. To paraphrase a soft voice that spoke to an Iowa corn farmer in the movie "Field of Dreams"—if you build the benefits, they will come.

---

* From education-portal.com. Reprinted by permission.

News Releases Deserve Fresh Leads, Especially for Annual Events

Standing heads are fine for stories that appear regularly in print or online. These standard headlines, which remain unchanged each time they appear, help readers find opinion columns or blog posts. Standing heads are OK. Standing leads are not.

A standing lead is one that could be used last year, this year or next year with only minor changes. Avoid this: "The Eighth Annual Orientation Extravaganza, sponsored by the Student Government Association, will be held at 6:30 p.m. Wednesday in Abney Hall on campus." Boring. Find out what will be different about the event this year. Focus on what makes this orientation worth attending. Look for the news instead of focusing on the "olds." Lead with an interesting element: "The Dangerous Duo, a band featuring twins playing harmonica and ukulele hits, is scheduled to open the Eighth Annual Orientation Extravaganza at 6:30 p.m. Wednesday in Abney Hall on campus."

Note that an event cannot be held, as in the palms of your hands, so substitute "is scheduled." That way if bad weather forces cancellation of the extravaganza, your lead is still correct.

Some of the skills involved in public relations could be compared to those of a detective or a conflict resolution mediator. Imagine answering a barrage of questions from clients, public figures and journalists. High on the list of your daily tasks most likely would be writing news releases and feature stories. Add to that scheduling press conferences, receptions, exhibits and tours. Then, as you continue to develop helpful contacts, you find yourself writing and editing company newsletters or planning a PR campaign. Getting experience writing for a university newspaper can boost your chances of success as you begin your PR career.

Juggling a variety of jobs at one time in a calm, organized way is essential in public relations. So many people depend on your ability to be creative, persistent and persuasive in addition to being able to communicate your plans clearly to diverse audiences.

You also need to have enough business savvy to understand that your work has to support the agency's goal of making a profit. Think about it. Is PR for you?

Now that you have convinced the young woman that good writing is essential to a successful PR person and you are convinced that she is still curious, you know another question is coming.

Media Writing vs. PR Writing

What is the difference between media writing and public relations writing? How can someone tell the difference between them? Why do companies hire public relations writers?

Both media and public relations writing share many of the same qualities. Writing for the media and public relations involves finding an angle about your topic—regardless of the format—that is relevant, interesting and timely to your target audiences. It has to pass the "so what?" test to capture readers' attention.

Capturing attention requires writing clearly and concisely. Focusing on what's important. Relating the message to your audience. Telling people why this matters to them. How will a proposed change alter their lives?

Media writing seeks to present an objective view about a topic; public relations writing represents the views about the company, product, event or service. Media writers generally write stories that are produced through print, broadcast or online news services directly to the public. Public relations writers are often hired

The "So What?" Test

Planning and thinking are important parts of the writing process that is often overlooked. Before you put your fingers on a keyboard, consider two questions that relate to anything you write:

- What is this story about?
- Who am I writing this for?

An easy way to focus on the main point of a story, news release, media pitch or whatever you may be writing is to think about how you would tell a friend what you are writing about. This answers the question—What is this story about?—in a simple, easy-to-understand way. That's a good way to create a lead.

Think about who you are writing for. Go beyond categories such as golfers, artists, college seniors, runners or soccer players. Think about a particular person who fits that category. If you are writing about a future lawyer who could possibly become a political candidate, put a visual image of a person in your mind to try to set the stage as you write the story.

Now, ask yourself these final questions:

- Why would someone be interested in this story?
- What difference does the information in your story make in the lives of potential readers?
- How does this story relate to what it is important to the people who read it?
- Why would a news medium want to use this story?

Put yourself in the place of your readers by asking yourself the tough question -- So what? -- to try to determine what makes your story interesting.

---

to write primarily for an internal audience through in-house publications or work for an agency hired by external organizations to handle their PR.

Media writing passes more directly from the writer to news consumers. Public relations involves writing messages that are acceptable to a client as well as a news source that will disseminate the information. Many public relations stories are written as feature stories, news releases or other format and then are edited or rewritten by media writers.

News editors often complain that public relations writers send them press releases that do not contain interesting or timely news. Often, though, a release that produces genuine news interest is not distinguished from other releases, and the terms news release and press release are used interchangeably.

Here are examples of how the same information might be written in different styles. Remember that public relations writers may have to change the way they present information by revising it to please clients.
A sample public relations lead:

CEO Ted Tango, the leading entrepreneur for Go Get 'Em Autos, the newest car company in Utopiaville, announced Wednesday the development of a passenger automobile that gets 43 miles a gallon in freeway driving, which will change the driving habits of commuters across the United States.

The car is expected to be on display at Tango's dealership at 108 S. Porter St. in Utopiaville by September after a nationwide naming contest is completed.

A sample media writing lead:

A four-door car designed to get more than 40 miles a gallon in stop-and-go traffic may be on display at a Utopiaville car dealership by September, owner Ted Tango of Go Get 'Em Autos said Wednesday.

Other information about the car and its name would follow probably with quotes from Tango, other business owners and drivers in Utopiaville.

A Sample of Online Resources for PR Practitioners

- PRweb.com
- publicityinsider.com
- prnewswire.com
- ereleases.com
- prsa.org
- helpareporter.com
- vocus.com
- emergingtechpr.com/prlingo.html
- bls.gov (search "public relations")
- writing-world.com/promotion/hanes.shtml
- prurgent.com/press_release_donts.htm
- blog.journalistics.com/2010/use-news-releases-for-more-than-PR/
- anthillonline.com/tag/public-relations/

PR Writers and Quotes

One of the main differences between quotes that media writers and public relations writers might include in their writing is the source of those quotes and the way they are gathered. Media writers use direct quotes, exactly what a person said, and indirect quotes, paraphrased language to express the intention of what a person said, to explain a topic.

Public relations writers are expected to develop relationships with their clients, so they can represent the clients' thoughts in writing. For that reason, public relations writers are allowed to create quotes for their clients. This often helps busy clients who trust public relations practitioners to portray them with well-crafted quotes to express their opinions.

Public relations writers need to establish this practice and sometimes get client approval for created quotes before they are released. PR people are expected to express ideas clearly and concisely in addition to taking into consideration how the public will perceive the quotations. This is a major responsibility for a public relations writer, who also may write speeches or op-ed columns with the client getting all the credit.

Questions to Consider before You Write a Press Release

- Who is your preferred audience?
- What do you want readers to take away from your release?
- What is the support or justification for the information in your release?
- What is the tone of your release?
- Are you aware of possible pitfalls or areas to avoid?
- What do you want to accomplish with your release: increase business, disseminate information, or both?

Copyright © eReleases ® (www.ereleases.com) All Rights Reserved. Reprinted by permission.

Press Release Formats

Formats for news releases vary according to the company represented. Generally a news release follows a company's letterhead at the top of a page. A sample press release format is presented here and can be used by groups to present the best image for an organization along with the new developments. New releases may be printed on letterhead or a specially designed letterhead to reinforce the brand.

Triple Tootsie's Chocolate Treats (company logo)

Contact: Jenn Lee
454-532-4627 (I LIKE CHOCS)
Jennifer@likechocs.org
Date of news release

FOR IMMEDIATE RELEASE

Triple Tootsie's Rolls Out App to Find Local Food Trucks

FORT WORTH, Texas (February 14, 2012)—Chocolate lovers soon can find food trucks in their cities that sell Triple Tootsie's desserts by using a free app scheduled for release on Valentine's Day.

"Triple Tootsie's wants to make it easier for our fans to find their favorite treats conveniently in their neighborhoods aboard food trucks," owner Jenn Lee said. The entrepreneurial owner, who often discusses award-winning chocolate desserts in her blog, says food truck vendors welcome the connection the app will provide.

Using an app, or applications software for mobile devices, is considered one of the most innovative ways to streamline the process of searching for Triple Tootsie products, said W.E. Deliver, president of Food Trucks of America.

Pilot tests of the new app have been tested in several Texas markets including Austin, Waco, Fort Worth, College Station and Lampasas, Deliver said.

"We believe this app appeals directly to our target market and provides benefits for our product and service by getting the chocolate treats to customers sooner and at a time when they want the desserts," Deliver said.

Information about pre-ordering a free app is available at Triple Tootsie's website, likechocs.com, or by calling I LIKE CHOCS (454-532-4627).

###

About Triple Tootsie's: After beginning your news release with information about why the news is important to your target audience, give some background information in general terms avoiding company jargon. Use quotes to add interest to your news release. This is a good way to increase visibility and name recognition for the company's executives. Finally, describe the company history briefly along with a description of products and services you sell. This is called boilerplate information.

Type *end* or ### at the bottom if this is the last page, or type — *more* — if there will be other pages. Identify each additional page with a number and a short phrase that relates to the content, such as Triple Tootsie's or Sweet New App, so there is no question about the order of pages for a release.

The order of these items in a press release may be moved and rearranged to fit the current format used by an organization, preferences of the public relations practitioner or company executives.

> **FOR IMMEDIATE RELEASE:**
>
> ## Competition Is Healthy Says Lemonade Stand Queen
>
> Hamilton, New Zealand—Nov. 12, 2004—Increased competition in the local lemonade stand market should be welcomed, says the operator of popular lemonade stand, "Shelly's Pure Lemonade."
>
> Twelve-year-old Shelly Smith has been selling her homemade brand of lemonade from the footpath in front of her parents' North Street home for 18 months and has seen the highs and lows of the trade.
>
> "Stands come and go," Smith said, "but when there are more stands around, the vendors are more serious. They try harder and make a better product. That gives our customers confidence, and sales go up."
>
> In recent months the number of lemonade stands on North Street has risen from three to five. Experts believe this trend will continue, with the possibility of two or even three new stands before the end of summer.
>
> Smith feels that a stable supply of lemonade will also benefit the street's economy.
>
> "People know that if they are thirsty, North Street is the place to come. With plenty of lemonade stands on this street, it doesn't matter if some of the vendors take a day off. The customer is never disappointed so they always come back."
>
> Shelly Smith is a sole trader of lemonade and occasional cookies. Her stand at 223 North Street is usually open weekdays after school and weekends, except when she is playing with her friends or watching a movie. (This last paragraph is similar to boilerplate information, which is standard information about what a company is, when it started, what it does and so on that provides context for understanding a news release.)
>
> Contact: Shelly Smith
> my@email.co.nz
> 233 North Street
> Hamilton, New Zealand
> Phone: +64-877-9233
>
> ###
>
> Copyright © www.mediacollege.com. Reprinted by permission.

News releases deal with a variety of topics. Above is an example of the elements of a news release, implemented in a different order, about an entrepreneurial venture in New Zealand in 2004. The example (Mediacollege.com n.d.) has been edited to conform to AP style.

Formats for press releases are similar, but the method of delivering releases has changed as the technology evolves. News releases have been delivered by snail mail and fax machines, but now many are posted online for news editors and reporters to find easily or sent by email.

Social media have caused dramatic changes on the media landscape. Differing opinions have been expressed about the importance of and need for social media news releases. As the results of research studies are released, it is likely that the debate will continue.

Public relations professional Peter Shankman understands that media writers often need information from PR writers and PR people need help delivering their clients' messages to target audiences through the media. Shankman founded HARO, Help A Reporter Out, in 2007 to help reporters find expert commentary without having to spend time searching blindly for information by calling various PR sources. He sold HARO in 2010, but continues to generate content for the company.

Press Releases about Coming Events

One of the most common press releases is one announcing an upcoming event—a speech, a seminar, a political rally, a concert or a fundraiser. When you write these stories, remember that you are writing a news story about an event, not an ad. If you want to write a glowing invitation to an event, buy an ad. If you're writing news, just give the facts.

Don't ever invite the public to attend. Instead of saying "The public is invited," write "The event is open to the public." Instead of "Donors are urged to leave canned food for the homeless," make it "Donors may drop off canned food between 8 a.m. and 5 p.m. at the church."

Shankman thinks the status of public relations today (Leggio 2012) involves anticipation by PR practitioners regarding what a journalist might want and need to help the journalist finish a story. Shankman often tells PR people they need to make journalists happy first because if they do that, the client will be happy by default.

As mentioned earlier in this book, using quotes adds zest to your writing whether it is a story, news release, proposal, letter, feature story, brochure, newsletter, column or op-ed piece. Inserting quotes is a legitimate way to include opinions in your writing, but media writers and PR writers do this in different ways.

Representing a Point of View

Media writing seeks to present information that is true, fair and balanced. That does not mean that public relations writing is false and biased. But public relations writing intends to represent a certain viewpoint. PR focuses on advocating or promoting goodwill for a client. This means that a story from a public relations practitioner may omit information that is uncomplimentary to the client or might cause legal action against the client.

Good public relations should not involve lies. Not telling the whole story is far different from lying. Sometimes PR practitioners cannot release information immediately because they must follow the wishes of company officials or consider possible legal liability on the advice of lawyers representing the same client.

The consequences of giving false information to news sources are not quickly forgotten. Once the news media or the public realizes a PR person has misled them, you have damaged your client's image and your own reputation. It is not worth it to try to gain immediate favor for a client by misleading the news media or others.

In a crisis, if you don't know what happened yet, don't guess and say something you might regret later. Saying nothing, with an explanation about why you cannot talk then, will not come back to haunt you as can partial, hastily gathered information or a lie.

Tell the media you are gathering information and say when you will have information. Then, be sure to give that update, even if you have to say it still will be later when you have complete information. Keep the media informed as you promised.

If you know what happened, but your client does not want to release that information, tell the media you cannot explain the situation now. Tell the truth, but keep in mind that your client is your major responsibility when you are working as a public relations practitioner.

A time may come when the company executives or lawyers allow you to give more information, but sometimes your efforts may be restricted. That is what you agree to do when you begin to represent a client. It's not always easy, but it's your role.

What to Remember about News Releases

- Everything that's true about media writing is true about PR writing. Don't think that because you are writing a press release you can insert an opinion or deviate from AP style.
- If you want to sell something, buy an ad.
- Remember news deadlines. Don't send out a story on an upcoming event, for instance, two days before it is to occur.
- No excuses for inaccuracy. Double-check all names and titles and dates and times and locations.
- Don't leave out key information; media writers won't call about it; they'll just junk the release.
- Don't try one size fits all; localize and tailor to specific media.
- Write short.
- Figure out whom to send it to at each media outlet.
- Don't use company or organizational jargon; that's insider language.
- The gatekeeper you must pass is the editor. The people in your organization typically won't understand this. They will want you to send out longer releases or slip advertising copy into the story or include opinion. Explain how news operations work. Your clients won't know; they haven't taken a media writing course.

The Bottom Line

The Public Relations Society of America states that public relations has been defined in many ways since the formal practice, dating back to the early 20th century, began and now has evolved alongside public relations' changing roles and technological advances. The earliest definitions emphasized press agentry and publicity, while more modern definitions incorporate the concepts of engagement and relationship building. PRSA led an international effort in 2011-2012 to replace the definition of public relations adopted in 1982 with this updated version:

> *Public relations is a strategic communication process that builds mutually beneficial relationships between organizations and their publics.*

This means you will find public relations practitioners working within organizations, which are often called an internal or in-house PR staff, and external public relations professionals at PR firms who are hired to produce a variety of messages or materials to stimulate interest in an organization.

Public relations helps people make connections that may deal with promoting better understanding between groups or solving an existing problem or one that occurs suddenly. PR students may begin their professional careers practicing public relations in a variety of work settings.

Both public relations and advertising are used to promote an organization because they complement each other, but public relations and advertising are different ways of communicating information.

Simply put, advertising is paid for by the sponsor, which means the client controls the message. Public relations involves asking someone else, generally the media, to present your message for you. Advertising has the advantage of message control. It is presented exactly the way it is written or created, and the client controls where or when it will be delivered, and how many times it is presented. Advertising comes with no extended warranty. It is delivered as is.

Some parents even find it difficult to describe what work their children will do after studying public relations. When Joan Lunden appeared on "Good Morning America" recently, she was asked at the end of an interview what her children are doing now. She answered the question in detail until she mentioned one of her daughters, who she said is working in public relations. Now, perhaps, we understand why she gave a short answer.

References

Dietrich, Gini. "PR's Perception Problem." *Sparksheet*. April 10, 2012. http://sparksheet.com/prs-perception-problem-redefining-public-relations/.

Editors. "20 Jobs That Are Much Better (or Worse) Than You Thought." *HR World*. April 11, 2012. http://www.hrworld.com/features/20-jobs-better-worse-than-you-think-012808/.

Leggio, Jennifer. "How NOT to Do Public Relations: An Interview with Peter Shankman." *Forbes*. February 15, 2012. http://www.forbes.com/sites/jenniferleggio/2012/02/15/how-not-to-do-public-relations-an-interview-with-peter-shankman/.

Mediacollege.com. n.d. "Format." *MediaCollege.com*. http://www.mediacollege.com/journalism/press-release/format.html.

Exercise 16.1

What's the difference between media writing and PR writing? Good examples of both types of writing should be similar in several ways. They attract readers with interesting story lines, demonstrate proper AP style and present information in an easy-to-understand style.

The main difference is that media writing is objective and public relations writing is designed to promote goodwill for the client, organization, product, service or event. Media writing presents information in an objective style without opinion or value judgments from a reporter. PR writing advocates a certain viewpoint while observing ethical practices. PR writing also may try to persuade readers to adopt a certain stance about a particular topic.

In political campaigns, for example, public relations writers and advertising copywriters often work together closely to try to deliver similar messages in different ways.

Look online to find a press release about a particular topic that is interesting to you. You may have to look at several before you find one that has a captivating lead. You can frequently find these news releases by going to a company or organization's website and looking for a tab called News, or some other heading that includes the words *news, press* or *media*. You can often find these by highlighting a few grafs of the press release and pasting them into a search engine—that will show you how other media have used the news release.

Then, look for a news or feature story about the same topic that probably was written as a result of the press release. There will be similarities between the two. The press release generally has an earlier release date, but the Internet provides a source for a press release and a news or feature story to have the same date. Also some of the language from the press release will be picked up in the news or feature story. Describe that in your evaluation.

Print copies of both the press release and the news story or feature. Compare and contrast the approaches used in both pieces. List the similarities and differences. What is contained in the press release that grabs the attention of a reporter or editor, who wants to pass along that news or information in a news or feature story?

Look at the direct quotations in the press release and in the news story. Do quotations in the press release seem more subjective than those in the news or feature story? How much of the original press release is contained in the news or feature story? Does the news or feature story explain the topic in a more developed way or is the press release used almost exactly as it was written? Think about other questions you can ask to help explore the differences and similarities of both styles of writing.

Exercise 16.2

Find some news releases from local organizations that violate what you have already been taught about media writing—maybe their leads are awful or they don't use AP style or their grafs are too long or they leave out important information. Rewrite those news releases to make them more professional and reader-friendly.

Exercise 16.3

Interview a local editor about what he or she thinks about news releases. Consider questions like these:

- What is your impression of the quality of most news releases you receive?
- Do you ever use a news release verbatim in your publication?
- Do you often pick up news tips from news releases and report and write the story yourself?
- Do you trust the accuracy of news releases?
- What, in your opinion, is the difference between a good and bad news release?
- Do you think most PR practitioners understand the needs of the media they send their news releases to?

Chapter Seventeen

Writing for the Web: Stories for People Who Skim and Scan

To understand how to write for the Web, you have to understand how people read on the Web. For that, we turn to Jakob Nielsen, whom The New York Times called "the guru of Web page usability." His answer?

"They don't."

Most of the time, when your readers are on the Web, they're skimming and scanning, so you have to adjust your writing style to compensate for that. It's not impossible to get people to read your stories online, but you do have to structure your writing so you hook them first.

Understanding how to write for the Web is increasingly important. Among all news media, digital is gaining audience faster than any other sector. The digital audience grew by 7.2 percent from 2011 to 2012, according to the 2013 State of the News Media report from the Pew Research Center's Project for Excellence in Journalism. Every other platform—except cable news, which only gained 0.8 percent—saw its audience shrink. That doesn't mean that other platforms don't matter. Those other platforms are still important profit centers for news companies and have substantial audiences. But the competitive nature of the Web means that for your content to stand out, you'll need to understand how to tweak your writing for maximum impact.

There are two types of online readers whom we're trying to target with the techniques in this chapter. The first is the "browser," people perusing the Web, looking for something to pique their interest enough to spend a few minutes reading it. We try to draw them in with snappy headlines and interesting display type.

The other reader we're trying to hook is the "information seeker." Information seekers are on a mission to find some specific piece of information or learn about some story they've heard about. When you go to Google to find out what time the Super Bowl is going to be on TV and search for "Super Bowl time," you're an information seeker. So are the people who hear someone talking about a news story they've never heard about and go straight to the Web for some background. For these readers, we're going to put as much information as possible on the surface of the story so they can easily find what they're looking for, even if that nugget of information is buried deep in the story. We write headlines and leads that tell them exactly what the stories are about so they can decide whether to read them.

Because reading on the Web is so different, the whole topic of how to write for the Web has become popular. Fortunately for media writers, writing for the Web should be pretty easy. Good Web writing and good newswriting have a lot in common. In fact, newspaper readers already skim and scan and resemble the "browser" discussed above, and newswriting already reflects that.

With that in mind, let's walk through how a typical news story needs to be altered to better serve Web readers and conform to the conventions of the Internet.

Headlines

Because the Web changes the way people consume content, it also changes the way we write. That often means slight tweaks to everything from headlines to attribution.

Headlines on the Web aren't all that different from the headlines you've learned to write in this book. Most of them are straightforward, active-voice headlines. The key difference is that Web headlines often use proper nouns and other hooks that would typically be left out of a newspaper or press release headline. This is helpful for Web info seekers. It's also important for search engine optimization, most often known as SEO.

SEO is important for public relations and advertising professionals who depend on getting a message out and for journalists whose companies' bottom lines are tied to the number of eyeballs they can draw to a page. In both cases, SEO is a big deal, and it's in your interest to understand the basics.

Much of the SEO you'll do for the stories you write will be in headline writing. We'll explain SEO basics as they relate to headlines. There are two types of optimizations that are part of SEO.

Optimizing for the machine. Every search engine has secret algorithms that determine how pages are ranked on the search engine results pages. For a writer, optimizing for the machine is all about keywords. So when you're writing a headline for your story, think about what you'd search to find that story. That often means including proper nouns in headlines when you normally wouldn't. Let's say you're writing headlines for the university newspaper at Texas Christian University and you have a story about the basketball team beating neighboring Southern Methodist University. You could write something like:

Basketball team beats Mustangs, 65-52

The problem with that headline is that most people who search for your story will likely type something like *TCU SMU basketball* into a search engine. You have only one of those three keywords. The Web version of that headline isn't as elegant, but it's far more effective:

TCU basketball beats SMU Mustangs, 65-52

This headline is now more likely to rank at the top of the most popular search queries for your story—the ones with the keywords *TCU, basketball* and *SMU*. Even if the refined headline means the same thing to most of your readers, it's far better for search engine algorithms.

Optimizing for the user. Getting to the top of the search engine results page is only the first half of SEO, though. You still need to get people to actually click through to your page if you want to show up in the No. 1 slot. That's the more human part of SEO, and it's where good, clear writing comes in. Just having the keywords doesn't do everything for you. If you had the keywords in your headline but it was unreadable, you're not likely to have much luck. A descriptive, engaging, well-written headline is still important in getting users to click through. Because of this, you'll always be balancing packing keywords into your headline while maintaining its readability.

One of the best strategies for writing Web headlines is to think about the way you usually search the Web. What would you Google if you were going to search for the story you're writing about? There are keyword research tools out there, and that's what SEO professionals use. Many companies employ professionals who do nothing but search engine optimization. You're likely not going to work with an SEO expert at your first job, though, and that means the best keyword research tool you have access to is yourself.

Aside from SEO, headlines have one other important role on the Web. On most modern websites, the headline is also the link that's used when your story is linked to throughout the site. Unlike in newsletters, newspapers and other printed pieces, on the Web you don't know how your headline will be presented on screen. In print, a headline may be made to play off a nearby photo or even off the lead of your story. On the Web, your headline is likely to be decoupled from the story and spread around your site and onto search engine results pages and social networks. That means it needs to stand on its own, independent of photos, subheads or anything else you may have on the page with it.

These reader-focused headlines will also help with social media optimization—often known as SMO—which will help your stories gain traction on social networks. Just like with SEO, SMO requires you to balance SMO concerns with providing the reader a clear, effective headline. For example, extreme SMO often means leaving important pieces of information out of a headline so a reader will click through, generating an additional pageview. Such headlines are often called "linkbait." For an example of extreme SMO, check out @HuffPoSpoilers on Twitter, a parody account that retweets Huffington Post linkbait and fills in the missing information.

Quotes and Attribution

The Web has its own unique form of attribution, and it's one of the best forms there is. Attribution online is done with the link. Unlike simple text attribution, the link actually can take the reader straight to the source you're referencing.

This increases the credibility of your writing significantly. In most writing you're simply telling the reader, "Here's what was said, according to me, the writer." When you link it's as if you're saying, "Here's what was said, and if you don't believe me, check it out for yourself. Just click the link." You may link back to a press release that has information you used in your story or you may link to a past story that has information you're reusing.

In some rare cases, links can even substitute for traditional attribution. For online-only news organizations, that's becoming common practice. Roy Peter Clark, an expert on newswriting at the Poynter Institute, has even argued that linking allows the writer freedom by getting unnecessary attribution out of the way. Read his opinion here: http://bit.ly/10pWiSM. That viewpoint is still considered pretty nontraditional among most news organizations, but it's important to think about how linking will likely shape how we write news in the future. For now, keep in mind that links can't substitute for traditional attribution, but they can certainly enhance it.

Subheads

It's important to remember that when people read your content on the Web they're not always on a desktop computer. Many are reading on mobile phones or tablets.

All good stories have a central idea and focus on an important topic or action. However, many stories have minor events and less important elements that still make it into the story, often low in the story after the main idea has been addressed. When you decide to focus on one important element and address it first, an assumption you make is that this is the most important, interesting thing in the story to the majority of your readers. There may be others out there who are more interested in something that you classified as a minor item in your story.

Let's say that your town's city council meets and passes a sweeping reform of the city's pension system. It's big news and will save the town tens of millions of dollars annually. The city council takes several other actions, including funding new sidewalks for a neighborhood—let's call it Highland Heights.

To most people in town, the pension reform is the big news. But for residents of Highland Heights, the sidewalks may be the biggest story. You can't reslant your story as that neighborhood represents only a small slice of your audience, but you can call attention to it so that people who live there can easily find that information if they're looking for it.

The easiest way to draw attention to this piece of the story is with a "subheadline." Subheadlines (or subheads) are similar to headlines, but are usually displayed in smaller type. In this chapter, the words "Headlines," "Quotes and attribution," and "Subheads" are all subheadlines. They let you, the reader, navigate to the specific part of the chapter you're looking for. When you're reading the chapter from beginning to end, subheadlines may not help much. But if you're returning to the chapter to remind yourself about Web headlines, the subheads allow you to go straight to that section. If you're flipping through the whole book, trying to find something about Lists, that subheadline will help you find it. Subheads work the same way in your news stories.

The most important thing you can do with your Web subheads is to load them with keywords, just like with your headlines. That lets readers skim the story to find what they're looking for. Your subheadline for the sidewalks piece of the above-mentioned story, for example, would be written something like *Sidewalks for Highland Heights approved*. Something that's clever, witty and engaging but without those keywords wouldn't have the same impact for the many people who are going to skim the story looking for that information.

Lists

Sometimes as media writers we're inclined to turn everything into a paragraph-form story. In some cases, a mature media writer needs to separate the *story* from the *information*. Not everything you write about is best presented in paragraph form. Paragraphs are great tools to guide a reader through a story, presenting things in the exact order you want and painting a picture. They allow you to present conflict, explain complicated issues and provide important color and observation.

Sometimes, though, things are just information. Let's take the city council story again. Let's say the council spent most of its time discussing a half-dozen big items and approved another 20 in less than a half hour. There may not be much story behind those 20 items. They're routine actions that may not need much explanation, don't have quotes associated with them and have relatively no supporting material. That means they're perfect for a list.

Rather than trying to write those many items into paragraph form, wasting screen space and the reader's time with unnecessary transitions, attribution and other writing devices, a mature writer may simply put those items in a list. Here's an example of what that might look like.

In other business, the council:

- *renewed the contract of City Manager Mike Smith*
- *decided to set the annual city picnic for the weekend of March 5*
- *passed a resolution honoring the football team's state championship victory*

And the list would go on in that fashion. Imagine those items in paragraph form; it's not pretty and it's not any more informative than the list.

The Bottom Line

The reality is that media writers are already pretty well trained as Web writers. The inverted pyramid is the perfect story form for the Internet. In fact, many guides that teach people how to write for the Web point them to the work of media writers. That said, there's always room for improvement.

Doing the assignments in this chapter seem like extra work, over and above the hours you're already putting in. However, the goal of any media writer is to get as many eyeballs on your writing as possible. The tools in this chapter will help you do just that. The Internet has the ability to spread content like no medium before it. Your stories, as soon as they hit the Web, can be read across the globe. But the Web is also competitive.

The hypothetical story about the city council may be written, in different forms, by a half-dozen others and also posted to the Web. And whether you're the public information officer for one of the members of the city council or a journalist covering the story, it may not be the best-written story that wins. That's because the best-written story may not get read if the writer wasn't able to draw readers in because of a flat headline or because the reader was looking at a giant, gray block of text. Sometimes the best writer doesn't always win if the presentation isn't right—especially on the Web where competition is fierce.

Skills Development: Practice in Media Writing

Exercise 17.1

First, write a headline for the story below. Then, insert subheads to make the story easier to scan. The story below has three ideas in it. It has, in a way, three inverted pyramids, each of which is smaller than the one before it. Use that organization to help you write the subheads.

Headline: _____

Members of the House of Student Representatives approved a bill Tuesday evening that allocated the rest of its budget, $22,506, to fund a student memorial on campus to remember and honor students who have died. House members passed the bill by a vote of 25–0 with three representatives not voting.

Student Government Association Vice President of Operations Josh Simpson said a student's death had a large impact on the student body, and the memorial would be part of a healing process. Students should be honored in all stages of life, he said.

The memorial would have a bronze statue similar to the lily pads on top of Frog Fountain in the middle, he said. The exact location of the memorial has not yet been determined.

According to the legislation, there was no central place for students to remember and honor students who have died, and the student memorial would create a place for individual and collective remembrance.

The Physical Plant estimated the student memorial would cost at least $50,000, according to the legislation.

In other business, House members unanimously passed a resolution thanking the university faculty for the 2011-2012 academic year.

The Academic Affairs Committee would present a letter to the Faculty Senate at the end of the academic year thanking faculty for their commitment and dedication to the university, according to the legislation.

House members also voted to reject a bill that would have allocated $2,500 to buy a one-year trial of Rida-roo.com, a carpooling website. House members rejected the bill by a vote of 12-20.

Opponents of the bill said SGA could be held responsible if an accident occurred and that students might not use the website often. Supporters said the bill was a good opportunity to try a program that could be successful.

The meeting was the last one of the 98th House session, which occurred during the 2011-2012 academic year.*

The story above is a good example of the organizational style that benefits from subheads. Find some stories from your student newspaper or from some other local source that you think could use subheads. Print them and insert the subheads where you think they should go.

Tip: For an example of how to build the story around the subheads, instead of adding the subheads to the story, check out the story at http://tc360.co/InRuk7—an example of a classic online story form, which has been adapted from magazines.

---

* From TCU360, 2012. Reprinted by permission.

Chapter Eighteen

Writing Advertising Copy: Oz, Magic, Rock 'N' Roll

By Carol Glover

I honestly believe that advertising is the most fun you can have with your clothes on.

~ Jerry Della Femina

Say goodbye to Kansas. Take one last look at Muggleville. Give up your symphony seats. Advertising is Oz, magic and rock 'n' roll all crammed into one big roller coaster ride.

Great advertising is outrageous, contagious and, at its best, courageous. Sure, you'll come across some flying monkeys and a Voldemort or two—you might even end up looking like Keith Richards—but you'll never work through same day twice and you'll never get tired of seeing your work out in the world.

People don't read ads. They read what interests them. And sometimes it's an ad.

~ Howard Luck Gossage

Advertising is a little bit magic and a little bit rock 'n' roll. In this chapter, we'll teach you a little bit about the ad industry and explain what goes into writing effective advertising copy.

Advertising is tough. No one opens a magazine or powers up an iPad to read ads. People don't drive down the road to look at billboards. You don't watch TV for the commercials (unless it's the Super Bowl). But every once in a while, an ad grabs you. It makes you say, "Hmm." Or think, "Oh." It might even make you laugh. And eventually you do something because of the ad—you try a new toothpaste, join a gym, give money to cure cancer or buy the Super Grande Burrito at 2 in the morning. If convincing people to do stuff against all odds sounds cool to you, you just might be a copywriter.

Advertising Is a Team Sport. Meet the Team.

Account executives are the liaisons between the ad agency and the client. They develop strategies and put together Creative Briefs. They also handle billing and budgeting and they help with client presentations.

Account planners focus entirely on consumers. They dig out insights for the account service and creative teams.

Creative directors manage the creative department. They work with art directors and copywriters to come up with The Big Idea, and they decide which campaigns get presented. They also pitch the creative work to clients. Creative directors usually start out as copywriters or art directors.

Copywriters come up with Big Ideas and write headlines, body copy and scripts. They typically team up with an art director or designer to create campaigns.

Art directors come up with Big Ideas and create the overall look of a campaign. They figure out visuals, put layouts together and work with copywriters to pull everything together.

Hey, You. Buy This

Good ads do two things:

- Grab attention
- Make people do something

Sounds simple, right? Well, grabbing people's attention isn't as easy as it used to be. We're bombarded with more than 5,000 marketing messages a day. That's a lot of clutter to break through. Besides that, people have learned to tune out ads. Grabbing someone's attention today takes more creativity than ever. And that's only half the battle.

Ads also have to persuade people to do something—buy, give, join, learn more, believe. Not in a slimy used car salesman way, but in an interesting way. The best ads never talk about tires or beer or insurance. The best ads talk about what tires and beer and insurance *do for* people.

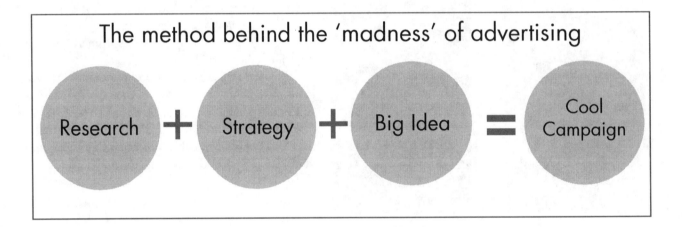

Writing Great Ads Starts with Research. Wah, Wah.

That's right. Put away your cool sunglasses and pick up a shovel. You've got some digging to do. Good advertising solves problems for people, and research helps you figure out what problem your product solves. Focus your research on three things: the product, the consumer and the competition.

The Product Let's say you have to create an ad campaign about tires. Start by learning everything you can about the tires. Find out how they're made, what's innovative about them, what makes them better than other tires. Read the product manual, the website, brochures, old ads, customer reviews online and anything else you can get your hands on. Go to the tire store, and don't forget to talk to the salespeople. People on the front lines usually have the best insights. They know why people buy stuff. And, more important, why they don't.

Figure Out the Product's Features and Benefits "Features" are specific qualities about a product. For example, Volvos have side air bags. Southwest Airlines has cheap fares. Nike shoes have Air insoles. Every product or service has features.

"Benefits" are the emotional satisfaction people get from the features. Because of side air bags, Volvos make Moms feel safer about driving their kids around. Since Southwest has cheap fares, families have the freedom to take vacations and make great memories. Guys who wear Nike Air sneakers have a competitive edge—like Kobe or LeBron.

Good advertising always turns features into benefits—benefits that mean something to moms or dads or wanna-be hoop stars. Benefits answer the "What's in it for me?" question for people.

The Consumer Every product has a "target audience"—the people most likely to buy it. Usually you get a description of these people in the Creative Brief. The description might read something like: women, 35-40, household income of $70,000+, living in the Midwest, married with two kids. Those are "demographics."

They're important, but you also want "psychographics"—deeper insights into what makes these women tick. You want the TV shows they watch, the websites they visit, the magazines they read, the causes they support, their pet peeves, what keeps them up at night, their secret hopes and dreams.

At big advertising agencies, these insights come from an account planner. Account planners figure out what makes consumers tick. Other times, agencies work with research firms to get into consumers' heads. If budgets don't allow for big-time research, it's up to you. But before you pull on your black jumpsuit and start stalking women 35-40 in the Midwest, try these less creepy methods:

- **Ask questions through social media.** A product's Facebook page is the quickest way to get insights from devoted customers.
- **Survey a company's email list.** Online surveys with tools like Survey Monkey or Zoomerang can deliver good information quickly and affordably.
- **Talk to people who fit the demographic profile.** Start with people you know. If you've got more time or money, pull together a focus group.

Research techniques vary, but whatever you do, listen hard when you get the chance. You won't believe how many times a headline will pop right out of someone's mouth—just like it did for Bud Robbins. Bud's story is legendary among ad copywriters.

Bud was hired in the '60s to write copy for Aeolian pianos, and his first assignment was to write an ad that would be placed in The New York Times. He knew he needed information on the pianos if he was to write ad copy, so he asked for a tour of the Aeolian factory.

Robbins had to write copy that would sell a $5,000 piano (remember, this was the 1960s, so that was more money than that it is today)—and he couldn't even play a piano, much less write about what made one piano worth a $5,000 investment.

So he went to upstate New York and spent two days touring the Aeolian factory. He learned pretty much everything there was to know about building a quality piano.

After the tour, he was taken into a showroom, where he saw an Aeolian, a Steinway and a Baldwin piano. His first reaction was that they all looked quite similar.

The sales manager giving the tour agreed, and told Robbins that one major difference was the shipping weight—the Aeolian was significantly heavier than the Steinway and the Baldwin.

Like any good copywriter, he wanted to know why. The reason for the extra weight, he was told, was the capo d'astro *bar.*

Huh?

Robbins and the sales manager climbed under the piano to see what a capo d'astro *bar was. The manager explained that all pianos began to warp within 50 years. But Aeolian had a* capo d'astro *that was made of heavier metal, and thus it wouldn't warp. The manager explained that this was why the Metropolitan Opera in New York used Aeolian pianos.*

Robbins then talked with the people at the Met, who at that time were moving to the newly built Lincoln Center in New York. He was told that the only thing the Met was taking to the Lincoln Center was its Aeolian piano.

Robbins built the Aeolian campaign around the fact that this piano was the only thing the Met was taking from its old location. The result: a six-year wait to receive an Aeolian piano after an order.

This story is frequently told by copywriters, who look for the equivalent of a *capo d'astro* bar whenever they do research for a new product.

The Competition Understand the product's archrivals. Find out how competitors position themselves in the market. Visit competitor websites, check out their Facebook pages and get familiar with their advertising. The last thing you want is to present a campaign and have the client say, "Oh yeah, that's exactly what our biggest competitor says."

What Comes First? The Chicken? The Egg? No, the Strategy

Long before you call Steven Spielberg to direct your bacon commercial, you'll have to figure out a strategy to sell the bacon. "Strategy" is a way to sell something before you create the campaign to sell it. A good strategy stakes out a position in the marketplace. Years ago, Volvo decided to own safety, while BMW focused on being the ultimate driving experience. Today, Corona touts escape, while Bud Light delivers a good time.

At advertising agencies, account executives develop strategies. They analyze the market and pore over research on the product, its competition and the consumers. If you end up working at a really small agency or an in-house marketing department, you might work on the strategy and write the ads. Either way, when the strategy gets nailed down, it becomes part of the Creative Brief.

In the factory we make cosmetics. In the drugstore we sell hope.

~ CHARLES REVLON

Advertising Is Like Matchmaking

Say you have two friends, a guy and a gal. They're both single and you think they'd be great together. Before you talk one up to the other, you take a minute to jot down a little about each person. It might look something like this:

GUY	GAL
24 years old	25 years old, blonde hair
Tall, brown hair	Played volleyball in college
Born in California	Teaches math
Works in accounting	Just moved back from Florida
Likes surfing, cooking	
Went to college on academic scholarship	Likes yoga, runs marathons
	Brother is a chef
Democrat	Republican
Kind of serious	Great sense of humor

You're going to meet your guy friend for lunch. What's the first thing you're going to tell him about your other friend? Maybe you mention she's a math teacher since he's an accountant. Or maybe you mention she has blonde hair because you know he dated a lot of blondes in California. Or maybe you mention she's into yoga because you know he likes surfing. Or, even though he's kind of serious, you might mention she's fun to be around because you know he appreciates friends who lighten things up.

The point is, you decide what to mention first based on what you know about him. You don't lead with her politics since they're on opposite sides of that fence. But you don't make anything up either. You just talk about the stuff you think he'd like best about her. It works the same way with products and consumers. So:

~~Guy~~ Consumer   ~~Gal~~ Product

What's the Big Idea?

The Big Idea brings an advertising strategy to life. It's the Chick-fil-A cows, or Snickers using Betty White to show how cranky hungry guys get. Big Ideas, or concepts, hold campaigns together—from magazine ads and billboards to TV commercials and online banner ads. They grab people's attention and give them the little "aha" moments that make ads memorable. But "aha" alone isn't enough.

Big Ideas need to be relevant and revolutionary—relevant to the product, consumer and strategy and **revolutionary**, or different enough, to break through the clutter.

A Big Idea that's revolutionary will be interesting in a heartwarming, funny, surprising, shocking or entertaining way, but if it's not relevant, it won't get the job done. The reverse is true, too. An ad that's relevant but not revolutionary will look like a walking strategy statement—the living dead of the ad world—and it won't stand a chance of getting noticed or remembered.

Creative Briefs

Creative briefs have nothing to do with underwear, unless Fruit of the Loom is the client.

Account executives write Creative Briefs to give creative teams a game plan. Think of it like football. Based on their players and their next opponent, the coaches decide, "OK, this Friday we're going to focus on passing. Not running or option plays. Passing—short passes—will work best." That's the strategy. When the creative team gets that direction, they figure out a bunch of short passing plays. Not tired, boring short pass plays, but surprising, kick-ass, short pass plays. Those are the ads.

How to Become an Idea Factory

Getting to that "aha" moment requires putting a lot of ideas on paper. The idea generation process in this chapter can help you identify your "big idea", which is a must-have for any advertising copywriter.

The scariest thing in advertising is a blank page. You need to start filling it up with words, phrases and sketches as soon as possible. The first step? Kick your inner critic to the curb. You know the one. The little voice in your head that whispers, "Wow. That's your idea? Maybe the Burger Shack is hiring." That voice is the enemy of creativity. Mute it. Then start with something simple to get your creative juices flowing.

Write Down Every Word or Phrase You Can Think of That Has to Do with What You're Selling Let's say your ad campaign is about shampoo, so you write: Hair, clean, clean as a whistle, squeaky clean, water, shower, naked, stark naked, naked as a jaybird, the naked truth, 1-900-NAKED— OK, OK, move on. Then think about images: bubbles,

Creative Connections? There's an App for That.

The Creative Whack Pack app by Roger von Oech can jumpstart your brainstorming with great exercises like these:

Exaggerate. Imagine a joke so funny that you can't stop laughing for a month. Paper stronger than steel. An apple the size of a hotel. A jet engine quieter than a moth beating its wings. Try exaggerating your idea. Think big: What if it were a thousand times bigger, louder, stronger, faster or brighter? Now think small: What if it were only one-thousandth as powerful, fast, costly or complicated as before? How can you exaggerate your idea?

Make a Metaphor. The key to metaphorical thinking is comparing unrelated concepts and finding similarities between them. Example: What do a cat and a refrigerator have in common? They both have a place to put fish; they both have tails; they purr; they come in a variety of colors; and they both have a lifetime of about 15 years. What similarities does your idea have with cooking a meal? Conducting an orchestra? Building a house? Raising a child? Waging war? What can you compare your idea to?

Download the Creative Whack Pack app with this QR code, or go to:

http://www.creativewhack.com/product.php?productid=64

wet hair, fluffy towel, the shampoo bottle, hands scrubbing, clean hair, shiny hair, spiky hair, sexy messed up hair and so on. Use all your senses, so think about smells: flowery, spring rain, eucalyptus, berries, clean hair smell, someone smelling clean hair. Imagine sounds: scrubbing, gurgling water, shower spray, dripping, blow drying, sniffing. Fill the page with words and then start looking for unexpected connections.

Unexpected Connections Are the Secret Sauce in Advertising Make a list of your 10 favorite ads. Odds are you'll see some crazy connections—like a baby promoting stock trading for E*TRADE or LMFAO's "Sexy and I Know It" introducing brown M&Ms. How about Dean Winters playing Mayhem for Allstate?

Always try to relate your product to something unexpected. Go back to the shampoo example and start making crazy connections. Shampoo and history. Shampoo and food. Shampoo and wild animals. Shampoo and ballet or opera. Shampoo and war or the military. Shampoo and sports or sex—oh, wait, those have already been done.

Making these kinds of connections takes guts, the guts to think, "What if …" and to keep going until it makes sense—until your Big Idea becomes relevant *and* revolutionary.

The Road to Big Ideas Is Paved with Stupid Stuff Give yourself permission to have bad ideas. That's part of the process. Advertising isn't like math where you're plugging away to find The Answer. Giving yourself permission to fail—permission to entertain ideas that might not work—is an important part of the creative process.

Keep Going Back to What Your Product Does for People Remember features and benefits? Keep going back to the benefits. What does your product really *do* for people? How do people use it to make their lives better, easier, more fun? It's tempting to get bogged down in details like the increased power and energy efficiency of the carbon-bonded, multichamber, stainless steel what-cha-ma-call-it, when all you really need to say is that it chops onions in half the time.

Tell a Story After you stretch your creative muscles by making unexpected connections, change gears. Think about the most basic truths about your product. Forget being clever or funny, and just find the pure human story at the heart of your product. Google did it beautifully with a series of TV spots. They might be the greatest product demonstrations of all time.

Stop Writing. Start Drawing What? That's right, ditch the words. You know the adage "A picture's worth a thousand words." So imagine how much time a great visual will save you. No one wants to write a thousand words. (And, frankly, no one wants to read them.) So try to tell the story with a single visual. Preparation H—a glamorous product if there ever was one—did a great series of ads that didn't even need headlines.

Go Away Stumped? Frustrated? Filling out your application for Burger Shack? Walk away. Go do something else. Run, drive, take a shower—whatever. After you've spent hours filling your head with information and ideas, getting away lets you think about it sideways. And very often that's just what you need to shake loose The Big Idea.

Good Ideas Make You Nervous It doesn't mean they're crazy or outrageous, it just means you haven't seen them before. When you land on a good idea you'll feel a little twinge. The idea might make you laugh out loud or tear up or cringe. The point is, it made you feel something. Good ideas pull at strings that don't get plucked a lot. That's why they work.

If you can't turn yourself into your customer, you probably shouldn't be in the ad business at all.

~ LEO BURNETT

The Bottom Line

Never forget you're writing to real people. Not *for* real people, *to* real people. And those people aren't women, 45–55 with 2.5 kids. Those people are your mother, your aunt, or your favorite teacher from third grade.

Of course, sometimes you're writing to people so outside your life experience they might as well be Martians. Can you put yourself in the Martian's shoes (assuming they have shoes)? Can you understand what it feels like to be from Mars? Can you care about what Martians care about?

Good copywriters do it every day.

Tips for Writing Great Advertising Copy

- Write like you talk. Have a conversation, not a sales pitch.
- Use "we" and "our"—you are the brand.
- Use "you" and "your"—like you're talking to a friend.
- Use contractions. You aren't writing an English paper.
- Avoid ellipses… especially in headlines. Gross. Seriously.
- Ditch the jargon and buzz words. Even brain surgeons use regular language at home.
- Cut the fat. Keep the meat. People read less. You need to cut more.
- Read it out loud. Does it sound natural? Be honest.

Skills Development: Practice in Media Writing

Exercise 18.1

Find five print ads you really like. What is the unique selling point of each ad? Analyze each of the five using the copywriting principles contained in this chapter.

Exercise 18.2

Write two print ads for the academic department that offers this media writing course. The target audience is high school seniors interested in majoring in journalism or advertising or public relations. Use the principles in this chapter to find a selling point for each ad. Your ads should be between 100 and 150 words.

Chapter Nineteen
Is That Legal? What Writers Need to Know About Media Law

By Chip Stewart

Every time you write something, you expose yourself to legal risk. You are responsible for what you write, so if it turns out to be untrue and hurts the reputation of another person, or if it infringes on the intellectual property rights of its owner, you face potential criminal sanctions and civil liability.

Terrified? Don't be. This chapter provides you with the basics of libel and copyright law. Coupled with an appropriate level of caution and responsibility, you should be able to avoid legal dangers, or at least have an idea of how to protect yourself in case somebody out there is displeased with what you wrote or how you wrote it.

Of course, the First Amendment provides broad safeguards for speech and publication: "Congress shall make no law ... abridging freedom of speech, or of the press." This primarily protects you from government interference with what you want to publish. The First Amendment makes it difficult for the state to prevent you from publishing things, as the Supreme Court noted in 1971 when it refused to allow the Nixon administration to ban The New York Times from publishing articles about the Pentagon Papers.

The high court also disfavors such prior restraints in the form of gag orders issued by judges to prevent publication or discussion of matters that may violate a criminal defendant's right to a fair trial, as was noted in the *Nebraska Press Association v. Stuart* case in 1976.

However, libel actions are largely unprotected by the First Amendment (more on this later). Copyright protection is built into the Constitution, providing creators of original works with strong legal protections that have largely withstood First Amendment challenges.

The first part of this chapter is a briefing on the libel law and related areas to help you avoid unfairly damaging somebody's reputation when you write. The second part focuses on copyright law, providing you with an understanding of what materials are safe for you to use as a writer and what should be treated with caution.

Libel

Libel is a daily danger for publishers. The Media Law Resource Center, which has been tracking lawsuits involving publishers since 1980, reports that 588 lawsuits involving media defendants went to trial between 1980 and 2011. The "vast majority" of these claims were for libel, and if the case actually went to trial, the results weren't pretty.

Publishers lose nearly 60 percent of cases at trial, with juries awarding an average of $2.86 million. After retrials and appeals, those numbers are somewhat better, with publishers winning about 56 percent of cases and damages reduced to about $675,000. But even if you win a libel lawsuit, you likely have done so after incurring tens of thousands of dollars in legal defense fees. So unless you have a spare million bucks or so lying around, it is unwise to take the risk of libel lightly.

A former newsroom colleague of mine, Fred Vultee, now a professor at Wayne State University, once compared dealing with libel to dealing with snakes. It is better, he said, to step over the snake than to have to deal with the snakebite. And, I like to add, if you know you're going to tangle with a snake, you want to protect yourself the best you can. Think of this chapter as providing both a guide for spotting snakes in the underbrush as well as a thick pair of snake handling gloves.

What Is Libel?

Every time you publish you're opening yourself up to the legal risk. Some topics are riskier than others, though. Throughout this chapter we'll help you identify topics that are often problematic.

In short, libel is publication of a false and defamatory statement of fact that harms the reputation of another. Classically, libel was under the umbrella of "defamation" law, which included both libel (for the printed word) and slander (for the spoken word). Today there is no practical distinction between them.

Libel is usually a matter of civil law—that is, it involves one party suing another party in civil court for money damages. Libel can also be a crime. According to the First Amendment Center, about half the states have criminal libel statutes on the books (http://www.firstamendmentcenter.org/criminal-libel-statutes-state-by-state). Such statutes allow the government to investigate and prosecute the publication of defamatory statements, with potential fines and jail time as punishment.

Thankfully, prosecutions of such cases are rare, typically used, for example, in cases involving domestic issues such as posting harassing sexual posts on the Web by aggrieved former lovers. In the odd case in which a prosecutor goes after legitimate news publication, the courts have not been friendly.

Before Colorado's criminal libel statute was repealed in 2012, an overeager prosecutor used it to investigate a college student who had written an unfriendly parody of a professor in an independent student newspaper. A federal court found that the prosecutor had violated the student's civil rights under the First Amendment and that the prosecutor would owe damages (see *Mink v. Knox*, U.S. District Court, District of Colorado 2011).

Most often, libel lawsuits are civil in nature, brought by people or businesses that believe a statement published about them is false, defamatory, and hurts their reputation. The good news for you is that courts have erected a number of safeguards over the years to avoid what is known as the "chilling effect," publishers' fear that they may be punished for writing things that may inadvertently lead to lawsuits. One of these safeguards is that libel plaintiffs (those who bring lawsuits against publishers) must prove each of the following elements of a libel lawsuit.

Publication. This is the easiest part for plaintiffs to prove. Publication simply involves one person communicating information to another. Publication need not be widespread; simply mailing a letter including a false and defamatory statement is enough to trigger liability.

More troublesome for publishers is the "republication doctrine," which makes publishers liable for the defamatory statements they repeat. It is not a valid defense to argue that you were accurately repeating what somebody else said. Let me repeat with added emphasis: *It is not a valid defense to argue that you were accurately reporting what somebody else said.* With very few exceptions (discussed later in this chapter), you are responsible for everything you publish. Courts impose a duty on publishers to get things right.

You must check and verify that statements you publish are accurate, or else you will be held responsible for the harm they cause. It is accepted in U.S. law that, as a number of legal scholars and judges have repeated over the years, "Tale-bearers are as bad as tale-makers." Indeed, by repeating a libelous statement to a larger audience, a publisher may be on the hook for even more damages for exacerbating a libel defendant's harm.

Perhaps the most famous libel case in U.S. history is *New York Times v. Sullivan*, decided by the Supreme Court in 1964, in which an Alabama city commissioner sued the Times for libel on grounds that it published a defamatory advertisement about him. While Sullivan ultimately lost the lawsuit, it was unquestionable that the Times was responsible for advertisements it published, even if the content of the ad was drafted by somebody else.

As the saying goes, "If your mom says she loves you, check it out." Do not let assertions of fact made by sources go unverified. Look to additional sources to corroborate what the first said. Seek public records and other news articles to verify harmful allegations.

There is, however, one huge exemption to the republication rule. In 1996, Congress recognized the risks that Internet service providers were assuming when they hosted bulletin boards and chat rooms, some of which included false and defamatory postings by users. To encourage online innovators to continue to make the Web a home for free and open exchange of ideas, the federal Communications Decency Act was enacted. Section 230 of the act provides a safe harbor for "users and providers" of "interactive computer services" to shield them from liability for repeating or hosting the harmful statements of others.

This has proven to be a virtually impenetrable shield for Internet publishers and hosts. For example, if a user posts a defamatory comment on Facebook, Facebook is not legally responsible for any damages caused by the post. It's important to remember that the original poster *is* responsible, but not the Web service or host.

Similarly, if you write on a blog or for an online news publication, you are responsible for the contents of your posting. But the blog host or the company that hosts your online news site is not.

For example, the notorious blogger and author Tucker Max, of "I Hope They Serve Beer in Hell" fame, once wrote on his blog about a botched party of a noted blueberry heir. Several readers posted comments about the disastrous party in the comments section of the post. A federal court found that, under Section 230's safe harbor, Max could not be held responsible for the defamatory posts. The commenters themselves were responsible for their posts, not the web host (see *Dimeo v. Max*, U.S. Court of Appeals for the Third Circuit 2007).

This shield extends to Twitter as well. If somebody writes a false and defamatory tweet, that writer is unquestionably responsible for it. For example, Associated Press basketball reporter Jon Krawczynski, writing from the sidelines about what he thought was an improper make-up call by an NBA referee, posted a tweet that ultimately cost him and the AP $20,000. But Twitter could not be held legally responsible because they were "providers" of an "interactive computer service." Interestingly, people who retweeted Krawczynski's offending statement also are protected by the shield, which covers "users" of the "interactive computer service" who repeat the content of others as well.

Remember, this shield applies *only* to digital publishers and users who repeat or host the digital statements of others. Otherwise, the general rule is: If you publish it, you are responsible for it.

Falsity. The libel plaintiff has the burden to prove that what you published was, in fact, false. As a general rule, the First Amendment protects truthful communications. This policy derives from the classic situation involving John Peter Zenger, the New York colonial publisher who was found not guilty for seditious libel in 1738 when it turned out that his defamatory statements about the governor were, in fact, true.

In most civil cases, the plaintiff must show, by a preponderance of the evidence (that is, it is more likely than not), that the statement in dispute is substantially false. Truth remains your best defense as a publisher.

Further, it is not enough for a libel plaintiff to prove that what you published was false. Such errors must be substantial, and they must be the cause of the claimed harm. For example, in the aforementioned *New York Times v. Sullivan* case, one of Sullivan's allegations of falsity was that the ad in question said that students protested by singing "My Country 'Tis of Thee," when, in fact, they actually sang the National Anthem. This statement was unquestionably false—and also unquestionably harmless to Sullivan.

Falsity can include misquoting people, if the misquote makes it appear that a person said something that could call him or her into disrepute. The New Yorker magazine and reporter Janet Malcolm got in hot water for an article published in 1984 about psychoanalyst Jeffrey Masson when he claimed that the article included misquotes or fabricated quotes, such as when he referred to himself as an "intellectual gigolo."

The Supreme Court ruled in 1991 that if these quotes were indeed inaccurate and caused Masson harm, he could collect libel damages (see *Masson v. New Yorker*). Ultimately, a jury found in favor of Malcolm, awarding no damages; however, this came after nearly a decade of litigation and appeal.

Defamatory. The libel plaintiff must also prove the statement is defamatory. This is often easy to determine based on the nature of the statement. In fact, libel law recognizes four major categories of defamatory statements, known as "libel per se." These kinds of statements are so obviously defamatory on their face that the plaintiff does not need to prove how they may be harmful.

The four libel per se categories are:

1. **Criminal behavior.** Accusing somebody of having committed a crime or having participated in some level of criminal activity. If it's in the penal code, don't write that somebody did it (or stands accused of doing it) without good sources. Remember that a person is innocent until proven guilty. Further, remember that people are not "arrested for" doing something, they are "arrested on suspicion of" committing an offense. "Arrested for" implies that they committed the act in question.

2. **Sexual misconduct.** Generally, this involves adultery, but also includes deviate sexual behavior. In most jurisdictions, accusing somebody of being homosexual when they are not is also libelous per se.

3. **Business misconduct.** An allegation that one is mismanaging one's business affairs can harm a person's business reputation. While this may also imply criminal behavior—for example, embezzlement or fraud—it also includes accusations that a businessperson mistreats employees, does not honor contracts or is delinquent in paying bills.

4. **Loathsome disease.** "Loathsome" means something that has negative public connotations, particularly diseases often connected to moral turpitude. Classically, this involved syphilis. Today, it includes sexually transmitted diseases, mental illness and addiction to drugs or alcohol.

Statements that are not libelous on their face may still be actionable for libel if the context or circumstances of the words harm a person's reputation. Such statements, known as "libel per quod," require the plaintiff to show exactly how the words in question caused harm. For example, suppose Jane Smith was a candidate for a U.S. Senate seat in Massachusetts, and she discovered the following factually baseless sentence in an otherwise glowing profile story about her: "Smith, despite growing up in Boston, is a lifelong New York Yankees fan. Her home features a personal shrine to legendary shortstop Derek Jeter." Now, as much as we may find it disagreeable, it is not a crime to be a fan of the New York Yankees, nor is it a disease or any other form of misconduct. Nevertheless, you could see how Smith would feel aggrieved by such a statement—and how those would very likely damage her chances at election in Red Sox Nation.

As such, writers should be on the lookout for particular kinds of words that may make people feel that they have been wronged. While it is impossible to know what statements will trigger liability in every circumstance, you should understand that when you write something false about a person, even what you consider to be a minor error, that person might consider it to be the biggest deal in his or her life. And the law says that you are responsible for plaintiffs as you find them.

Thus, be very careful when you are writing about anything that a person may find to be harmful. In particular, be wary of allegations of wrongdoing or bad behavior. The following words or phrases should set off warning sirens:

Abused, abuser	Burglary	HIV
Addiction	Came out of the closet	Homosexual
Adultery	Charged	Illegal
Affair	Cheat, cheated	Illicit
AIDS	Convicted	Ill, illness
Alcoholism, alcoholic	Cover up	Immoral
Arrested	Deviate, deviant	Infringed
Assaulted	Drinking, drunk, drunken	Killed
Attacked	Drug problem	Lesbian
Bankrupt, bankruptcy	Embezzled	Lied
Beat	Fraud, fraudulent	Mismanaged
Bisexual	Gay	Mistreat
Breached	Harass, harassment	Molested

Murdered	Sex	Theft
Perjury	STD	Trespassed
Prostitute, prostitution	Slept with	Underage
Rioted	Smuggled	Waste, wasted
Robbed, robbery	Spied	
Scandal	Steal, stole, stolen	

Before you publish these words or phrases or others like them, double-check to make sure you are accurate and can substantiate the statement with evidence. Treat your sources as if you will need to call them as witnesses in a libel case—would you, as a member of a neutral jury, trust this person to be telling the truth?

And a final warning: Using the word *allegedly* will not save you from libel responsibility. Nor does *reportedly*, nor phrases such as *it is believed that*. These weasel words do little besides show that you cannot properly attribute an accusation to a source. As mentioned before, repeating the libels of others makes you responsible for them, so if somebody else is "alleging" something, then you are too by repeating it. It is better to attribute properly and write what you know as fact—"Police arrested Mrs. O'Leary on suspicion of arson"—than to write that Mrs. O'Leary allegedly burned down the city of Chicago through her improper cattle handling practices.

Statement of Fact. For a statement to be actionable for libel, it must be a statement of fact, not one of opinion. Opinion is protected under the First Amendment. As such, judgmental words—best and worst, delicious or disgusting—that express your opinion about a subject cannot properly be the basis of libel claims. However, this does not mean that all opinion statements are protected. You cannot couch a statement of fact in an opinion to shield it from libel.

For example, if you were to write, "It's my opinion that the mayor is a child molester," you would be making an objectively verifiable claim. If a publication includes mixed statements of fact and opinion, a jury can decide whether a statement of fact has been made that would be subject to a libel claim. This happened in *Milkovich v. Lorain Journal Co.*, a case that involved a sports columnist writing about a fight that broke out at a high school wrestling match. The columnist, based on his own eyewitness account of the fight, wrote that the wrestling coach had lied under oath at an investigative hearing about the matter.

When the coach sued for libel, the columnist claimed he was merely expressing his opinion about what he witnessed. The Supreme Court, ruling on the case in 1990, said that whether this was a statement of fact or not should be determined by a jury. As another cautionary tale—the wrestling match in question happened in 1974, and the case was not completely disposed of via settlement until after the high court's ruling more than 15 years later.

Fault. In most cases, if you publish something and it turns out to be untrue, you are responsible because you acted with negligence, that is, a reasonable person in your position should have known the statement was false and that it would hurt someone's reputation. If you breach your duty to fact-check harmful statements before you publish them, that is all a libel plaintiff needs to establish your fault to the court.

However, as I mentioned earlier, the First Amendment does provide some breathing space for factual errors when you are writing about public figures or public officials. This was established by a string of cases beginning with the Supreme Court's Sullivan decision in 1964. In that case, the court held that despite the inaccuracies contained in the advertisement published in The New York Times that may have harmed Sullivan's reputation, the newspaper had not acted with "actual malice," and thus it could not be held liable for damages. Because Sullivan was an elected public official and because we want to have what Justice Brennan referred to as "robust, uninhibited, wide-open debate" about public affairs, the court placed this burden on public officials.

The legal meaning of "actual malice" is publishing with knowledge of falsity or reckless disregard for the truth. It is *not* merely regular malice, that is, dislike of another or intent to harm their reputation. Instead, libel plaintiffs in these cases must establish that the writer knew that what was being published was false, or that the writer acted recklessly in publishing it, by (for example) ignoring evidence to the contrary, not checking facts with a reasonable level of diligence, or refusing to talk to sources who may present a different take on the facts.

The "actual malice" requirement has been extended to most government employees as well as public figures such as celebrities, professional athletes, and anyone seeking widespread fame or notoriety through their public actions. This burden, in theory, makes it harder for such people to win libel lawsuits, and it should discourage them from bringing libel lawsuits except in the most egregious instances.

Does this mean you should feel comfortable publishing harmful statements that are potentially untrue about public figures and officials? Of course not. But it does mean that you have some room for honest errors that can happen when you are operating on a tight deadline or when you are being deceived by sources.

Damages. Finally, libel plaintiffs must prove that they have actually been harmed. Courts will not presume a damage award based on the publication of a false and defamatory statement. Instead, plaintiffs must establish their actual damages—lost wages, harm to reputation, emotional pain and suffering—by presenting evidence and calling witnesses to testify.

More troublesome to publishers are punitive damage awards. Punitive damages go above and beyond actual harm, serving as a tool for juries and courts to punish bad behavior and to deter others from acting in a similar manner. When libel judgments reach the millions of dollars, it is most often because a jury intended to send this kind of message.

In such instances, good faith behavior is your best defense. If you acted without actual or regular malice, it is harder for a judge or jury to punish you in this fashion.

Additionally, publishers should look to mitigate damages when possible. Timely corrections, clarifications or retractions of false or misleading information can limit the amount of damage you may be responsible for. If you believe you have acted in error, it is best to respond as quickly as possible to limit your liability.

Libel defenses

Suppose you have not managed to step over the snake or you know that no matter what you do, the snake will strike. How can you best defend yourself?

A number of defenses have emerged to help publishers who face libel lawsuits:

Truth. Always your best defense. While you do not have the burden to prove the truth of your statements (remember, the plaintiff must prove the statements are false), if you can establish truth, you win. Courts do not want to punish truthful speech.

Fair Comment/Criticism. Critical reviews of a creation or performance of another (consider movies, art, the theater, music, restaurants, etc.) are protected as statements of opinion. As long as your criticism is fair, that is, it is based in fact and your own actual experiences, you can assert this defense.

Fair Report. Under the "Fair Report privilege," which is recognized in nearly every jurisdiction, if you accurately and truthfully repeat statements made by public officials in public records, meetings and other forums, you will not be responsible for those statements if they turn out to be false or defamatory. This is limited to government affairs, however. Reporting on matters of great public interest, such as businesses activity, are not covered by the Fair Report defense. The Fair Report privilege is a conditional one. You must show that the statements involve government matters and that you reported the statements in a fair, accurate and unbiased manner.

Absolute Privilege. Sworn testimony, such as statements made under oath in court or affidavits made out of court, are bulletproof for libel purposes. For example, a police report or statement made by law enforcement officials at a press conference would likely trigger the Fair Report privilege mentioned above. But an even better defense would be the use of absolutely privileged materials such sworn testimony or statements made on the floor of legislative bodies.

Anti-SLAPP. In response to the proliferation of frivolous or meritless filings of libel lawsuits, several jurisdictions have enacted laws providing added protection for publishers. Sometimes, a person or business may bring a libel lawsuit merely to harass a publisher. As mentioned before, libel litigation is time-consuming and expensive, and many libel defendants may prefer to retract or withdraw their statements or otherwise settle with libel plaintiffs to avoid the hassle.

Such actions are called "strategic lawsuits against public participation," or SLAPPs. The goal is to silence publishers by threatening to drag them through the legal process. Anti-SLAPP laws provide a weapon for publishers facing such actions. If the publisher can establish that the lawsuit is without merit, for example, by showing that the statements in question are matters of opinion or could not have caused actual harm, then early in the case, the publisher can ask the judge to dismiss the action and sanction the libel plaintiff. Media defendants have been awarded damages and attorney fees in such cases as a way to compensate them for having to deal with a harassing lawsuit.

Copyright

Federal copyright law provides creators of original works of authorship the right to control copying, sale, distribution and other uses of their works for a limited time. Today, that limited time is the life of the author plus 70 years, meaning that most works created in the 20th century are still protected by copyright.

For you, as a writer, this means you should be cautious about how you use passages that you find in other sources. Just because you find something on the Web, or because somebody is voluntarily sharing it without making copying difficult or putting it behind a paywall, does *not* mean you are free to use it.

This section focuses on how copyright law works and how you can protect yourself to ensure that you do not infringe on the rights of other authors.

What Does Copyright Protect?

Original works of authorship are eligible for copyright, including literary works (such as books or news articles), music and lyrics, film, sound recordings, dance choreography, dramatic works such as plays, photography, graphic art, sculpture, even works of architecture. Facts and ideas are not copyrightable, but the tangible expression of them—that is, once they are fixed in a medium of expression, as the law puts it—is eligible for copyright.

Today, copyright automatically attaches at the second the work is created. One does not have to file for a copyright in order to claim it. A copyright owner can file and backdate the filing to the moment the work was created to later enforce his or her rights in court. This creates a strong presumption that anything new has or can quickly have copyright protection.

Some things are not copyrightable. Short phrases, slogans and names may be eligible for trademark, but not copyright because trademark law provides news reporting with a fair use exemption, you may use trademarked slogans, logos or phrases if relevant to your writing. Recipes and lists of ingredients may not be copyrighted, though as mentioned before, the way in which they are expressed or written can be protected. Works created by the government, such as the 9/11 Commission Report or court opinions, are not eligible for copyright. It is always safe to use these uncopyrightable works in your writing, as well as works that have fallen into the public domain after their copyrights have expired.

Infringement

Copyright holders have several exclusive rights in their works. They have the right to make copies, to distribute or sell copies, to permit or create derivative works based on the original, such as writing a sequel or allowing a book to be turned into a movie, and to perform or display the work publicly.

Unless you have a license or other permission to use a copyrighted work, you may be infringing on these exclusive rights. Under federal law, copyright holders can seek civil damages against you, the greater of either their actual losses or in damages provided by the Copyright Act. In 2012, minimum statutory damages were set at $750 per infringing use, with statutory damages of up to $30,000 per infringing use. That means that if you are found to be infringing on someone's copyright, he or she can seek at a minimum $750 in damages from you.

A cautionary tale: In 2010 and 2011, the Righthaven Company sought to enforce the copyrights of news publishers in Las Vegas and Denver by bringing a string of lawsuits against online publishers and bloggers. They sought the maximum $30,000 damage award in each case, extracting settlements in several cases before judges began dismissing cases on either fair use or other technical grounds over whether Righthaven actually had enough ownership in the copyrighted works to create a right to sue.

Fair Use

The Fair Use defense permits people to use copyrighted works in limited amounts for certain qualifying purposes. The idea is that copyright law is supposed to both (a) provide economic incentives for authors and (b) stimulate creativity by the public, allowing some uses of works without permission will stimulate creativity, as long as it doesn't cause significant harm to the original copyright holder.

Under the Copyright Act, if a use is for news reporting, criticism or commentary, teaching, scholarship or academic research, it may qualify as Fair Use. This is good news for writers, who most often are engaged in these favored activities.

However, just because a work qualifies for Fair Use doesn't mean it automatically is a fair use. Courts apply a four-part test to determine whether a use is fair:

1. They examine the purpose of the secondary work; if it is for profit, that weighs against a finding of Fair Use;

2. They look at the nature of the original work, use of works of fiction and fancy are less likely to be found to be Fair Use than use of nonfiction and historical works;

3. Courts look at the "amount and substantiality" of the use: how much of the original work was taken and how much of the secondary work is made up of the portion taken from the original;

4. Courts examine the effect on the market of the original; if the secondary work has a negative economic impact on the original, that weighs against a finding of Fair Use.

Courts most often focus on amount and substantiality and harm to the market. For example, when The Nation magazine published a leaked excerpt from Gerald Ford's memoirs, it was found not to be Fair Use, even though it was news reporting of nonfiction with great public interest and only 300 to 400 words were taken from a manuscript hundreds of pages long. In that case, *Harper & Row v. Nation Enterprises* (1984), the Supreme Court found that The Nation had taken the "heart" of the work—Ford's description of why he pardoned Richard Nixon—and that they had caused financial harm because the use caused another magazine to cancel its $25,000 contract to publish an exclusive excerpt.

The aforementioned Righthaven cases show, however, that courts can be forgiving of less harmful uses. In one case, a federal district court found that a not-for-profit organization in Oregon qualified for Fair Use, even though the organization posted an entire 33-paragraph article from the Las Vegas Review-Journal on its website (see *Righthaven v. Jama*, U.S. District Court for the District of Nevada 2011). In other cases, courts found that copying eight full sentences on a realtor's blog was Fair Use because the sentences were largely factual, even if the blog had commercial interests (see *Righthaven v. Realty One Group*, U.S. District Court for the District of Nevada 2011).

These cases reflect a shifting understanding of Fair Use of news articles on the Web. However, you should not lightly use long passages from other sources. Remember that Fair Use means you have a right to hire a lawyer to defend yourself only against a copyright action, which can get expensive.

It is wise to limit your borrowing of passages to the most essential information. Use one or two sentences and attribute to the original source by name, providing a hyperlink to the original if possible. Attribution and hyperlinking are evidence that you are acting in good faith, which will help you if you ever wind up in court. Avoid "scraping," that is, copying and pasting the complete article of another person.

When in doubt, don't be afraid to ask. If there's an article that serves as a perfect example of an idea you are trying to communicate, ask the author for permission to use it. Get permission in writing or via email to show that you are not infringing.

The Bottom Line

I once attended a panel discussion of media lawyers in Washington, D.C. One of the attorneys was asked what advice he offered to journalists to avoid legal trouble. His answer was stunningly simple: "Be a good journalist." Check everything out. Don't print something if you have any indication that it's not true. Don't spread rumors. Be diligent. Do your homework. Keep good records. Don't copy.

These media law basics apply as much to advertising and public relations writing as they do to journalism. Remember that the landmark case in libel law, *Times v. Sullivan*, was based on an ad in The New York Times, not a news story.

Media Law Resources

Here is a list of free media law resources for more details on legal issues that you may face as a writer.

- U.S. Copyright Office: www.copyright.gov
  Good primer on the basics of copyright law, including registration and Fair Use
- Electronic Frontier Foundation: www.eff.org
  San Francisco-based organization, strong advocates for digital publishers who run into legal trouble
- Media Law Resource Center: www.medialaw.org
  Great resources for publishers about media law, particularly libel and privacy issues
- Citizen Media Law Project: www.citmedialaw.org
  Provides legal information about digital media law and can help with legal training and defense; connected to Harvard University's Berkman Center for Internet and Society
- Reporters Committee for Freedom of the Press: www.rcfp.org
  Washington, D.C.-based nonprofit resource for journalists and the media law challenges they face

Skills Development: Practice in Media Writing

Exercise 19.1

This online site allows you to think about what you would do in several types of media law cases. Go to this website: http://medialibel.org/wwyd/.

The site provides several sample situations to role-play the decisions media professionals make every day, some based on real cases. These situations will give you a chance to explore the kinds of decisions media writers frequently have to face.

Chapter Twenty

Final Thoughts: On Learning to Write for the Media

There's an inherent problem with media writing textbooks. They can't teach you to write.

What we *can* do is to give you some good examples of writing. We can share some principles of clear writing and even give you some steps to follow. But that's about it. Ultimately, you have to incorporate those ideas into your writing.

And the only way to learn to write, is to write. Even if you learned a lot—and maybe even aced the course—your greatest learning will be in actually "doing it." Several hundred news stories or ads or blogposts from now, you'll probably feel like you're becoming a media writer.

That's the way it is with any skill. Perhaps you have taken a cooking class and now you're experimenting in the kitchen. You try to remember what you learned and you probably check your recipes many times to make sure you're doing it right. But eventually, cooking will become second nature to you. The learning becomes practice and the practice becomes habit. And the habit is repeated many times until the cooking is an expression of who you are and how you think.

Media writing is like that. You know the basics now, and there's probably nothing wrong with your media writing style that a few years of practice won't cure. Our advice is to write, write, write. Take other writing courses. Indeed, take writing courses outside of mass communication. Take an essay course or a poetry-writing course in the English department. Keep a writer's notebook. Start a blog. And never turn down the chance to write: news stories, ads, op-eds for the university newspaper, brochure copy for your favorite nonprofit.

Most important, look for the opportunity to make writing your job, if only part-time. Internships are great, but don't get hung up on earning academic credit for your job. If you have the opportunity for a job that gives you credit hours, take it. But you also may be able to work a few hours a week in a school or charity PR office. Newspapers are always looking for people to cover high school sports one night a week. Churches need help with newsletters. And great copy editors are always in demand. Get credit or money if you can, but even if you can't … just write.

Science fiction writer Ray Bradbury said it best: "You only fail if you stop writing."

Good luck as you continue to develop a skill that will assure your future success in the mass media.

Appendix A Media Writer's Guide to Grammar

The Big Four

So let's say you went to a football game with a friend who didn't know the game. On the opening series of downs, facing a third and long, your quarterback hit his tight end on a slant for a 42-yard touchdown.

"What just happened?" your football novice friend asks.

And you try to explain. But you realize that he doesn't know what a quarterback is. Or a tight end. Or a slant. This is going to be tougher than you thought. Kind of like writing.

Now do you see the importance of understanding a little basic grammar? Partly, of course, it's to avoid subject-verb agreement errors and pronoun-antecedent errors and comma splices. But beyond that, knowing some basic grammar helps you identify the elements you work with as a writer.

You may remember the eight parts of speech from junior high. The Big Four of that eight are nouns, verbs, adjectives and adverbs. And maybe you remember doing worksheets where you put a line under a noun subject and two lines under a verb and circled the direct object, if there was one. But often we do those types of exercises mindlessly and never think about what those parts of speech mean to writers.

So let's review the Big Four, not as your junior high English teacher might, but with a view toward what they mean to writers.

Nouns

From 'The Sound of Music' to Tom T. Hall

Media writers use nouns to pull readers into their writing by naming people and pointing to places and things and even concepts. We know the favorite things (really, the favorite nouns) of Oscar Hammerstein II, who wrote "These Are a Few of My Favorite Things" in "Sound of Music" (see http://bit.ly/12tZP if you have forgotten those memorable lyrics … or they were way before your time). Those "things," all nouns, put word pictures in the minds of listeners; you actually see the raindrops and mittens and sleigh bells when you hear the song.

Country music writers have done the same thing. Take Tom T. Hall. His song "I Love" tells you exactly what he loves: ducks, trucks, trains, rain, streams, sleep, Sunday School, hay, and more. All nouns! Look back over the list; they're things you can picture. As writers typically do, Hall has added adjectives to sharpen the focus of the nouns. We discover, for instance, that it's not just ducks he likes. They should be little baby ducks. And not just trucks. He loves pick-up trucks. His trains? Tom T. likes them slow-moving.

All this leads us to one of the primary distinctions among nouns: abstract and concrete. *Abstract nouns* are things you can't visualize, or things that are so indefinite that it's hard to visualize. Let's say Tom T. Hall's song said he liked transportation or conveyances. That puts no pictures in your head. So he used a specific noun—trains—something you can immediately see in your mind's eye. And to help you see it better, he added adjectives to help you see slow-moving trains.

Media writers know that one of the keys to readability is using nouns that bring the writing alive. An inexperienced writer might say:

The man parked his vehicle in front of his house.

Writers will point out that the sentence doesn't work because it evokes no images. Or in other words, it suffers from poor noun choice. The man? Doesn't he have a name (a proper noun)? The vehicle? Is it a car or truck or van or limousine? And what's the front? In the yard or on the sidewalk or on the street? They're all typically in front of the house. Look at this revision:

Ralph Franklin parked his classic 1966 red Mustang in his driveway.

There are only a few changes, but they are significant. Not a man, but Ralph. Not a vehicle, but a Mustang. And not in front, but in the driveway. Those three simple noun substitutions bring the sentence to life. And not content with a noun substitution of Mustang for vehicle, we have added three adjectives (classic, 1966, red) to give you a still better picture of the car in Ralph's driveway.

Writers see nouns like construction engineers see the steel skeleton of a skyscraper. Nouns give writers the images and concepts—the skeleton—around which they build action and ideas and elaboration. The most frequent definition of a noun is that it's the name of a person, place, thing or idea. Whatever exists can be named, and that name is a noun.

If it's the name of a specific person, place or thing—Roberto Salazar, France, God, the Constitution, Buddhism, Mississippi, the Nile River, the Republican Party—it's called a *proper noun*.

If it's less specific—a student, a country, a religion, a river, a political party, and the like—it's called a *common noun*.

There are other nouns that can't be touched or felt or even easily seen. These nontangible nouns include concepts like patriotism or love or grief or friendship or patience. Writers frequently deal with these abstractions by giving readers a picture that helps them see the concept, not just take the writer's word for it.

For instance, you might use the noun *patriotism* like this:

Joe Graham loves his country and his patriotism is obvious to all who know him.

The sentence is correct grammatically, but the abstract noun patriotism is difficult for the reader to picture. So how about this rewrite:

Tears came to Graham's eyes and he stood a little straighter when the flag passed by in Arlington's Fourth of July parade.

Obviously, this sentence is more visual because it paints a word picture of Graham's patriotism with an illustration, rather than just labeling it.

Writers Stewart O'Nan and Stephen King (yes, *that* Stephen King) wrote a book about the 2004 baseball season, when their beloved Boston Red Sox broke the Bambino's Curse (if you didn't get that reference, it's because you aren't a baseball fan!) to win the World Series. That book, *Faithful: Two Diehard Boston Red Sox Fans Chronicle the Historic 2004 Season* (2004), begins with O'Nan's explanation of his background as a Sox fan. Let's say O'Nan didn't understand the power of the noun. He might have written something like this:

I would pay for a ticket and sit in the outfield seats near the camera of a local TV station, where I had a good view of the game and could heckle opposing outfielders.

But O'Nan *did* understand how nouns could bring a sentence to life, so this is what he actually wrote:

... game after game I happily shelled out my three bucks at the barred ticket window outside Gate C and staked my claim to Section 34 in straight center, right beside Channel 38's camera, you could call balls and strikes and let the opposing center fielder know he was on the road. (p. xiii)

Want still another example? Check out John Grisham's book about high school football, *Bleachers* (2004). You won't have to read further than the opening paragraph, where Grisham uses specific nouns to paint a word picture for the reader:

The road to Rake Field ran beside the school, past the old band hall and the tennis courts, through a tunnel of two perfect rows of red and yellow maples planted and paid for by boosters, then over a small hill to a lower area covered with enough asphalt for a thousand cars. (p. 1)

To get a better appreciation of what nouns bring to a piece of writing, occasionally take a sentence like this and rewrite it, substituting more general nouns for the specific nouns. You might come up with something like this:

The road to the football field ran past the school and other buildings and facilities owned by the school district, past trees planted by football fans, and eventually to a paved parking lot.

Nouns can be used in a sentence in many ways. They can be subjects or direct objects or appositives or objects of prepositions. Sometimes writers seeking to improve their work identify *noun phrases*, the noun and all its modifiers (like a *22-piece high school jazz band*), or *noun clauses*, a subject and a verb used as a noun (*What media writers do* is paint word pictures for readers.)

It isn't necessary for media writers to be able to identify every type of noun and classify their uses. But being aware of the types of nouns helps writers look for ways they can use nouns to bring writing to life.

Verbs

The Key to Good Writing

If you want to start a lively conversation with a bunch of writers, don't bring up grammar. Writers use grammar as a tool, but it isn't exactly exciting to talk about.

The possible exception to that piece of advice is the topic of verbs. Writers realize that verbs, perhaps more than any other part of speech, are key to their writing. That's because verbs tell what a noun—or its substitute—is doing or being: He runs, he thinks, he is, he seems. It can express an action (runs and thinks) or a state of being (is and seems). And it can even stand alone as a complete sentence: Stop!

Verbs are so important to writers because there is a lot they can do in a sentence. Verbs carry the following qualities:

- **Tense.** This refers to time: when the action or the state of being the verb represents takes place.
- **Action or state of being.** Does the verb represent an action, or does it link a subject with another word that re-names or describes it?
- **Transitive or intransitive.** "Transitive verbs" have a direct object (the receiver of the action) that tells to whom or for whom the action was done; "intransitive verbs" do not take a direct object. Intransitives themselves are of two types: "complete verbs" (action but no direct object) or "linking verbs" (a state of being). Here are some examples:
  > Jack ran his bike into a tree. (transitive with action verb and direct object)
  > Jack ran into a tree. (intransitive with action verb and no direct object)
  > Jack is a bicyclist. (intransitive, linking with a predicate noun renaming the subject)
  > Jack is careless. (intransitive, linking with a predicate adjective renaming the subject)

  Note how these verbs are reflections of *writers' choices*. If the writer wants to tell readers what Jack *did*, she chooses an action verb. If the writer wants to share something about Jack's *nature* or *characteristics* or *personal attributes* (what the textbooks call "state of being"), she chooses a linking verb. In other words, she links up the subject—Jack—with an adjective or a noun. The writer chooses an adjective to describe Jack in some way (careless) or a noun to rename him (bicyclist) and thereby helps the reader to see one of Jack's characteristics more clearly. The sentence "Lady Gaga is a singer" links the subject with a noun (singer) that extends the reader's understanding of Gaga.

- **Voice.** All verbs are either in the active or passive voice. "Active voice" stresses the doer of the action by making the doer the subject of the sentence. "Passive voice" stresses the receiver of an action by making the receiver the subject.

Here are some of the things good writers look for in their verb choices:

Preferring action over state of being. Sometimes writers edit out verb choices that are technically correct, just to make their verbs more powerful. Some writers do a word-search for "is" and "was." Nothing wrong with these state-of-being verbs, but they can often be strengthened. A sentence like "Javier is the city's most-honored football player" might become "Javier earned all-district honors as a junior tailback." Note the editing affected both a verb and a noun: The verb *was* became *earned*, and the noun phrase *football player* became *junior tailback*. Writers who do the word-search for *is* and *was* don't change all usages of those verbs; they simply make sure that those are appropriate uses, not weak substitutes for a better verb.

Preferring specific verbs over weaker verbs with an adverb. The most effective verbs are specific. Good writers look for stronger verbs, rather than adding an adverb to a weaker verb. For example:

- *devoured*, not ate heartily
- *slouched*, not sat lazily
- *ambled*, not walked slowly
- *bellowed*, not announced loudly
- *shrieked*, not screamed piercingly

Good writers don't use adverbs that needlessly extend a verb, like *totally destroyed*. By definition, the verb *destroyed* is total. There is no such thing as partial destruction. Other examples: *wander away* for *wander*, *mercilessly tortured* for *tortured* and *absolutely sure* for *sure*. Adding the needless adverb bloats your writing.

Preferring the active voice to the passive voice. The passive voice carelessly used slows the pace of the story. When verbs are active, so is the sentence. When verbs are passive, the sentence also loses its punch: Instead of doing something, the subject has something done to it. Look at these sentences:

Passive: The football was passed by the quarterback to the wide receiver.
Active: The quarterback passed the football to the wide receiver.
Note the differences between the active and the passive voice:

- Passive voice sentences are longer because you have to add an auxiliary verb (*was passed* in the passive voice instead of *passed* in the active). Also, the doer (the quarterback, in this case) becomes the object in a prepositional phrase you have had to add.
- Passive sentences allow the writer to leave out the actor altogether. The sentence could have read, "The football was passed to the wide receiver." Innocuous enough here, but imagine a doctor's statement: "A surgical tool was left inside the patient during surgery" to "I left a clamp inside the patient." In other words, passive voice is used to help avoid a lawsuit.
- The passive voice slows down the action, with the verb guiding the reader backward toward the subject of the sentence rather than forward toward the object.

This doesn't mean that passive-voice sentences are wrong. It does mean that writers need to be aware of the differences between active and passive. Many grammar teachers would be satisfied if their students could identify the differences between active and passive voice sentences and change active to passive and passive to active. In fact, that's typically what students have to do on tests to demonstrate "mastery" of voice. But some students make A's on those tests and still don't "get it." When you can identify voice and rewrite sentences from one voice to another, all that means is that you have the tools you need to begin to understand the voice of verbs the way writers do.

Writers look at their verbs to see if they have chosen the appropriate voice. In passages where they are trying to move along the action, they prefer the active voice. In passages where they are trying to slow down the action, or focus on the action rather than the doer of the action, they choose the passive voice. A detective novelist, for instance, might write, "The bloody dagger *had been left* near the body." That's passive, but you wouldn't want to change it. The writer doesn't want to emphasize the person who left it; after all, in a detective novel, we don't even know who the murderer is yet. Instead, the writer wants to emphasize the dagger—the object, what had been left.

Media writers are so much in love with the active voice that when you hear some speak, you might come away thinking active is good and passive is bad. But don't confuse their preference for active verbs with disdain for passive verbs. When you need to emphasize the object, or when you want to slow the action down, the passive voice can be used.

Adjectives

The Rodney Dangerfield of Grammar

Young writers love adjectives. More mature writers approach them warily, like Mark Twain: As to the adjective: When in doubt, strike it out (quoted in Safire and Safir, 1992). And in an 1880 letter, he says:

> *I notice that you use plain, simple language, short words and brief sentences. That is the way to write English—it is the modern way and the best way. Stick to it; don't let fluff and flowers and verbosity creep in. When you catch an adjective, kill it. No, I don't mean utterly, but kill most of them—then the rest will be valuable. They weaken when they are close together. They give strength when they are wide apart. An adjective habit, or a wordy, diffuse, flowery habit, once fastened upon a person, is as hard to get rid of as any other vice. (Letter to L.D. Bowser, quoted on http://www .twainquotes.com/Adjectives.html)*

Journalism professor Ben Yagoda (2004) summed up the attitude of many professional writers toward adjectives:

> *As far as not getting respect goes, adjectives leave Rodney Dangerfield in the dust. They rank right up there with Osama bin Laden, Geraldo Rivera, and the customer-service policies of cable-TV companies. That it is good to avoid them is one of the few points on which the sages of writing agree. (p. B13)*

The traditional definition of an "adjective" is a word that modifies (slightly alters the meaning of) a noun or a pronoun by describing it, identifying it or quantifying it. In English, adjectives usually precede the noun or pronoun they modify. In the following paragraph from "Jurassic Park" (Crichton 1990) the underlined words are adjectives:

> *They moved into a <u>green</u> tunnel of <u>overarching</u> palms leading toward the <u>main</u> visitor building. Everywhere, <u>extensive</u> and <u>elaborate</u> planting emphasized the feeling that they were entering a <u>new</u> world, a <u>prehistoric tropical</u> world, and leaving the <u>normal</u> world behind.*

Note that the boldfaced words meet the definition of an adjective in every way. There are no quantifying adjectives in the "Jurassic Park" paragraph, but you can see how the boldfaced words either describe or identify their nouns. You can also add the *a's* and *the's* to the adjectives in that paragraph; grammarians consider the articles *a, and* and *the* to be adjectives. Note what happens when you leave the adjectives (except for the articles) out of the "Jurassic Park" passage:

> *They moved into a _____ tunnel of _____ palms leading toward the _____ visitor building. Everywhere, _____ and _____ planting emphasized the feeling that they were entering a _____ world, a _____ _____ world, and leaving the _____ world behind.*

The adjectives Crichton used in those two sentences were not long, obscure words, but note what you lose when you leave them out, the difference between a tunnel of palms and a tunnel of overarching palms, for instance. You probably did not notice the first time you read the sentences that Crichton had used the word *world* three times at the end, twice as the direct object of "were entering" and once as the direct object of "[were] leaving." But note how the adjectives *modified* the *world* each time. He contrasts a *new* world with a *normal* world, and after the first use of *world*, he throws in another *world* as an appositive, but this time he adds two adjectives that sharpen the word's focus.

Of course, adjectives are not limited to the types of describing words we have already mentioned. There are other types:

Nouns that function as adjectives. Sometimes a noun can be used to extend the meaning of another noun and thereby function like an adjective. Take the word *visitor*, a noun. But in the paragraph from "Jurassic Park" above, note that *visitor* modifies another noun, *building*. Though we did not underline it as an adjective in the original passage, in effect this noun does serve as an adjective.

Pronouns that function as adjectives. Like nouns, pronouns can also extend the meaning of nouns. In the phrase *My seldom-used grammar book*, note that the noun *book* is modified in several ways, all of which extend the meaning of *book* and help the reader to picture it. We learn that it is *seldom-used*, an adjective that may tell us that the book looks almost new. It is a grammar book. *Grammar* is a noun, but is used here as an adjective, again modifying the meaning of *book* to tell us about its contents. The phrase begins with the pronoun *my*, here used as an adjective to indicate possession. So the noun tells us there is a book, adjectives tell us whose it is, something about its possible condition and what kinds of content it contains, all vital information to the writer who is trying to paint a picture of this book in the reader's mind.

So it looks like adjectives can be useful in helping the reader picture a noun. But didn't all those writers say that adjectives weakened writing? Who's right? Are adjectives good or bad?

Neither, of course. Let's say the newlyweds were having a meal together and the husband tells his new wife that she has put too much salt in the casserole. If she is insecure about her cooking, she may say, *"Well, if that's the way you feel, I will never use salt again!"*

He didn't say that salt was bad, or that she should not use it. He said that in this particular dish only, there was too much for his taste. She reacted by saying she would cut out salt altogether. That is similar to the debate over adjectives. Many writers perhaps overreact to inexperienced writers' heavy reliance on adjectives. Experienced writers might say, as Mark Twain did, that you should catch adjectives and kill them. But notice the first sentence of the Twain quote cited earlier in this chapter. We have boldfaced the adjectives: "*I notice that you use **plain, simple** language, **short** words and **brief** sentences.*" Twain used four adjectives in the beginning of his rant against adjectives! Twain and other writers are not literally saying that adjectives are bad; they are saying that good writers avoid over-use of adjectives and prefer using a noun that contains the meaning carried by the adjective when possible.

Writer Judy Delton (1985) made her case against overdependence on adjectives this way:

> *There was a time when strong writing depended on adjectives. Or at least adjectives were very popular. And many beginning writers (and some "ending" writers) still believe that the strength of effective writing is lining up modifier after modifier in front of a noun, that the more pretty, descriptive words, the better. Actually the exact opposite is true. Adjectives weaken; the fewer you use in an article or story, the better. If you are describing a man and say, "The tall, dark, handsome, virile young man..." we don't know much more about him than we did before you described him. It is better to choose one strong adjective that is more specific than several weak, general ones. Try "the dapper young man" or compare him to someone everybody knows. And it is better to use no adjectives at all. Save your strength for verbs. The strength of all good prose (and even poetry!) is in verbs.*

Experienced editors view adjectives warily, because reporters often use them to cover up a lack of hard facts. Journalists covering a candidate, for instance, might attach adjectives like *slick, disciplined, detached, careful, cautious* or *calculating*. But notice that all of those are evaluations, an opinion.

So use adjectives, but select specific nouns and verbs whenever possible.

Adverbs

Useful ... if really needed

A fan magazine recently referred to a television show as an "incredibly popular, groundbreakingly racy sitcom."

Obviously the writer was in love with adverbs. But that sentiment is not shared by most experienced professional writers. In fact, you can apply everything you read in the previous section about adjectives to adverbs. Here is Stephen King's (2000) take on adverbs:

> *Adverbs, like the passive voice, seem to have been created with the timid writer in mind. With the passive voice, the writer usually expresses fear of not being taken seriously; it is the voice of little boys wearing shoepolish mustaches and little girls clumping around in Mommy's high heels. With adverbs, the writer usually tells us he or she is afraid he/she isn't expressing himself/herself clearly, that he or she is not getting the point or the picture across.*
>
> *I believe the road to hell is paved with adverbs, and I will shout it from the rooftops. To put it another way, they're like dandelions. If you have one on your lawn, it looks pretty and unique. If you fail to root it out, however, you find five the next day ... fifty the day after that ... and then, my brothers and sisters, your lawn is <u>totally</u>, <u>completely</u>, and <u>profligately</u> covered with dandelions.*

The road to hell? Come on Stephen, don't mince words; tell us how you *really* feel. (Oops! Stephen probably wouldn't like the "really" in the previous sentence.)

King, and many other writers, believe that a well-chosen action verb needs no adverb. Adverbs that end in -ly are probably the best known. Those adverbs begin with an adjective—like *quiet*, as in the quiet student. Add -ly and you have *quietly*. Now you can write: The student spoke quietly. But why not improve the weak verb to come up with one that includes both the idea of speaking and the idea of quiet: The student *whispered*. Here are some more -ly adverbs that should be dropped in favor of a stronger verb:

- He ran swiftly. vs. He sprinted.
- He spoke harshly to her. vs. He berated her.

Sometimes, as with adjectives, the adverb needlessly repeats something already included in the verb. Why say the music *blared loudly* in the next room? Can music blare softly? Can you be *totally* flabbergasted, as opposed to partially flabbergasted? Or can you be *absolutely* sure? As opposed to *partially* sure?

Writers who criticize adverb use are not suggesting that they be dropped, only that we be aware of them and look for opportunities to strengthen verbs instead of adding adverbs.

Adverbs are a versatile tool for writers. Look at all we can do to extend a verb by adding an adverb:

- Adverbs can tell us *how* something happened: He waited *patiently* for her to return. The town grew *quickly* after the new plant opened.
- Adverbs can tell us *where* something happened. The search team looked *nearby*. Please go *home*. The child went *indoors*.
- Adverbs can tell us *when* something happened, *how often* or *for how long*: She returned to school *yesterday*. *Later*, she went back to pick up her keys. He *often* spends the morning in the weight room. I'm *still* hungry.
- Adverbs can express our *certainty* of an event: He *probably* finished the book. He will *certainly* finish the book. *Surely* you jest.

- Adverbs express the *intensity* of an action, an adjective or another adverb. He was *extremely* cold. He *hardly* noticed. The coffee was *too* hot.
- Adverbs can *ask questions*: *Why* did you do that? *When* will you arrive? *How* are you? *Where* is it?

That is only the beginning of the way writers use adverbs. Many writers do not know as much about adverbs as we have reviewed in this chapter, and use them only by what "feels right." Those writers who can find adverbs and identify the ways in which they are used will certainly be more adept at looking for ways to strengthen those adverbs or even to leave them out in favor of a better verb.

Paula LaRocque

A VISIT WITH YOUR WRITING COACH
Shattering Some Myths

When to follow the rules

http://snd.sc/LoVKj7

References

Crichton, Michael. *Jurassic Park*. New York: Ballantine Books, 1990.

Delton, Judy. *The 29 Most Common Writing Mistakes and How to Avoid Them*. Cincinnati: Writer's Digest Books, 1985.

Grisham, John. *Bleachers*. New York: Dell, 2004.

King, Stephen. *On Writing*. New York: Scribner, 2000.

O'Nan, Stewart, and King, Stephen. *Faithful: Two Diehard Boston Red Sox Fans Chronicle the Historic 2004 Season*. New York: Scribner, 2004.

Safire, William, and Safir, Leonard. *Good Advice on Writing*. New York: Simon and Schuster, 1991.

twainquotes.com. "Directory of Mark Twain's Maxims, Quotations, and Various Opinions." twainquotes.com. n.d. http://www.twainquotes.com/Adjectives.html.

Yagoda, Ben. "The Adjective—So Ludic, So Minatory, So Twee." *The Chronicle of Higher Education*, 2004.

Skills Development: Practice in Media Writing

The Internet has all the resources any media writer would ever need to improve his or her grammar. So if you need help on something specific like comma splices or identifying passive constructions, or you need a start-from-scratch guide because you slept through all those grammar lessons in elementary and junior high and high school, you can find what you need online.

The following sites will get you started. But remember, all you have to do is go to a search engine to find the answer to all your grammar problems. The first site below is an online grammar diagnostic test, but there are lots of those online. If you want to take another one, just go to a search engine and type in "online grammar diagnostic test" and take your pick. You can do that with any grammar problem you're having, from punctuation of appositives to pronoun-antecedent agreement.

Here's the bottom line: You have chosen a field where you need excellent grammar skills. If you wanted to become an artist or a research chemist or a rancher or a police detective or any one of a thousand other professions, you would need good, but not necessarily excellent, grammar skills. But lucky you—you have chosen a word field. People in advertising and journalism and public relations need far-better-than-average grammar and punctuation skills. If that's not you, then you need to get to work to improve those skills.

The good news is that most of the problems college media writing students have trouble with were actually taught in the seventh grade or before. This isn't new stuff or advanced-level skills. It's the rules and principles that were taught before. And maybe you were bored then and thought you'd never use this stuff, so you memorized enough to pass the test and then did a memory dump.

The bad news is that most college journalism and ad/PR programs don't devote courses to teaching you the grammar you missed in previous years. The good news is that it's all online and searchable, so you can pick up everything you missed.

Start with the diagnostic test to see where you may have weaknesses. Then move on to other areas where you might need help. The list of sites below is not exhaustive by any means. If you look at the information on, say, compound sentences and still don't think you get it, type compound sentences into a search engine and you'll find all the information you need.

An online grammar-diagnostic test http://www.kristisiegel.com/grammartest2.html

Grammar skills

- Help with indefinite articles *a* and *an*: http://owl.english.purdue.edu/owl/resource/591/01/
- Help with adjectives: http://owl.english.purdue.edu/owl/resource/537/01/
- The difference between adjectives and adverbs: http://owl.english.purdue.edu/owl/resource/536/01/
- Prepositions of direction: http://owl.english.purdue.edu/owl/resource/594/02/
- Prepositions of location: http://owl.english.purdue.edu/owl/resource/594/03/
- Prepositions for time, place and introducing objects: http://owl.english.purdue.edu/owl/resource/594/01/
- Using pronouns clearly: http://owl.english.purdue.edu/owl/resource/595/01/
- Pronoun case: http://owl.english.purdue.edu/owl/resource/595/02/
- Appositives: http://owl.english.purdue.edu/owl/resource/596/1/
- Dangling modifiers: http://owl.english.purdue.edu/owl/resource/597/01/
- Independent and dependent clauses: http://owl.english.purdue.edu/owl/resource/598/01/
- Subject-verb agreement: http://owl.english.purdue.edu/owl/resource/599/01/
- Sentence fragments: http://owl.english.purdue.edu/owl/resource/620/01/
- Active and passive verbs: http://owl.english.purdue.edu/owl/resource/539/01/
- Apostrophes: http://owl.english.purdue.edu/owl/resource/621/01/

Punctuation skills

- Commas after introductions: http://owl.english.purdue.edu/owl/resource/607/03/
- Commas and semicolons in compound sentences: http://owl.english.purdue.edu/owl/resource/607/04/
- Comma splices: http://owl.english.purdue.edu/engagement/2/1/34/
- Hyphens: http://owl.english.purdue.edu/owl/resource/576/01/
- Punctuating essential and non-essential elements: http://owl.english.purdue.edu/owl/resource/607/05/
- Overview of comma use in sentences: http://owl.english.purdue.edu/owl/resource/607/02/
- Punctuating different types of sentences: http://owl.english.purdue.edu/owl/resource/604/01/

An AP Styleguide

The style rules in this section of the appendix are adapted from the "Associated Press Stylebook." Everything below can be found in the stylebook, but it's scattered throughout the book, literally from A to Z. What we've done is to mine the Stylebook for the most relevant rules for new writers and group them for (we hope) easier learning.

There are more rules for capitalization, abbreviation, and the like in the Stylebook than what you will find here. But we think you'll agree that this is a more effective introduction for people new to media writing.

Remember: While this is the best-known and most useful style for new writers, this is only one of several styleguides. For example: This styleguide tells you not to use courtesy titles (Mr., Ms., etc.), but The New York Times stylebook mandates their use. Or the medium you work for may choose to put magazine and newspaper titles in italics, rather than only capitalizing them. Still, AP style is a good place to start. Typically, newspapers or websites or PR offices with their own stylebooks base them largely on the AP Stylebook.

Part 1: Capitalization

1.1 **Directions.** Lowercase north, south, southwest, etc., when they indicate directions. Capitalize them when they indicate geographical regions and specific places. Examples: Go two blocks and then turn north. Tennessee is south of Kentucky. The wagon train headed west. The Pacific Northwest has a more temperate climate than you might think. He moved to West Texas. She has a Southern accent. For more examples, see the **directions and regions** entry in the "Associated Press Stylebook."

1.2 **Brand names.** Capitalize brand names, but use them only if they are necessary for a story. See the **brand names** entry in the "Associated Press Stylebook."

1.3 **Buildings.** Capitalize the names of buildings, including the word *building* if it is a part of the name: the Moudy Building, the Empire State Building. Capitalize named rooms, like the Oval Office. Capitalize *room* when it is used to designate a specific place: His office is Room 165.

1.4 **Government and politics.** Capitalization rules related to government:

   a) Capitalize *U.S. Capitol* and the *Capitol* when referring to the building in Washington, D.C. Or: *The governor's office is in the Capitol in Austin. Capital* refers to the city where the seat of government is located.

   b) Capitalize *U.S. Constitution* and or any reference to the *Constitution* with the U.S. modifier. Capitalize the First Amendment or any specific segment of the Constitution. When referring to a state constitution, capitalize only when it is used with the name of the state. *The Texas Constitution is much longer than the constitutions of most other states.* Lowercase *federal*.

   c) Capitalize *Senate, House of Representatives, U.S. Congress* and *Congress*. Lowercase *congressional, congressman, congresswoman* and *congressional representative*.

   d) Capitalize *city council* when it is a part of a proper name: *the Fort Worth City Council*. Also capitalize if it refers to a specific city council, even though the name of the city may not be attached. Lowercase when it refers to several city councils: *the Fort Worth and Dallas city councils*.

   e) In identifying the party affiliations of members of Congress, use this short form: John McCain, R-Ariz., Barbara Boxer, D-Calif.

   f) Capitalize office when it is part of an agency's formal name: *the Office of Management and Budget*.

g) Capitalize *county* when it is a part of a name of a governmental unit: *Tarrant County*. Without the name of the county before it, lowercase it: *He said county roads were poorly maintained* or *Dallas and Tarrant counties established a joint task force to study gang crime*.

h) Lowercase *first lady, administration, government, presidential* and *federal* (unless it is part of a specific name, like the *Federal Trade Commission, the Federal Reserve, the Federal Bureau of Prisons*).

i) Capitalize the names of political parties. If you are just writing the word *party* without Democratic, Republican, etc., in front of it, lowercase it: *Democratic Party, Republican Party. The Republican analyst said his party had moved too far to the right.*

j) Lowercase political philosophies. This can be tricky, because sometimes a philosophy can also be the name of a party, like socialism and the Socialist Party. Example: *He said Obama is a socialist*. In that sentence, you have to ask yourself what the speaker meant. Was he saying that the president is actually a member of the small Socialist Party in the United States, or just that he had adopted some of the political philosophy of socialism?

1.5 **Interstate highways.** Make it Interstate 20 on first reference and I-20 after that.

1.6 **The military.** Capitalize the names of U.S. armed services: the U.S. Army or Army (if it refers to the U.S. Army); the Navy; the Air Force. Lowercase the armed forces of other nations: the Brazilian air force, the Chinese army.

1.7 **Race, ethnicity, nationality.** Capitalize the proper names of races: Arab, Eskimo, Asian. Lowercase black and white. Capitalize nationalities: French, Chinese, Angolan.

1.8 **Proper nouns.** Capitalize nouns that name specific persons, places or things: the Mississippi River, Amon Carter Stadium, Plymouth Rock, Cooper Street, Central Park. But when common names (river, stadium, street, park) are not used as a part of the proper name, they are lowercased: The Mississippi River flooded because of the spring rains. An Army Corps of Engineers spokesperson said the river was higher than it has been for a decade. When common nouns are used to form plurals with proper nouns, they are lowercased: Matlock and Cooper streets, lakes Ray Hubbard and Tawakoni, the Democratic and Republican parties.

1.9 **Seasons.** Lowercase spring, summer, winter, fall, autumn, along with springtime and other derivatives. But uppercase if they are part of a name: Winter Olympics.

1.10 **Police.** Lowercase police in most uses. The exception would be when you use the formal department name. The Fort Worth Police Department has a new chief. But Fort Worth police are investigating.

Part 2: Abbreviations

2.1 The first time an organization is mentioned, spell out the name. After that, abbreviate it only if you think it would be obvious what the abbreviation stands for. You would spell out the Organization to Eliminate Boring University Lectures on first mention, but you would not call it the OEBUL on second reference. Instead, refer to it as *the group* or *the organization*.

2.2 There are exceptions to rule 2.1. Some organizations are so well known that you can refer to them by their initials on first reference: CIA, FBI, YWCA, NASA, the NFL in sports stories, and of course, your university's abbreviation.

2.3 Never abbreviate these words: associate, assistant, attorney, building, professor, president, superintendent. Never abbreviate the days of the week.

2.4 Never use the ampersand (&) in place of *and* in news copy.

2.5 Abbreviate states if they are used with a city. Write out state names when they stand alone. He was born in Little Rock, Ark. He was born in Arkansas.

2.6 Use traditional state abbreviations, not ZIP code abbreviations. You can look up state abbreviations in your "Associated Press Stylebook." Eight states are never abbreviated: Idaho, Iowa, Maine, Ohio, Texas, Utah, Alaska and Hawaii.

2.7 Both U.S. and U.N. take periods. The European Union is abbreviated EU and the United Kingdom (England) is abbreviated UK, without periods. USA does not take periods. You also drop the periods for US in headlines, though you would use them as U.S. in news copy.

2.8 Abbreviate company, incorporated, corporation, limited and brothers (Co., Inc., Corp., Ltd. and Bros.) when they follow the name of a business entity.

2.9 Here are the abbreviations for common academic degrees: Ph.D., Ed.D., J.D., B.A., M.A. When possible, avoid degree abbreviations in text. Use this instead: Smith, who holds a doctorate in art history …

2.10 Abbreviate Jr. and Sr. after a person's name, but do not set it off with a comma: The new memorial honors Martin Luther King Jr.

2.11 The abbreviation mph is acceptable on all references. You can use mpg only on second reference.

Part 3: Numbers

Basically, there is one style rule for handling numbers: Spell out everything under 10 (including zero); beginning with 10, use numerals. Animal control officers found nine puppies and 27 cats in the abandoned house. There are lots of exceptions. They include the following:

3.1 Always spell out words at the beginning of sentences. Fifteen students were enrolled in the class. Avoid starting sentences with larger numbers. Not: 218 votes separated the two candidates. Instead: The two candidates were separated by 218 votes.

3.2 Always use numerals for money: 5 cents, $5. Note that the word cents is spelled out, but the dollar sign is used for dollar amounts. When you have even dollar amounts, do not use a decimal and zeros: $5, not $5.00.

3.3 Spell out million, billion, trillion, etc. Take larger numbers out two decimal points: The philanthropist gave the university $6.23 million for academic scholarships.

3.4 Always use numbers for ages. The 7-year-old boy returned seven overdue books to the library. When an age is used as an adjective, hyphenate it: Ruth, who had a 7-year-old brother, was 9 years old. The rule for ages includes all ages, not only human and animal ages. Thus: a 2-year-old building, an 8-year-old car.

3.5 Use numbers for weights and measurements: 5 inches; 5 pounds. Spell out the units of measurements: inches, feet, yards, pounds, etc. The seventh grader was 6 feet 1 inch tall.

3.6 Always use numbers for years. When numbers are left out (the '60s instead of the 1960s), use an apostrophe to indicate the omitted numbers. Also, make numbers used in dates plural the way you make any noun a plural: add *s*. Tax rates were lowered in the 1980s.

3.7 Use figures for percentages: 5 percent; 5.23 percent. Always spell out the word *percent* and avoid the % symbol. For percentages less than 1 percent, use zero and a decimal: 0.5 percent.

3.8 Use figures for temperatures, except for zero. Spell out the word *degrees* and the word *minus* in temperatures under zero: The temperature, in Minot, N.D., was minus 30 degrees.

3.9 Other rules for numbers:

3.91 Spell out fractions: four-fifths; seven-eighths.

3.92 Report votes as numbers. If there are more than 1,000 votes, use "to" instead of a hyphen between the numbers: He won 3,233 to 2,355.

3.93 When indicating rank, make it No. 1, No. 5, etc. Capitalize *N*, even if it's in the middle of the sentence: He finished No. 3 in the voting.

3.94 Use figures for scores: The Rangers beat the Angels 4-3. Tiger Woods shot a 4 on the final hole.

3.95 To make a number plural, add *s*: There are two 6s in his street address. To make a single letter plural, add *'s*: Does he give many A's in that class?

3.96 Do not use parentheses in telephone numbers: 817-257-7000.

3.97 Do not begin sentences with numerals. Except you can begin a sentence with a year, but always look for a way to avoid doing that.

Part 4: Punctuation

4.1 Commas

4.11 For items in a series, omit the comma before the conjunction. The class includes first-year students, sophomores and juniors. Note that this is a journalism convention; when you write papers in other disciplines, your professors will probably want that comma to be inserted before the conjunction.

4.12 Set off ages with commas: Franklin Hodge, 28, was among those killed in the crash.

4.13 Set off states with commas. If the state does not end the sentence, put a comma after the state's name. He moved from Nashville, Tenn., to Birmingham, Ala.

4.14 Set off hometowns with commas: Susan Richardson, Amarillo, and Mandy Morris, Houston, were named to the starting lineup. It's less confusing, however, to use the preposition *of* and omit the commas: Susan Richardson of Amarillo and Mandy Morris of Houston were named to the starting lineup.

4.2 Semicolons

4.21 You won't find many semicolons in the mass media. Instead of using a semicolon and adding another independent clause, mass media writers are more likely to stop the sentence with a period and add a new sentence. However, there is one place that we do use semicolons: as a souped-up comma to separate elements that already include commas. Here's an example: The chancellor appointed the following faculty members to the new committee: *Martha Randall, professor of art history; Betty Yarborough, instructor in mathematics; and Mike Wood, lecturer in advertising.* In series like this, you retain the semicolon before the coordinating conjunction.

4.3 Colons

4.31 Avoid colons after a *be* verb.

No: The goals of the new plan are:

Instead: The new plan has three goals:

4.4 Quotations

4.41 Commas and periods always go inside quotation marks. "I am withdrawing from the race," Smith said. Or: Smith said her opponents had "engaged in a new low in campaign advertising."

4.42 Dashes, semicolons, question marks and exclamation points go within the quotation marks when they apply to the quoted material and outside when they apply to the whole sentence. Examples: *She asked, "Will you support me if I choose to run?" Do you remember "Leave it to Beaver"?*

4.43 Do not use a comma before an indirect or partial quotation. Example: *Perry said he would "definitely consider another presidential race."* No comma after *would* in that sentence.

Part 5: Dates and time

5.1 Always use Arabic figures for dates. Don't use *st, nd, rd* or *th*. Abbreviate these months: January, February, August, September, October, November and December. Fall registration is scheduled for Aug. 23.

5.2 When you use a month together with a year, do not separate them with a comma. You only abbreviate a month when you use the date with the month: She was born in October 1980. She was born on Oct. 23, 1980.

5.3 When the date includes a year, always put a comma after the year if the year does not end the sentence: She was born on Oct. 23, 1980, in Oklahoma City.

5.4 Use figures for times. Lowercase *a.m.* and *p.m.* and always use periods. For midnight or noon, do not use 12 midnight or 12 noon. For even clock hours, do not use zeros in the minute positions. Make it 7 p.m., not 7:00 p.m.

5.5 Avoid time redundancies like 10 a.m. this morning.

5.6 Do not use *on* before a day of the week unless you need it for clarity. The meeting will be held on Thursday. The team left for the bowl game on Wednesday.

5.7 It's daylight saving (no *s*) time. When referring to time zones, make it Eastern daylight time, Mountain daylight time, etc., omitting *saving*.

Part 6: Addresses

6.1 Use numbers for addresses: 4 Hawthorne Court.

6.2 For street addresses, abbreviate street, avenue and boulevard only. Any other thoroughfare designation (drive, alley, oval, court, terrace, point, place, etc.) is spelled out: 432 Parkmeadow Court, but 432 Morningside Ave.

6.3 Abbreviate points of the compass when they are used in addresses or quadrants of a city. But when numbers are not used in an address, do not abbreviate compass points: She lives at 432 E. Morningside Ave. NW. The factory will be built on East Mason Avenue.

6.4 Numbered streets follow the rule for numerals. Make it First Street, Ninth Street, but 13th Street, 21st Avenue. But: 232 First St., 232 N. First St., 232 S. 21st Ave.

Part 7: Titles and identifications

7.1 The first time you refer to a person, use the person's first and last name and title. On second reference, use the last name only.

7.2 A title used before a person's name is always capitalized. Titles used after name (and typically you put longer titles after names, not before them) are lowercase: TCU will be represented by Chancellor Victor Boschini. The featured speaker is Nowell Donovan, provost and vice chancellor for academic affairs.

7.3 Titles used in other places in text (not before a person's name) are always lowercase. So it's Dean David Whillock, but David Whillock is dean of the College of Communication.

7.4 Some titles must be abbreviated when they come before a name. Examples: Dr., Gov., Lt. Gov., Rep., Sen., The Rev. and certain military titles like Gen., Adm., Lt., Capt., Sgt. (see AP Stylebook for specific military titles). Exception: When a title is used before a name in a direct quotation, do not abbreviate it. When people are referred to by their titles, without their name, the title is spelled out and lowercase: Lt. Gov. David Dewhurst announced his candidacy for the Republican nomination for the U.S. Senate. The lieutenant governor should have a well-funded campaign.

7.5 Don't hyphenate vice. It's vice president, vice chairman, and so forth.

7.6 Some titles are really job descriptions. Don't capitalize them when they come before a name: second baseman Ian Kinsler, custodian Max Morris, actor Jack Nicholson, coach Gary Patterson.

7.7 When a title is used before a name but there is a comma after the title, do not capitalize it: He welcomed the secretary of state, Hillary Clinton. He welcomed Secretary of State Hillary Clinton. He welcomed Hillary Clinton, U.S. secretary of state.

7.8 Do not use courtesy titles: Mr., Miss, Mrs., Ms.

Part 8: Names

8.1 When you use a person's initials, don't put a space between them: O.J. Simpson.

8.2 On first reference, use a person's full name and title. After that, use the last name only. This applies even when the person is fairly well known. You wouldn't refer to Mayor Smith on first reference; make it Mayor John Smith. The same rule goes for the president; make it President Barack Obama, not President Obama, on first reference. After that, call him Obama, not President Obama.

8.3 Capitalize titles before names (and abbreviate them if they need to be abbreviated). Lowercase titles that follow names. Shorter titles can come before names, but put longer titles after names.

8.4 Put nicknames in quotation marks after a name: Paul "Bear" Bryant.

Part 9: Religion

9.1 Capitalize the names of monotheistic deities: God, Jesus, Allah, the Holy Spirit.

9.2 Capitalize the names of holy days for Christian, Jewish and Muslim feasts.

9.3 Capitalize Satan, but lowercase satanic. These are lowercase: devil, heaven, hell. But Hades.

9.4 Capitalize Mass, but lowercase any adjectives that modify it: a requiem Mass, a high Mass. Mass is *celebrated*, not *said*.

9.5 Pope is capitalized as a formal title before a name. It is lowercase in all other uses. Pontiff is not a formal title; always lowercase it. Pope John Paul II. The pontiff lives at the Vatican.

9.6 Capitalize Bible and do not use quotation marks around it. Capitalize Old Testament, New Testament, Gospel of John, etc. Lowercase *biblical* in all uses. Lowercase bible when it is used as a nonreligious term: His book is the bible of coin collecting.

9.7 Capitalize imam when it is used as a formal title before a name. Lowercase in all other uses.

9.8 When using the title *Rev.* before a name, always precede it with *the*. Make it *the Rev.* James Robinson, not *Rev.* James Robinson. On second reference, use only last names of clergy, as with anyone else.

Part 10: Education

10.1 Lowercase the names of academic departments unless they contain proper nouns: the history department, the department of sociology, the English department, the department of Spanish.

10.2 Capitalize the names of schools and colleges: the Schieffer School of Journalism, the College of Communication.

10.3 Never abbreviate professor.

10.4 GPA is acceptable in all uses for grade point average.

10.5 Do not refer to someone who holds a Ph.D. or an Ed.D. as Dr. Use Dr. only if that individual holds a doctor of medicine, a doctor of dental surgery, a doctor of optometry, a doctor of osteopathic medicine, or a doctor of podiatric medicine. For professors, do it this way: Bill Slater, who holds a doctorate in journalism, teaches the course.

10.6 It's professor of, but instructor in.

10.7 Use an apostrophe in bachelor's degree and master's degree. The most common degree abbreviations are B.A., B.S., M.A., M.S., Ph.D. and Ed.D. Make it Bachelor of Science degree or Master of Arts degree (no apostrophes). But the Master of Business Administration degree does not take periods: it's an MBA.

10.8 *Alumnus* is one male graduate; *alumna* is one female graduate; *alumnae* is a group of female graduates; *alumni* is either a group of male graduates or a group of males and females.

10.9 Avoid *coed*. Make it female student. But it is appropriate if you are talking about coeducational institutions.

Part 11: Books, periodicals, art, music

11.1 Put quotation marks around the following titles: books, musical compositions, TV programs, movie titles, poem titles, song titles, the titles of lectures and speeches and works of art.

11.2 Do not put quotation marks around the Bible and reference works (encyclopedias, almanacs, directories).

11.3 Do not put quotation marks around the titles of software.

11.4 Do not put quotation marks around the names of magazines. Lowercase the word magazine unless it is a part of the magazine's formal title: Time magazine, Image magazine.

11.5 Do not put quotation marks around the names of newspapers. Capitalize *The* in a newspaper's name if it is part of the name of the newspaper. A good way to know is to look at the nameplate of the newspaper on page one. Does it say Star-Telegram or The New York Times?

11.6 Never underline anything. Ever.

Part 12: Internet style

Here is the preferred spelling and capitalization style for common Web-related terms:

- the Web
- the World Wide Web
- Web page/Web feed
- website/webcam/webcast/webmaster
- wiki for the software, but Wikipedia for the website
- Internet
- email, but e-book, e-business and e-commerce
- Wi-Fi
- home page
- online

Part 13: Words: spelling and media usage

13.1 Spelling

Acknowledgment, not acknowledgement
African-American
All right, never alright
Ax, not axe
Adviser, not advisor
Backward, not backwards
Backyard is now acceptable in all uses, both as a noun and an adjective
Barbecue (no q!)
Best-seller
Gray, not grey
Judgment
Light, not lite
Sewage, not sewerage
Teen, teenager, teenage, not teen-age; avoid *teen-aged*
Toward, not towards
Through, not thru
ZIP code

13.2 Usage

13.21 **And, but at the start of sentences.** Don't put a comma after *and* or *but* at the start of a sentence unless you are punctuating something else in the sentence.
No: And, he told his employees that he was closing the plant.
Yes: And he told his employees that he was closing the plant.
No: But, he refused to drop out of the race.
But: But, hoping for an election-day miracle, he refused to drop out of the race.

13.22 **Beside, besides.** *Beside* means next to; *besides* means in addition to.

13.23 **Damage, damages.** *Damage* refers to destruction; *damages* are a court award.

13.24 **Ensure, insure.** *Ensure* is to guarantee; *insure* refers to insurance.

13.25 **Entitled, titled.** *Entitled* means you have a right to something; *titled* refers to a book. Never say a book was entitled.

13.26 **Girl, boy.** Both *girl* and *boy* apply until age 18. For people older than 18, use *men* and *women*.

13.27 **Half-mast, half-staff.** Flags on ships and naval stations are flown *half-mast*; other flags are flown *half-staff*.

13.28 **Injuries.** They are *suffered*, not sustained or received.

13.29 **Acquitted, guilty.** Use acquitted when writing about trials, rather than not guilty.

13.30 **Over, more than.** *Over* refers to spatial relationships (The cow flew *over* the moon). Use *more than* when you are talking about amounts (The deficit is more than $1 trillion).

13.31 **People, persons.** One individual is a person; use people in plural usage. *One person died in the fire. More than 100 people demonstrated in front of City Hall.*

About the Authors

Tommy Thomason

Tommy Thomason was the founding director of the TCU Schieffer School of Journalism and Strategic Communication. He is currently professor of journalism at TCU and director of the Texas Center for Community Journalism, one of only five such community journalism centers in the United States.

Thomason began his career in journalism in the early 1970s with the Associated Press, working as a sportswriter in Arkadelphia and Little Rock, Ark. He has also worked in public relations in Dallas and as a copyeditor for several regional magazines.

Thomason was co-director of the first national symposium on crime victims and the news media, which was televised nationally on C-SPAN, and a symposium on coverage of sex crimes, *Sex in the Media: The Public's Right to Know vs. the Victim's Right to Privacy*.

He maintains an interest in writing at all academic levels, and frequently speaks to elementary school teachers about writing workshops for children. He is the author of "More Than a Writing Teacher: How to Become a Teacher Who Writes," "Writer to Writer: How to Conference Young Authors," "Write On Target: How to Prepare Young Writers for Success on Writing Achievement Tests," "Absolutely Write: Teaching the Craft Elements of Writing," "Writeaerobics: 40 Exercises to Improve Your Writing Teaching" and "Tools, not Rules: Teaching Grammar in the Writing Classroom." He and Amiso George of the Schieffer School are co-authors of a textbook, "Race, Gender, and Stereotypes in the Media: A Reader for Professional Communicators." He is also co-author of one picture book for children, "O Is for Oil."

Andrew Chavez

Andrew Chavez serves as director of digital media for the TCU Schieffer School of Journalism and Strategic Communication, where he also teaches a class on new media Web tools. He is also the adviser for TCU 360 and The 109, a local news site that covers the 76109 ZIP code.

Before joining the Schieffer School, he worked at the Fort Worth Star-Telegram as a part-time night police reporter. Chavez is also the associate director of the Texas Center for Community Journalism.

Chapter Authors

Suzanne Huffman

Suzanne Huffman, professor of journalism, chairs the Division of News in the TCU Schieffer School of Journalism and Strategic Communication. She reported, anchored, and produced news at commercial television stations in Tampa, Fla., Santa Maria, Calif., and Cedar Rapids, Iowa. Her reports have appeared on NBC's "Today" show.

She is co-author of "Reporting from the Front: The Media and the Military," published by Rowman & Littlefield. She is also co-author of "Women Journalists at Ground Zero: Covering Crisis," published by Rowman & Littlefield and "Broadcast News Handbook: Writing, Reporting, and Producing in the Age of Social Media," published by McGraw-Hill. Huffman is a contributing author to "Indelible Images: Women of Local Television," published by Iowa State University Press. Her research centers on the practice of broadcast journalism and has been published in Journal of Broadcasting & Electronic Media and presented at regional and national symposia.

Chip Stewart

Chip Stewart, an associate professor of journalism in the Schieffer School of Journalism and Strategic Communication at TCU, holds a Ph.D. in journalism and a J.D. in law. He is currently editor-in-chief of Dispute Resolution Magazine, a quarterly publication of the Dispute Resolution Section of the American Bar Association. His journalism experience includes working as city editor of the Columbia Missourian. He is also a sports freelance writer and has worked as a sports public relations assistant at Southern Methodist University.

Stewart earned his law degree at the University of Texas and is licensed to practice by the Texas bar and the Missouri bar. He worked as an attorney in Killeen, Texas, in the late 1990s, practicing criminal, bankruptcy, and family law. He also clerked in the Travis County Attorney's office.

Maggie Thomas

Maggie B. Thomas, who covered the first heart transplant operations in Dallas as a medical writer for the Fort Worth Star-Telegram, teaches media writing and public relations courses at the TCU Schieffer School of Journalism and Strategic Communication. At the Star-Telegram, she also served as editor of a special section for teens. An avid sports enthusiast, she wrote high school football stories for the Star-Telegram and later for the Bryan-College Station Eagle.

As chair of the Professional Development Committee for the Greater Fort Worth Chapter of the Public Relations Society of America, she organized seminars about litigation journalism, desktop publishing, media coverage for organizations, and career development for public relations professionals. She consults with businesses and governmental agencies regarding written and oral communication methods.

Robert Bohler

Robert Bohler is an instructor in the TCU Schieffer School of Journalism and Strategic Communication, where he also advises TCU Student Media. He teaches a variety of journalism courses and advises the staffs of the TCU Skiff newspaper and Image Magazine.

He has worked in, written about, or taught how to practice journalism for more than 30 years. He began his journalism career as managing editor at a community newspaper, and he has worked as a general assignment and public affairs reporter for several mid-size to large metropolitan dailies, including The Greenville News in South Carolina and The Atlanta Journal-Constitution.

His commentary on the ethics scandals at newspapers and the deaths of Princess Diana and John F. Kennedy Jr. have been published in Editor and Publisher magazine, and other essays on news coverage and popular culture have appeared in the Atlanta Journal-Constitution.

From 2006 to 2012, he was editor of College Media Review, the flagship publication and magazine of popular and peer-reviewed articles for College Media Association, the nation's largest group of college journalism advisers. During that time, he led the quarterly review's transformation from a print to online-only publication.

Geoff Campbell

Geoff Campbell is a lecturer in journalism at the University of Texas at Arlington, where he teaches introductory media writing, reporting, and strategic communication.

Campbell is a two-time winner of the UT Arlington College of Liberal Arts Outstanding Adjunct Award (2011, 2013) and the author of seven nonfiction books. He has extensive professional writing experience that includes work for weekly newsletters, daily newspapers, magazines and a wire service. He worked in Washington for nearly 10 years, covering Congress, the executive branch, the U.S. Supreme Court and municipal finance. Campbell also wrote for the internal strategic publications of a global eye care company and served as senior writer for a public relations firm, where he specialized in articles, blog entries and literature pieces.

Carol Glover

Carol Glover leads a team of nationally recognized creative professionals at the Balcom Agency in Fort Worth.

Glover has won numerous awards for creative excellence, including more than 200 local and district Addy awards, several Best of Show Addy awards, Dallas Press Club Katie awards, Dallas Topps and Medical Marketing & Media honors.

Paula LaRocque

Paula LaRocque is a writer and writing consultant who has conducted workshops for hundreds of media, government, academic, and business groups across the United States, Canada, and Europe. She also has been a writing consultant for the Associated Press, the Drehscheibe Institute in Bonn and the European Stars & Stripes in Germany.

For 10 years, LaRocque taught technical communication at Western Michigan University's School of Engineering and journalism at Texas A&M, Southern Methodist and Texas Christian universities. And for the following 20 years, she was assistant managing editor and writing coach at The Dallas Morning News.

She has been a columnist for the Society of Professional Journalists' Quill magazine for more than two decades. Her commentaries air regularly on National Public Radio in Dallas. She is the author of three nonfiction books and one novel.